WOMEN SCIENTISTS FROM ANTIQUITY TO THE PRESENT: AN INDEX

WOMEN SCIENTISTS FROM ANTIQUITY TO THE PRESENT: AN INDEX

An International Reference Listing and Biographical
Directory of Some Notable Women Scientists
from Ancient to Modern Times

Caroline L. Herzenberg

LOCUST HILL PRESS
West Cornwall, CT
1986

LIBRARY OF CONGRESS CATALOGING-IN-PUBLICATION DATA

Herzenberg, Caroline L., 1932–
  Women scientists from antiquity to the present.

  Bibliography: pp. xxix-xxxvii
  Includes index.
    1. Women scientists—Biography—Indexes.
  2. Women engineers—Biography—Indexes. I. Title.
Q141.H475 1986   509'.2'2 [B]   85-23985
ISBN 0-933951-01-9 (lib. bdg.)

Quotation on pp. xxvii–xxviii of this
book from *Woman in Science* by H.J. Mozans.
Copyright 1913 by D. Appleton & Co.,
renewed 1941 by W.J. Doheny. A Hawthorn
book. Reprinted by permission of
E.P. Dutton, a division of New American
Library.

Printed on acid-free, 250-year-life paper

Manufactured in the United States of America

Contents

Preface

S ince antiquity there have been women scientists, physicians, engineers, and inventors contributing to knowledge and progress in their fields. Generally speaking, these women are not widely known, and such biographical material as exists is in most cases sparse, widely scattered, and in many instances difficult to locate. This biographical directory has been organized in an effort to make information on these women scientists more widely and readily accessible. We hope that it will enable readers to locate information on women scientists of the world easily and quickly.

This index provides information and biographical references for approximately 2500 of the many thousands of women who have worked in and contributed to the development of science, medical knowledge, engineering, and technology from the earliest recorded times to the present.

The main section of this book comprises an alphabetical index listing women scientists with attendant information on each. It is preceded by (1) a bibliography and source abbreviation key to approximately 130 works to which the reader is referred for further specific information on these women, and (2) a brief listing of coded notes dealing with specialized biographical information. The book concludes with a comprehensive index of women scientists rearranged according to fields of specialization.

In the main section, the primary listing of each individual's name is alphabetical, with cross references to accommodate variations in spelling, marital surnames, pseudonyms, etc. An additional unit of information provides scientific field identifications. (Because of space limitations, this has in most cases been limited to the two or three most significant areas of scientific work.)

Dates of birth or approximate dates of scientific activity are given for each scientist. In the case of many women scientists of the past, this information is of necessity imprecise, and in a number of instances only the century is listed. It should be noted in particular that the entry (1900s) refers to all of the twentieth century, and includes contemporary women scientists whose dates of birth were not readily available at the time of compilation of the index. In a number of cases, however, this information may be available in other reference sources.

For each woman scientist, nationality or nationalities are given as precisely as possible. Each entry also provides from one to at most five alphanumerically coded references to biographical information sources. The approximately 130 references to which these refer are listed following the Introduction.

Finally, some entries give coded notes that facilitate identification of certain subsets of women scientists (such as minority women scientists or women members of the National Academy of Sciences). A key to abbreviations for this information appears on page *xxxix*.

Most of the many thousands of women working in science today are obviously not included in this limited listing. Emphasis has been on historical coverage, including those early women scientists for whom some biographical information is reasonably accessible. Women scientists from the United States are more fully represented in this listing than women scientists from other countries because of more readily available biographical information on them. However, an effort has been made to incorporate an international representation of women scientists. A sampling of today's women scientists is also present. This includes some especially prominent present-day scientists, some minority women scientists, some disabled or handicapped women scientists, and some women scientists notable for particular achievements or unusual activities.

This biographical directory has been designed to be extensive, not intensive; that is, the objective has been to provide the user with several biographical references for each of a relatively large number of women scientists rather than giving comprehensive listings of biographical materials for a small number of more well-known women scientists. In regard to biographical material, I have referenced primarily those sources containing biographical or related material on many women scientists, and have not extended the bibliographical references to include many of the books and articles dealing with single scientists (e.g., full-length individual biographies). Accordingly, the biographical references generally provide starter material, and are in no sense complete. Some of the references contain biographies or biographical sketches; in other cases the reference is to a more limited account of some aspect of the life or scientific accomplishments of the individual. For those women scientists who are listed in this index with at least three references, there is in many cases an appreciable amount of additional uncoded biographical material in other books or articles listed in the references section.

In general I have attempted to refer the user to materials that are reasonably accessible in larger libraries, although some references to more recondite materials are included. In most cases the materials referenced are books rather than journal articles. I have intentionally included in the references several books suitable for younger readers, and also a number of popular books and articles as well as more scholarly studies.

Creation of this index has resulted from the confluence of several activities. These include the collection of materials on women scientists (particularly women physicists) while I was a member of the American Physical Society Committee on the Status of Women in Physics; preparation of systematized materials on prominent living American women scientists for the Association for Women in Science while I served as a national officer; and, most recently, development of information on women scientists in connection with an exhibit on women in science while I served as a member of the Museum Exhibit Committee of the Association for Women in Science Chicago Area Chapter. Had it not been necessary to keep track of the women scientists proposed for the museum exhibit, this index in all likelihood would never have been assembled.

I would like to express my gratitude to members of the Association for Women in Science Chicago Area Chapter and in particular to past and present members of the AWIS-CAC Museum Exhibit Committee, not only for stimulating and sustaining my interest in early women scientists, but also for bringing to my attention some of the initial entries that formed the original core of this listing. I am also very grateful to the members of my family and to many friends and colleagues for their continuing interest and helpfulness. I am especially indebted to colleagues in the Energy and Environmental Systems Division of Argonne National Laboratory for their continuing assistance and supportiveness in connection with this study.

It is clear that not all of the women scientists who might be included in an index such as this have been entered into this initial list. I would appreciate users bringing to my attention suggested additional entries as well as corrections, further information, and other suggested changes.

Caroline L. Herzenberg
Argonne National Laboratory
Argonne, IL 60439
August 1985

Introduction:
Early Women Scientists and Engineers

C ould you, if asked, identify several prominent contemporary women scientists? Could you identify a woman scientist who lived before the time of Marie Curie? Most people could not, and neither could many scientists or engineers.

There is thus a widespread impression that there were no women actively engaged in science or engineering prior to relatively modern times. It may therefore come as a surprise to learn that there have been women practicing science for well over 3000 years, and that among these women were included a number of prominent scientists, even world-class scientists.

Science during this long stretch of time, which in the past has usually been regarded as substantially devoid of women participants, actually benefited from the contributions of many women scientists. During recent years, over 1000 early women scientists have been identified, and they as well as some notable contemporary women scientists are included in this index, which we anticipate will help to provide information to permit us to start examining systematically some aspects of this previously largely overlooked chapter in the history of science.

The earliest evidence of women engaged in activities relating to science dates back about 6000 years. Very little is known of these women, in many instances not even their names, but many of them were physicians. (For example, in the Musée du Louvre, there is a stone carving depicting a Sumerian priestess–physician, dating from about 4000 B.C. An illustration of this is reproduced in *A History of Women in Medicine*, Reference K.) Most of these women lived in the Middle East (or Near East or eastern Mediterranean region), although there is some evidence of women engaged in activities relating to science in the Far East (chiefly in China and India) during antiquity.

Perhaps the earliest woman in the medical sciences to be recorded by name was Merit Ptah, who lived in Egypt around 2700 B.C. Her picture is in a tomb in the Valley of the Kings. Her son, a High Priest, described her as the "Chief Physician."

The earliest woman active in the physical sciences and engineering whose name has come down to us is Tapputi-Belatekallim, a Babylonian chemist (or perhaps we should refer to her as a chemical engineer), who lived around 1200 B.C. Her name, and what we know about her work, is recorded in cuneiform writing on clay tablets. Tapputi worked in the chemistry and chemical technology of perfume production in ancient Mesopotamia, and the second part of her name indicates that she was the chief chemist or chemical engineer, the authority in charge of the operations. The cuneiform records indicate that she had worked out the various steps of preparation by her own methods. Interestingly enough, Tapputi was not an isolated example of a woman chemist in Mesopotamia: other cuneiform records refer to another woman chemist in the perfume industry (who was the author of an ancient text on perfume production), whose name is partially obliterated on the clay tablets. It appears that there may have been an accepted role for women in chemical technology in Mesopotamia already by 1200 B.C. As we shall see, women have had a share in the development of chemistry from Babylonian times onward.

It may come as a surprise to many readers to find out that there is historical evidence to indicate that two of those great architectural and engineering structures of the ancient world, the Seven Wonders of the Ancient World, were built by women, and that women not only commissioned these structures, but may also have participated in their design. Some historical authorities credit Queen Semiramis, who lived around 800 B.C., with building the famous Hanging Gardens of Babylon, as well as with being associated with various other achievements in engineering and technology. Another great queen of antiquity, Artemisia of Caria, who lived around 300 B.C., built in Halicarnassus (in present-day Turkey) another of the Seven Wonders of the Ancient World, the monumental Mausoleum of Halicarnassus, in honor of her dead husband Mausolus. Artemisia was also one of the outstanding botanists of antiquity, as well as a medical researcher and a scholar. (She discovered a number of plants, and is even today remembered and honored in the name of the plant genus Artemisia, which includes sagebrush and tarragon among its better–known species.)

Information about the women scientists who lived during early antiquity is very scarce. But even recording systematically the names of these women scientists (and engineers, inventors, and physicians), together with their fields and approximate dates, as has been done in this index, enables us to obtain a count of the number of notable women scientists during every century. This provides us with a measure, albeit an unsophisticated one, of the participation of women in science as a function of time. As an introduction, we will look into the general trends and the specific features of the number of women scientists as a function of time in their historical and sociological context while also looking at the lives of some specific women scientists who lived during ancient and medieval times.

Throughout early antiquity up until about 500 B.C., at most one or rarely two women scientists have been identified during each century. The number of notable women scientists, after starting at these very low levels in early antiquity, went up dramatically at around 600 B.C., peaked at around 450 B.C., and dropped off again around 200 B.C. This reflects the rise in Greek science and culture, and specifically reflects the rise of the Pythagoreans, followed later by the Platonists. Both of these major groups encouraged the participation of women, and provided a social context in which women were able to engage in academic pursuits, including science. The falloff in the number of women scientists around 200 B.C. reflects the decline in classical Greek culture at that time.

Let us now look at some of the women scientists from the Hellenic period. During the sixth century B.C., the philosophical school of Pythagoras, which developed in southern Italy, created a favorable social climate in which at least some women could pursue an academic career. The Pythagorean school, in addition to being an academy for the study of mathematics, philosophy, and natural science, also developed an order with secret rites and observances. The Pythagorean order came to the conclusion early that numerical relationships were at the basis of natural phenomena, and thus mathematics was fundamental to their philosophy. In addition to their emphasis on mathematics, the Pythagoreans studied many other areas of knowledge, including astronomy, music and acoustics, and medicine. Women were substantially equal members (as scholars and teachers, as well as students) of the Pythagorean school. The Pythagorean women philosophers and mathematicians were so numerous that a book was later written about them by Philochorus the Athenian during the third century BC. (This, unfortunately, has been lost, like so many manuscripts of antiquity.) Prominent among the women of the Pythagorean school was Theano, wife and former student of Pythagoras, who became a teacher in the Pythagorean school. Like many Pythagorean women, she was interested in the study of mathematics, physics, and medicine, in addition to child psychology, and she wrote several treatises on these subjects. One of her treatises contained the principle of the "Golden Mean," celebrated as a major contribution of Greek thought to the evolution of social philosophy. Theano assumed leadership of the Pythagorean school following the death of Pythagoras, and some of their children, including two of their daughters, also carried on the work of the Pythagorean school, helping to spread the system of thought that was developed there. The customs and practices of the Pythagorean philosophy were thus spread to greater Greece and to Egypt by teachers of both sexes, and, as we shall see, had considerable influence, notably on the schools of such mentors as Plato and Aristotle.

At about the same time, at Sais in Egypt, by about 500 B.C. there was a fine medical school with a women's section dealing specifically with gynecology and obstetrics, and here women were faculty members as well as medical students.

Arete of Cyrene was a prominent scientist and a younger contemporary of Socrates who lived around 400 B.C. in North Africa. She wrote extensively on physics and other fields of science. Like many of the women scientists of antiquity, Arete was a member of a family of scientists and philosophers. Her father, Aristippos of Cyrene, was one of Socrates' pupils and was the founder of the Cyreniac school of philosophy. Her son, Aristippos the Younger, continued the family tradition of teaching hedonistic and rationalist philosophy. Arete became the head of the Cyreniac school of philosophy after the death of her father; historical records credit Arete with teaching science and philosophy for 35 years, and indicate that she wrote 40 books and counted among her students 110 philosophers. She was so highly esteemed by her fellow citizens that they had inscribed on her tomb an epitaph which declared that she was the splendor of Greece and possessed the beauty of Helen, the virtue of Thirma, the soul of Socrates, and the tongue of Homer. Such an outpouring of appreciation was phenomenal; although there were important exceptions, women scientists were not always highly regarded by their fellow citizens, and, as we shall see, some women scientists of antiquity and the Middle Ages even became martyrs.

While most Greek women were kept in enforced seclusion and did not participate in the intellectual fervor of the Hellenic age, there were a number of women active in science during the fourth and third centuries B.C. A number of these women were associated with Plato's Academy, which was founded on lines partly suggested by the Pythagorean societies that Plato had seen in southern Italy. Plato had a deep appreciation for the intelligence of women and attempted to give women a more equal position of responsibility; his writings indicate that he thought that women should receive an education, which should include subjects such as mathematics and astronomy. Plato's attitude made his school accessible and appealing to women. Women, in defiance of a law forbidding their attendance at public meetings, were numerous in Plato's Academy in Athens, where the most important mathematical work of the 4th century B.C. was done. These women include Diotima, Perictione, and Aspasia, who were primarily philosophers but also engaged in scientific work. Aspasia of Miletus was one of the most remarkable women of antiquity. Most of the famous philosophers and intellectuals of the period were friends and associates of Aspasia. She was one of Socrates' teachers, and it is believed that she strongly influenced his ideas and those of Plato. In addition, she convinced Pericles, ruler of Athens, that women should not be denied opportunity for intellectual development.

Another significant woman scientist of antiquity was Pythias of Assos, who was both the wife of Aristotle (384–322 B.C.) and an important marine zoologist of antiquity. Pythias was the niece and adopted daughter of Hermeias, a financier who became a student of Plato and a philosopher. Pythias' outlook must have been affected by the tragic life of her adopted father, who was a eunuch, and who met his death by crucifixion while Aristotle was staying with them in Assos.

Aristotle and his wife Pythias wrote an encyclopedia incorporating research in botany, biology, and physiology they had done while honeymooning on the island of Mytilene. (While Pythias did not specifically lend her signature to her part of these studies, Aristotle himself claimed that she was his assistant.) Pythias diligently gathered a wide spectrum of living things for examination, thereby nurturing a specialty in histology and embryology; she and Aristotle both took a keen interest in the study of generation as well. Together they wrote books on generation and histology, advancing a theory of the embryo and fertilization based on careful observation of the eggs of most vertebrates, as well as arachnids and insects. It is noteworthy that they conducted their studies with a depth of logic that largely made up for their lack of modern instruments such as the microscope. Aristotle and Pythias had a daughter who was also named Pythias; one wonders if she also became an active scientist like her parents.

The earliest woman astronomer whose name has come down to us is Aglaonice, daughter of Hegetoris of Thessaly. This Greek woman was able to predict eclipses by means of the lunar cycle referred to as the Saros, a period discovered by the Chaldean astronomers, which extends a little over 18 years, during which the eclipses of the moon and sun recur in nearly the same order as during the preceding period. The people among whom Aglaonice lived regarded her as a sorceress, but her accomplishments qualify her as an astronomer of antiquity.

As we have seen, the number of women scientists rose dramatically during those few hundred years of antiquity when some centers of learning were present which offered a social environment in which conditions of equal opportunity prevailed. Following this period of intellectual excitement and intellectual accomplishment, a drop in the number of women scientists began during the second century B.C. This decrease in the number of women scientists started at about the time of the decline of Hellenism and the rise of the Roman Empire (150 B.C.). Subsequently the number of women scientists rose again and reached a plateau (of about the same level as during the classical Hellenic period) which extended, dropping off slowly until about the fifth century A.D. This latter time period corresponds approximately to the period of the Neopythagoreans and Neoplatonists.

A notable feature of this period of antiquity was the many women alchemists who flourished from perhaps a century or so before the birth of Christ to about 300 A.D. Outstanding among these women alchemists was Mary the Jewess, also known as Maria of Alexandria. She was a world–famous alchemist in her day, and she is celebrated as the inventor of several types of apparatus for distillation and sublimation which revolutionized alchemy and possibly even preceded alchemy and made it possible. Maria was the first person to describe the still, the basic equipment for distillation, in the chemical literature, and thus to make the construction and use of stills widely known. Maria was highly inventive and deeply interested in chemical experiments and the instruments that made them effective and precise. She invented or elaborated all of the essential equipment with which alchemy or chemistry was to carry on for more than 1000 years. In particular, she seems to have invented the water bath, which even to this day honors her name in French-speaking countries, where this particular piece of equipment is called a *Bain-Marie*, and also in Spanish-speaking countries, where it is called *Baño de Maria*. Maria was a real instrumentalist and developing equipment was her forte. But in addition she seems to have made significant chemical discoveries, and she was a prolific author. Unfortunately, all of her many manuscripts have been lost, but they are referred to and quoted frequently in the writings of the other major alchemists of antiquity.

There were at least 25 other women alchemists active during the several centuries around the birth of Christ. These included a woman alchemist named Cleopatra, who played a significant role in early chemistry by her emphasis on the importance of weighing, so that she led the way toward quantitative work in chemistry. Cleopatra was the author of a treatise on weights and measures. (It is the portions of her manuscripts dealing with efforts to transmute other metals to gold that are usually reproduced or referred to in books on the history of early chemistry, however.)

During the thousand years centered on the birth of Christ, there were on the average about 13 notable women scientists per century. Lifetimes were shorter then, and if we take 40 years as an estimate of a life span, there would have been on the average about 5 notable women scientists alive simultaneously throughout the world. Clearly, that did not provide much opportunity for a mentor relationship between outstanding women. However, as we have seen, women scientists during antiquity tended to cluster in supportive social environments or were found in family groupings of scientists and philosophers.

The world population has been estimated to have been about 250 million at the beginning of the Christian era. Thus, notable women scientists were present at a level of the order of 0.02 parts per million in the population as a whole. (The population of women scientists was generally growing faster than the population at large—prior to the year 1750, perhaps at four times the rate of growth of the population as a whole. During the recent past, of course, the population of women scientists has increased extremely rapidly.)

One of the universal geniuses of antiquity, and the last great woman scientist of antiquity, was a woman named Hypatia, who was born around 370 A.D. in Alexandria, Egypt. Alexandria at the time was a great center of Greek intellectual life and was a cosmopolitan center of learning where scholars from all over the Roman Empire gathered to exchange ideas. Hypatia's father, Theon, was a distinguished professor of mathematics and astronomy at the University of Alexandria, and later headed the university. Hypatia's parents attempted to educate and develop their daughter to intellectual perfection. After a very thorough formal education, Hypatia travelled abroad and then returned to lecture on philosophy, mathematics, and astronomy at the University of Alexandria, where she attracted great numbers of students.

Hypatia was able to make contributions to the fields of mathematics, philosophy, physics, and astronomy, surpassing her famous father's accomplishments. She wrote several treatises of which only fragments remain. In addition to two mathematical works, a treatise on the Conics of Apollonius, and a commentary on the Arithmetica of Diophantus (which was actually a treatise on algebra), she also coauthored (with her father) at least one treatise on Euclid. Hypatia also wrote commentaries on the "Almagest," the astronomical canon of Ptolemy that contained his numerous observations on the stars. The philosopher Synesius of Cyrene, who was one of her pupils, credited her with the development of instrumentation and devices for astronomy and navigation, including a planesphere and an astrolabe; Synesius also requested her assistance in the construction of equipment including a hydrometer for measuring the specific gravity of liquids, and credited her with the invention of apparatus for distilling water and for measuring the level of liquids. In addition, Hypatia was recognized as the head of the Neoplatonist school of philosophy in Alexandria, and major scholars of the time corresponded with her and came to Alexandria to confer with her.

Hypatia's personal life was so dramatic that her life and times have been romanticized in a historical novel. She seems to have been not only an immensely learned woman, but also beautiful, eloquent, charming, and widely admired. Her home, as well as her lecture hall, was frequented by the most outstanding scholars and was, along with the library and the museum of Alexandria, one of the most remarkable intellectual centers in a city of great learning. She had connections in the highest circles, not only scientific and literary, but also among the ruling elite of Egypt. She moved among men with great freedom and had numerous love affairs but never married. (To the offers of marriage she received from princes and philosophers, Hypatia supposedly answered that she was "wedded to the truth.") As a Greek pagan philosopher and scientist, Hypatia was in a dangerous position in the Alexandria of her time, which was a city in officially Christian Egypt, a part of the Roman Empire. As the end of the Roman Empire approached, the pagan Greeks in Alexandria had become scapegoats for the growing frustrations of the Romans. Tensions and riots between Christians and non-Christians repeatedly racked Alexandria. Although Hypatia had

Christian friends and followers, most notable of whom was Synesius (who had become bishop of Ptolemais), she was highly visible as a pagan Greek intellectual, who was defiant of Christian theology. In 412 A.D., a new patriarch of Alexandria named Cyril was designated who regarded Neoplatonism as heretical, and he began a systematic oppression of the Neoplatonists. Because Hypatia was the head of the Neoplatonist school of philosophy in Alexandria (and perhaps also because of her friendship with Orestes, the ruler of Egypt, who was a power threat to Cyril), Hypatia was targeted and became a victim of the religious and political conflict. Hypatia's life had a violent end. She was killed brutally; while on her way to lecture at the university she was dragged from her chariot by a fanatical sectarian mob of Cyril's followers and was barbarously mutilated and tortured to death. Edward Gibbon described her end in *The Decline and Fall of the Roman Empire*: she was "inhumanly butchered by the hands . . . of a troop of savage and merciless fanatics: torn from her chariot, stripped naked, dragged to the church" and there "her flesh was scraped from her bones and her quivering limbs were delivered to the flames."

The death of Hypatia and the burning of much of the great library of Alexandria, which occurred at about the same time and resulted in great loss of knowledge about the science and technology of antiquity, marked the end of the Alexandrian period and of Alexandria as a center of intellectual culture, and also marked the beginning of the Dark Ages.

Following Hypatia's death, a world-wide decline in science and learning set in, and continued for several centuries through most of the western world. During this intellectually barren period known as the Dark Ages, which started with the fall of the Roman Empire in the fifth century, the last vestiges of the civilization of antiquity faded away, and Europe remained shrouded in intellectual obscurity for the next four centuries or so, until about 1000 A.D. This was a time of economic recession, of political discord and barbaric customs, during which civilization in Europe reached a very low ebb. The Dark Ages constituted the beginning of the Middle Ages.

During this period, when intellectual life in much of the civilized world almost came to a halt, the number of women in science dropped to a level almost as low as during the centuries of early antiquity before the classic Hellenic age. It is interesting that during those centuries of the Dark Ages when the representation of women in science was at its lowest, those few notable women we find were physicians, and no other areas of scientific or engineering activity than medical sciences were represented. Medicine seems to be a "beachhead" field in science both in time and space for populations of women with scientific inclinations; we find that many of the earliest women in distant antiquity were active in the medical sciences, as have been many of the earliest women in science in developing countries; and during the Dark Ages, medicine seems to have provided a transitional field for women when other areas of the sciences were at a low ebb.

In the eleventh and twelfth centuries, Europe roused from its intellectual slumber. There was a tremendous shift of populations, leading to the clearing of new land, the growth of towns, the establishment of religious orders, the Crusades, and the building of cathedrals. Commerce revived and led to international contact through which the West was made familiar with Arabic and Moslem science, as well as the Greek classics in science.

At around 1000 A.D. the number of notable women scientists started to increase again, marking the rise of European science from the Dark Ages. This increase in the population of women scientists started in Italy and gradually spread to northern Europe (as indeed was the case with science as a whole).

It was in Italy, in Salerno, that one of the most famous women physicians, Trotula, seems to have flourished around 1000 A.D. Trotula Platearius appears to have practiced and written in collaboration with her husband Giovanni Platearius and one of her sons, who was a surgeon. They compiled an encyclopedia of medicine, *Practica Brevis*, and a guide to the preparation of medicines, *De Compositione Medicamentorum*. Trotula was a leading gynecologist and obstetrician who also made a special study of dermatology and epilepsy. She seems to have been especially noted for a diagnostic method which depended upon skillful questioning allied to close observation and experience to recognize symptoms, since the rules of the chuch forbade dissection, and, therefore, precluded much knowledge of pathology. She was a widely acclaimed professor of medicine, considered one of the most knowledgeable members of the faculty at the university. Her world-wide fame developed in part because of her outstanding and much-copied book on obstetrics and gynecology, *De Mulierum Passionibus* (*On the Suffering of Women*), which was known and widely used throughout western Europe during the Middle Ages.

What have been called the greatest scientific works of the Middle Ages were written by Saint Hildegard of Bingen, a German abbess who lived during the twelfth century. Hildegard was an authority in the medical sciences and was the most distinguished naturalist of her century. She was also a religious visionary, a philosopher, and a politician.

Hildegard was born in the year 1098 at Boeckelhein, near the Rhine River. The youngest child in a large noble family, she was sent at the age of eight to a convent to study, convents being practically the only place where a girl could become educated during the Middle Ages. She spent almost her entire life in Benedictine convents, and as an adult she was abbess of a convent on a hilltop overlooking the Rhine River. From there she travelled on horseback, accompanied by groups of nuns and servants, throughout Germany and France to teach about science, medicine, and theology in monasteries and other church institutions. She corresponded with popes and emperors, sometimes influencing their actions. (She predicted the downfall of the Holy Roman Empire and also predicted the coming of the reformation as a consequence of the corruption of the clergy of the Catholic Church.) Hildegard was not only gifted with a phenomenal intellect but also possessed great energy. She was the author of 14 works, some in several volumes. Her books cover a wide range of topics: medical and psychological treatises, treatises on natural history, works on religious instruction, accounts of her visions and prophecies. She wrote in depth on subjects including zoology, botany, folk medicine, psychology, and human anatomy. Hildegard relied considerably upon her own direct observations, which in some instances were unusually accurate, and she set a precedent by dealing with earlier authorities in a somewhat cavalier manner. It is evident that her contemporaries regarded her with great reverence; otherwise she would have been accused of heretical teachings. Hildegard's work foreshadowed such later discoveries as the circulation of the blood, the causes of contagion and autointoxication, nerve action originating in the brain, and the chemistry of the blood. Some of Hildegard's books are beautifully illustrated, particularly those that deal with her visions, some of which incorporate scientific material. (In her work entitled the "Scivias," in which she wrote about and illustrated her visions, there is an impressionistic depiction of the solar system, which incorporates the planets of our solar system and the sun and the moon in a geocentric arrangement, which was the accepted astronomy of Hildegard's time. However, elsewhere in her writings Hildegard described the sun as "in the center of the firmament" and appears to have anticipated the heliocentric system.) After a long and extremely productive life, Hildegard died in 1178. She was known for centuries as the Sibyl of the Rhine and was called Saint Hildegard, although she was never canonized.

Herrade of Landsberg was a contemporary and friend of Hildegard and, like her, was noted for her culture and wide range of knowledge. Herrade was abbess of Hohenburg in Alsace. Her abbey was high in the Vosges mountains between Basel and Mainz and was surrounded by other monasteries and castles. In 1167, Herrade was already noted as a teacher of all medieval academic subjects, including medicine and other sciences. In 1187 she built a large hospital in her convent at which she was physician-in-chief. Herrade wrote one of the earliest encyclopedias, called *Hortus Deliciarum* or *Garden of Delight*. This was a remarkable work, encyclopedic in character, which was designed to embody in words and pictures the knowledge of her age. This extraordinary work, which has given us the finest record of the technology of the Middle Ages, was written in Latin on 324 pages of parchment with 636 colored drawings. It included topics from methods of measurement to agriculture, emphasizing plants and their uses, and exhibited the enormous range of knowledge of its author. This priceless volume was destroyed in 1870 during the siege of Strasburg, with the exception of a few pages; fortunately, it had been partially copied at an earlier time. Herrade's writings and illustrations provide us with much of our current knowledge of the technology of the Middle Ages.

The next outstanding woman mathematician and also probably the most learned woman physician in France during the twelfth century was Héloise. But most people who have heard of Héloise know her only as the heroine of one of the most famous love stories of all time. The story of the passionate love affair between Héloise, as an outstandingly brilliant 18-year-old student, and her tutor, the 40-year-old nobleman Abélard, is almost as well known as the story of Romeo and Juliet, and tends to overshadow the fact that, at the same time, Héloise was going through the equivalent of a graduate course in medicine, surgery, theology, and philosophy. Héloise and Abélard were in fact among the foremost intellectuals and scholars of the twelfth century. The love affair of Héloise and Abélard resulted in the birth of a child, whom they named Astrolabe. (That they considered this name of an astronomical instrument a suitable name for a child suggests a mutual interest in astronomy as well.) However, premarital sex was not looked upon permissively by their contemporaries, and Abélard was castrated in punishment. He subsequently entered a monastery, and Héloise entered a convent. For 20 years after the couple's separation, she taught and practiced medicine at the Paraclete, a hermitage for women in France, where she became abbess. Héloise, a woman of science as well as a romantic heroine, died in the year 1164.

During the 1300s in Italy there were numerous women scientists, particularly in the medical sciences, and they were frequently associated with universities. In Bologna, there were generally women on the staff of the university. Among the more famous of these was Dorothea Bucca, who in 1390 was appointed professor of medicine and moral philosophy, succeeding her father. She subsequently taught at the University of Bologna for forty years. Another famous woman at the university, who distinguished herself in anatomy during the early part of the fourteenth century, was Alessandra Giliani. She was the assistant of Mondino, the founder of modern anatomy. In addition to possessing great skill in dissection, Giliani devised a way of extracting the blood from even the smallest veins and arteries then filling them with variously colored liquids which solidified quickly. By this means she was able to exhibit the circulatory system in all its details and complexity and to have available, for purposes of instruction, an anatomical model that was absolutely true to nature. Perhaps Alessandra Giliani is the young woman who appears in a woodcut made in 1318 which shows the anatomist Mondino sitting in a high chair explaining a dissection on a table below, while a long-haired girl performs the dissection and demonstrates the organs of an anatomical subject. When Giliani died in 1326, a tablet to her memory and skill was placed in the hospital church of Santa Maria de Mereto in Florence; it tells us that her lover (himself an anatomist) was so grieved at her death that he also had a swift and lamentable death.

Following the time of Héloise and Hildegard, and the golden age of scholasticism during the thirteenth century, came the Renaissance, a period of great revival of art, literature, and science in Europe. The Renaissance, which overlapped the time period of the late Middle Ages, began in the 1300s and extended to the 1600s and marked the transition from the medieval to the modern world. The Renaissance started in Italy, where educated women of ability tended to be treated by men as equals, and continued into northern Europe, bringing a great resurgence in science. We might have expected a rapid rise in the number of women active in science during the Renaissance, but, somewhat surprisingly, the data do not show this. The number of women scientists in this index continues to rise after the time of Héloise and Hildegard and peaks during the golden age of scholasticism in the 1200s, but then it decreases again during the Renaissance and does not rise again appreciably for nearly 400 years. What could account for this apparent decline in the participation of women in science during a period of such a great resurgence in intellectual activity as the Renaissance?

We may speculate that there are several different effects here which relate to changes in the number of women scientists. For one thing, the Black Death, a form of bubonic plague, spread over Europe and killed an estimated one quarter to one third of the population during the 1300s. For another, the Hundred Years War, the series of wars between England and France, extended from 1337 to 1453 and may have contributed to a reduction in the level of scientific activity. The closing of convents reduced the opportunities for women to study and practice science, but this did not occur extensively until after the start of the Reformation during the sixteenth century. But a countervailing effect was the invention of printing: during the middle years of the fifteenth century, while Europe was recovering from the physical and spiritual shock of the Black Death, the then-recent invention of printing with movable type made it possible for scientific works to become much more widely available than ever before. The earliest printed book from western Europe is dated 1447, and by the end of the fifteenth century, over 30,000 editions of various works were available. Of these, few were scientific, but these few, coupled with existing manuscripts, provided a base for expansion.

Finally, and probably uniquely important to the participation of women in science, the persecution of women as witches occurred throughout Europe during the time period from about 1300 through the 1600s. It has been stated that the worst peril that women physicians were exposed to from the 1300s onward was that of being accused of witchcraft, and it would surely be surprising if women alchemists, for example, were in less peril. The pursuit of witches reached such intensity that it has been estimated that in the 1600s, no less than 40,000 women accused of witchcraft were executed and many more were tortured. It is against this background of religious bigotry and persecution as well as more mundane forms of sex discrimination that women worked in the sciences through the late Middle Ages and Renaissance, even well into the seventeenth century. Only the most brilliant and fortunate were able to survive and contribute to progress in science and technology, and even many of these outstanding women were not safe from persecution.

We now come to a final historical example of a woman who was both a scientist and an engineer, and who was a transitional figure between the late Middle Ages and the Enlightenment.

Martine de Bertereau du Châtelet was a French woman who was a mineralogist and a mining engineer during the early 1600s. She married Jean du Châtelet, Baron de Beausoleil in 1610 and became the Baroness of Beausoleil; they had a daughter, Anne. Martine de Beausoleil explored mineral deposits and visited mines and travelled with her husband in Germany, Sweden, and America for 16 years following her marriage. On her return to France, she wrote several important treatises on mining engineering. But the story of this extraordinary woman is told in perhaps the most interesting manner in the quaint language of a book published nearly 80 years ago (Mozans' *Woman in Science*, Reference Z):

> Yet as early as the first half of the seventeenth century, the Baroness of Beausoleil had achieved a great reputation by her investigations into the mineral treasures of France. Indeed, she may, strange as it may appear, be regarded as the first mining engineer of her native land. She details the qualifications of a mining engineer and tells us that he must, among other things, be well versed in chemistry, mineralogy, geometry, mechanics, and hydraulics. As for herself, she assures us that she devoted thirty years of study to these divers branches. To Mme. de Beausoleil is also attributed the glory of awakening her countrymen's interest in the mineral resources of France, and of showing them how their proper exploitation would inure not only to the credit of the nation abroad but also to its prosperity at home. She was the author of two works which prove that she was a woman of rare attainments combined with exceptional breadth of view and political acumen. She was deeply concerned in the development of the mineral resources of her country and foresaw how greatly they could be made to contribute to the augmentation of the nation's finances. Her work entitled *La Restitution de Pluton* is a report on the mines and ore deposits of France, and is a document as precious as it is curious. It was addressed to Cardinal Richelieu, and shows how the French monarch could, if the subterranean treasures of the country were properly developed, become the greatest ruler in Christendom and his subjects the happiest of all peoples. Another report by this energetic and enthusiastic woman is in the same strain. In it she proves how the king of France, by utilizing the underground riches of his country, could make himself and his people independent of all other nations. In these two productions Mme. de Beausoleil treats of the science of mining, the different kinds of mines, the assaying of ores and the divers method of smelting them, as well as of the general principles of metallurgy, as then understood. But, unlike the majority of

her contemporaries, this enlightened woman had no patience with those who believed that the earth's hidden treasures could not be discovered without recourse to magic or to the aid of demons. She was unsparing in her ridicule of those who had faith in the existence of gnomes and kobolds, or thought that ore deposits could be located only by divining rods or similar foolish contrivances which were relics of an ignorant and superstitious age.

It is sad that the end of Martine de Beausoleil's life provides a bitter and ironic commentary on the age in which she lived. Although Martine herself was an eminently rational, empirical, modern individual, most of her contemporaries were not. As mentioned earlier, during the early 1600s, there was still a widespread belief in witchcraft, and women who were different provoked fear and condemnation and often became the targets of hysterical witch hunts. In 1642, Martine du Châtelet was imprisoned for witchcraft in Vincennes, a suburb of Paris. She died in prison later that year.

Martine de Beausoleil's death marks a transition, not only in the history of women in science and engineering, but also in the history of science as a whole: the year in which she died in prison, 1642, is also the year in which Galileo died, and the year in which Newton was born. The world was changing, and becoming more rational, and within 50 years after Martine de Beausoleil's death, the societal craziness of witchhunting had diminished and largely ended. Women still had to contend with many less virulent forms of persecution, and the best education for girls was still widely regarded as no education at all. But as time went on there were more and more women educators and educated women, and during the 1700s there were a number of outstanding women scientists, the immediate predecessors of the many women scientists and engineers of the 1800s.

Today we can look back with appreciation to the early women pioneers of science and engineering who lived and worked during the difficult past. In all the diversity of their lives, their extraordinary activity, their individuality, their passion, they succeeded in establishing a presence and a tradition of their own in science and technology, and in contributing to progress in their fields, which has been continued by the many women scientists and engineers of today.

REFERENCES

Bibliography and Source Abbreviation Key

A   Jaques Cattell Press, ed. *American Men and Women of Science*. 15th ed. New York: R.R. Bowker Company, 1982.

A1   *American Men of Science*. Editions preceding 1944.

A2   Aykroyd, W.R. *Three Philosophers*. Westport, CT: Greenwood Press, 1970.

A3   Holmyard, E.J. *Alchemy*. Baltimore: Penguin Books, Inc., 1957.

A4   Lindsay, Jack. *The Origins of Alchemy in Graeco-Roman Egypt*. London: Frederick Muller Ltd., 1970.

A5   Taton, René, ed. *History of Science--Ancient and Medieval Science*. Trans. by A.J. Pomerans. New York: Basic Books, Inc., 1963.

B   National Academy of Sciences of the United States of America. *Biographical Memoirs*. Washington, D.C.: National Academy Press, 1877-1983.

B1   Macksey, Joan, and Kenneth Macksey. *The Book of Women's Achievements*. New York: Stein and Day, 1976.

B2   Hall, Diana Long. "Academics, Bluestockings, and Biologists: Women at the University of Chicago 1892-1932." In Briscoe, Anne M., and Sheila M. Pfafflin, eds. "Expanding the Role of Women in the Sciences." *Annals of the New York Academy of Sciences*, Vol. 323 (1979).

B3   Young, Herman A., and Barbara H. Young. *Scientists in the Black Perspective*. Louisville, KY: The Lincoln Foundation, 1974.

B4   Jorpes, J. Erik. *Jac. Berzelius: His Life and Work*. Berkeley: University of California Press, 1970.

B5   O'Hern, Elizabeth M. "Women Scientists in Microbiology."
      Bioscience, Vol. 23, No. 9 (September 1973), pp. 539–543.

B6   Whitrow, Magda, ed. *Isis Cumulative Bibliography*.
      London: Mansell/The History of Science Society, 1971.

C   Turkevich, John, and Ludmilla B. Turkevich. *Prominent
      Scientists of Continental Europe*. New York: Elsevier,
      1968.

C1   McDowell, Barbara, and Hana Umlauf, eds. *Women's Al-
      manac*. New York: Newspaper Enterprise Association,
      Inc., 1977.

C2   Peavy, Linda, and Ursula Smith. *Women Who Changed
      Things*. New York: Scribner, 1983.

C3   Noble, Iris. *Contemporary Women Scientists of America*.
      New York: Julian Meissner, 1979.

C4   Downs, Robert B. *Landmarks in Science--Hippocrates to
      Carson*. Littleton, CO: Libraries Unlimited, Inc., 1982.

C5   Houlihan, Sherida, and John H. Wotiz. "Women in Chemis-
      try Before 1900." *Journal of Chemical Education*, Vol.
      52, No. 6 (June 1975), pp. 362–364.

C6   Bishop, Lloyd O., and Will S. DeLoach. "Marie Meurdrac--
      First Lady of Chemistry?" *Journal of Chemical Education*,
      Vol. 47, No. 6 (June 1970), pp. 448–449.

C7   Armstrong, Eva V. "Jane Marcet and Her 'Conversations
      on Chemistry.'" *Journal of Chemical Education*, Vol. 15
      (1938), pp. 53–57.

C8   Read, John. *Prelude to Chemistry*. London: Oldbourne
      Book Co., Ltd., 1961.

C9   Levey, Martin. "Babylonian Chemists." In Farber,
      Eduard. *Great Chemists*. New York: Interscience Pub-
      lishers, 1961.

D   Gillispie, C.C., ed. *Dictionary of Scientific Biog-
      raphy*. New York: Scribner, 1970–1980.

D1   Lovejoy, Esther Pohl. *Women Doctors of the World*.
      New York: The Macmillan Company, 1957.

D2   Dampier, Sir William Cecil. *A History of Science*.
      Cambridge, Eng.: Cambridge University Press, 1949.

D3   Stearner, S. Phyllis. *Able Scientists--Disabled Persons*.
      Oakbrook, IL: John Racila Associates, Inc., 1984.

D4   Uglow, Jennifer S., and Frances Hinton, eds. *The
      International Dictionary of Women's Biography*. New
      York: The Continuum Publishing Company, 1982.

D5   Boorstin, Daniel J. *The Discoverers*. New York: Random House, 1983.

E   *Who's Who in Science in Europe*. Guernsey, U.K.: Frances Hodgson Publishers, 1978.

E1   Trescott, Martha M. "Women Engineers in History: Profiles in Holism and Persistence." In Haas, Violet B., and Carolyn C. Perrucci, eds. *Women in Scientific and Engineering Professions*. Ann Arbor: The University of Michigan Press, 1984.

E2   *The New Encyclopaedia Britannica*. 15th ed. Chicago: Encyclopaedia Britannica, Inc., 1979.

E3   Meislich, Estelle K. "The Eve of Chemistry." *Chemtech* (October 1978), pp. 588–592.

F   Fins, Alice. *Women in Science*. Skokie, IL: VGM Career Horizons, 1979.

F1   Arnold, Lois Barber. *Four Lives in Science*. New York: Schocken Books, 1984.

F2   Beard, Mary R. *Woman as a Force in History*. New York: The Macmillan Company, 1946.

F3   Schmidt, Minna Moscherosch. *400 Outstanding Women of the World*. Chicago: The Author, 1933.

F4   Hays, Mary. *Female Biography, or Memoirs of Illustrious and Celebrated Women of All Ages and Countries, Alphabetically Arranged*. Philadelphia: Fry and Kammerer, 1807.

G   Hoyt, Mary Finch. *American Women of the Space Age*. New York: Atheneum, 1966.

G1   Goodell, Rae. *The Visible Scientists*. Boston: Little, Brown and Company, 1977.

G2   Lefkowitz, Mary R., and Maureen B. Fant. *Women's Life in Greece and Rome*. Baltimore: The Johns Hopkins University Press, 1982.

G3   Lefkowitz, Mary R., and Maureen B. Fant. *Women in Greece and Rome*. Toronto: Samuel-Stevens Publishers, 1977.

G4   Marlow, Joan. *The Great Women*. New York: A & W Publishers, 1979.

H   Schacher, Susan, Coordinator. *Hypatia's Sisters: Biographies of Women Scientists—Past and Present*. Seattle, WA: Feminists Northwest, 1976.

H1   Murray, Janet Horowitz. *Strong Minded Women and Other Lost Voices from Nineteenth Century England.* New York: Pantheon Books, 1982.

H2   Hughes, Muriel Joy. *Women Healers in Medieval Life and Literature.* Freeport, NY: Books for Libraries Press, 1968.

H3   Blashfield, Jean F. *Hellraisers, Heroines, and Holy Women.* New York: St. Martin's Press, 1981.

H4   Gascoigne, Robert M. *A Historical Catalogue of Scientists and Scientific Books.* New York: Garland Publishing, Inc., 1984.

H5   Sarton, George. *A History of Science.* Cambridge, MA: Harvard University Press, 1952.

I   Asimov, Isaac. *Asimov's Biographical Encyclopedia of Science and Technology.* Garden City, NY: Doubleday & Co., Inc., 1964.

I1   Minai, Naila. *Women in Islam.* New York: Seaview Books, 1981.

I2   *International Who's Who in Energy and Nuclear Sciences.* Detroit, MI: Longman Press, 1983.

I3   Barr, E. Scott. *An Index to Biographical Fragments in Unspecialized Scientific Journals.* University: The University of Alabama Press, 1973.

I4   Spender, Dale. *Women of Ideas.* London: Routledge & Kegan Paul Ltd., 1982.

I5   Ireland, Norma Olin. *Index to Scientists of the World from Ancient to Modern Times: Biographies and Portraits.* Boston: The F.W. Faxon Company, Inc., 1962.

I6   "Women in Science: A Man's World." *Impact of Science on Society,* Vol. 25, No. 2 (April–June 1975).

I7   "Women in the Age of Science and Technology." *Impact of Science on Society,* Vol. 20, No. 1 (January–March 1970).

I8   "Some Ideas from Women Technicians in Small Countries." *Impact of Science on Society,* Vol. 30, No. 1 (January–March 1980).

I9   Baig, Tara Ali. *India's Womanpower.* New Delhi: S. Chand & Co. (Pvt.) Ltd., 1976.

J   James, E.T. *Notable American Women 1607–1950.* Cambridge, MA: Harvard University Press, 1974.

J1   Friedenwald, H. *The Jews and Medicine*. Baltimore: The Johns Hopkins University Press, 1944.

J2   Welt, Ida. "The Jewish Woman in Science." *The Hebrew Standard*, April 5, 1907, p. 4.

K   Hurd-Mead, Kate Campbell. *A History of Women in Medicine from the Earliest Times to the Beginning of the Nineteenth Century*. Haddam, CT: The Haddam Press, 1938. Rpt. Dover, NH: Longwood Press, 1978.

K1   Boynick, David K. *Women Who Led the Way--Eight Pioneers for Equal Rights*. New York: Thomas Y. Crowell Co. (Harper & Row), 1959.

K2   Kundsin, Ruth B., ed. *Women and Success*. New York: William Morrow & Co., Inc., 1974.

K3   Hurd-Mead, Kate Campbell. *Medical Women of America*. New York: Froben Press, 1933.

L   Opfell, Olga S. *The Lady Laureates*. Metuchen, NJ: Scarecrow Press, 1978.

L1   Dash, Joan. *A Life of One's Own*. New York: Harper and Row, 1973.

L2   McHenry, Robert, ed. *Liberty's Women*. Springfield, MA: G. & C. Merriam Co., 1980.

L3   *The World of Learning 1982-83*. London: Europa Publications Ltd., 1982.

L4   Meyer, Gerald Denis. *The Scientific Lady in England 1650-1760*. Berkeley: University of California Press, 1955.

L5   Duveen, Dennis I. "Madame Lavoisier." *Chymia*, Vol. 4. Philadelphia: University of Pennsylvania Press, 1953.

L6   Lipinska, Mélanie. *Histoire des femmes medicins depuis l'antiquité jusqu'à nos jours*. Paris: Librairie G. Jacques & Cie., 1900.

L7   Levey, Martin. *Chemistry and Chemical Technology in Ancient Mesopotamia*. New York: Elsevier Publishing Co., 1959.

M   Perl, Teri. *Math Equals*. Menlo Park, CA: Addison-Wesley Publishing Co., 1978.

M1   Kumagai, Gloria L.; Linda Garrett; Anita Faber Spencer; and Kathleen M. Blair. *Minority Women in Math and Science*. St. Paul, MN: St. Paul Public Schools Urban Affairs Department, 1980.

M2   Power, Eileen, and M. Poscon. *Medieval Women*. Cambridge: Cambridge University Press, 1976.

M3   Materials held in MIT Archives.

M4   Crombie, A.C. *Medieval and Early Modern Science*. Garden City, NY: Doubleday & Co., Inc., 1959.

M5   Dubreil-Jacotin, Mme. Marie-Louise. "Women Mathematicians." In Lelionnais, F., ed. *Great Currents of Mathematical Thought*. New York: Dover Publications, Inc., 1971.

M6   Coolidge, Julian L. "Six Female Mathematicians." *Scripta Mathematica*, Vol. 17, No. 1 (March-June 1951), pp. 20-31.

M7   Grinstein, Louise S. "Some 'Forgotten' Women of Mathematics: A Who Was Who." *Philosophia Mathematica*, Vols. 13/14 (1976/77), pp. 73-78.

M8   Campbell, Paul J., and Louise S. Grinstein. "Women in Mathematics: A Preliminary Selected Bibliography." *Philosophia Mathematica*, Vols. 13/14 (1976/77), pp. 171-203.

M9   Kramer, Edna E. "Six More Female Mathematicians." *Scripta Mathematica*, Vol. 23, Nos. 1-4 (1957), pp. 83-95.

N   Osen, Lynn. *Women in Mathematics*. Cambridge, MA: M.I.T. Press, 1974.

N1   Yost, Edna. *American Women of Nursing*. Philadelphia: J.B. Lippincott, 1947.

N2   James, Edward T., ed. *Notable American Women: 1607-1950; A Biographical Dictionary*. Cambridge, MA: Harvard University Press, 1971.

N3   Sicherman, Barbara, and Carol Hurd Green, eds. *Notable American Women: The Modern Period*. Cambridge, MA: Harvard University Press, 1980.

N4   Smith, Eng. Capt. Edgar C. "Some Notable Women of Science." *Nature*, Vol. 127 (1931), pp. 976-977.

N5   Woodsmall, Ruth Frances. *Women and the New East*. Washington, D.C.: The Middle East Institute, 1960.

O   Other biographical source--clippings, correspondence, etc.

O1   O'Neill, Lois Decker, ed. *The Women's Book of World Records and Achievements*. New York: Da Capo Press, Inc., Plenum Publishing Corporation, 1979.

O2   Ruddick, Sara, and Pamela Daniels, eds. *Working It Out.*
New York: Pantheon Books, 1977.

P   Haber, Louis. *Women Pioneers of Science.* New York:
Harcourt Brace Jovanovich, 1979.

P1   Sheldon, H. Horton, and S. Edgar Farquhar, eds. *The
Progress of Science; A Review of 1941.* New York: The
Grolier Society, Inc., 1942.

P2   Johnson, Diane. "Women in Meteorology: A Small Glimpse
at the Large-Scale Pattern." *Weatherwise,* Vol. 28,
No. 2 (June 1975), pp. 108-113.

P3   Meitner, Lise. "The Status of Women in the Professions."
Physics Today, Vol. 13 (August 1960), pp. 16-21.

P4   Weeks, Dorothy W. "Women in Physics Today." *Physics
Today,* Vol. 13 (August 1960), pp. 22-23.

P5   *The Lives of the Ancient Philosophers.* London: J.
Nicholson, 1702.

P6   Pledge, H.T. *Science Since 1500.* London: His Majesty's
Stationery Office, 1947; also reprinted New York:
Philosophical Library, 1947.

P7   Brush, Stephen G. "Women in Physical Science." *The
Physics Teacher* (January 1985), pp. 11-19.

Q   *Biographical Memoirs of Fellows.* London: Royal Society
of London, 1955-1971.

Q1   Partnow, Elaine. *The Quotable Woman.* Garden City, NY:
Anchor Press/Doubleday, 1978.

R   Rebière, A. *Les Femmes dans la science.* Paris: Nony &
Cie., 1897.

R1   Rossiter, Margaret W. *Women Scientists in America.*
Baltimore: The Johns Hopkins University Press, 1982.

R2   Rossiter, Margaret W. "'Women's Work' in Science, 1880-
1910." *Isis,* Vol. 71, No. 258 (September 1980), pp.
381-398.

R3   Maulde la Clavière, R. de. *The Women of the Renaissance.*
Trans. by George Herbert Ely. London: Swan Sonnenschein
& Co., Ltd.; New York: G. Putnam Sons, 1900.

R4   Bainton, Roland H. *Women of the Reformation: From Spain
to Scandinavia.* Minneapolis, MN: Augsburg Publishing
House, 1977.

R5   Wightman, W.P.D. *Science and the Renaissance.* Edin-
burgh, Scotland: Oliver and Boyd, Ltd., 1962.

S   Telberg, Ina, comp. *Who's Who in Soviet Science and Technology.* New York: Telberg Book Co., 1960.

S1   Dorland, W.A. Newman. *The Sum of Feminine Achievement.* Boston: The Stratford Company, 1917.

S2   Visher, Stephen Sargent. *Scientists Starred 1903-1943 in "American Men of Science."* Baltimore: The Johns Hopkins Press, 1947.

S3   Sabin, Dr. Florence R. "Women in Science." *Science,* Vol. 83, No. 2141 (1936), pp. 24-26.

S4   Schafer, Alice T. "Women and Mathematics." In Steen, Lynn Arthur, ed. *Mathematics Tomorrow.* New York: Springer-Verlag, 1981.

T   Turkevich, John. *Soviet Men of Science.* Princeton, NJ: D. Van Nostrand Co., Inc., 1963.

T1   Dark, Sidney. *Twelve Great Ladies.* London: Hodder and Stoughton, 1928.

T2   Deuel, Leo. *Testaments of Time: The Search for Lost Manuscripts and Records.* New York: Alfred A. Knopf, 1965.

T3   Singer, Charles; E.J. Holmyard; A.R. Hill; Trevor I. Williams; Y. Peel; and J.R. Pelty, eds. *A History of Technology.* London: Oxford University Press, 1957.

T4   Musson, A.E., and Eric Robinson. *Science and Technology in the Industrial Revolution.* Manchester, Eng.: Manchester University Press, 1969.

U   *Black Contributors to Science and Energy Technology.* U.S. Department of Energy Publication DOE/OPA-0035(79), 1979.

U1   Boulding, Elise. *The Underside of History: A View of Women Through Time.* Boulder, CO: Westview Press, 1976.

V   Rossiter, Margaret W. "Women Scientists in America Before 1920." *American Scientist,* Vol. 62, No. 3 (May-June 1974), pp. 312-323.

V1   Trescott, Martha Moore, ed. *Dynamos and Virgins Revisited: Women and Technological Change in History.* Metuchen, NJ: The Scarecrow Press, Inc., 1979.

V2   Fraser, Antonia. *The Weaker Vessel.* New York: Alfred A. Knopf, 1984.

W   Debus, Allen G., ed. *World Who's Who in Science.* Chicago: Marquis-Who's Who, Inc., 1968.

W1   Rayner, William P. *Wise Women*. New York: St. Martin's
      Press, 1983.

W2   *Who's Who of American Women*. 13th ed. Chicago: Marquis-
      Who's Who, Inc., 1982.

W3   *The World Who's Who of Women*. 7th ed. Cambridge, Eng.:
      International Biographical Center, 1983.

W4   Marks, Geoffrey, and William K. Beatty. *Women in White*.
      New York: Charles Scribner's Sons, 1972.

W5   Ireland, Norma Olin. *Index to Women of the World from
      Ancient to Modern Times: Biographies and Portraits*.
      Westwood, MA: F.W. Faxon Co., Inc., 1970.

W6   Roscher, Nina Matheny. "Women Chemists." *Chemtech*,
      Vol. 6 (December 1976), pp. 738-743.

X   Yost, Edna. *American Women of Science*. Philadelphia:
      J.B. Lippincott, 1943.

Y   Yost, Edna. *Women of Modern Science*. New York: Dodd,
      Mead & Co., 1966.

Z   Mozans, H.J. *Woman in Science*. New York: D. Appleton
      and Company, 1913. Rpt. Cambridge, MA: M.I.T. Press,
      1974.

BIOGRAPHICAL NOTES

AE U.S. Atomic Energy Commission Former Chairperson

AS Astronaut or Cosmonaut

FR Fellow of the Royal Society of London

HA Disabled or Handicapped

MI Minority

NB U.S. National Science Board Member or Former Member

NE U.S. National Academy of Engineering Member

NL Nobel Laureate

NS U.S. National Academy of Sciences Member

SS U.S.S.R. Academy of Sciences Member

THE INDEX

A

ABBOTT, MAUDE E. Physician	(1869–1940) Canadian	[D1,I5,D4]
ABELLA Physician/Educator	(1300s) Roman/Italian	[K,Z,W4,L6]
ABERLE, SOPHIE BLEDSOE Anthropologist	(1899–) American	[A,O1] [NB]
ABETE-SCARAFIOTTI, ANNA ROSA Mathematician	(1900s) Italian	[E]
ABIDH, STELLA Public Health Physician	(1900s) Jamaican	[D1]
ABOUCHDID, EDNA Physician	(1900s early) Lebanese	[D1,W5]
ABROTELIA Natural Philosopher/Mathematician	(BC 400s) Greek/Italian	[P5]
ACCAME-MURATORI, ROSANNA Biologist/Zoologist/Ichthyologist	(1934–) Italian	[E]
ACKERMAN, BERNICE Meteorologist	(1924–) American	[A,O1]
ACOSTA-SISON, HONORIA Physician	(1888–) Philippine	[W,D1,W5]

ADAMS, A. ELIZABETH: *See* ADAMS, ELIZABETH A.

ADAMS, ELIZABETH A. Zoologist	(1892–) American	[R1,S2,A1]
ADAMS, GRACE Psychologist	(1900–) American	[Q1,F2]
ADAMS, MILDRED Chemist	(1899–) American	[W]
ADAMS, SARAH E. Physician	(1779–1846) American	[W4]

ADELBERGER, ABBESS: *See* BERTHAGYTA, ABBESS

ADELBERGER OF LOMBARDY   (700s late)   [K]
Medical Practitioner   Italian

ADELLE OF THE SARACENS   (1100s)   [K]
Physician   Italian

ADELMOTA OF CARRARA, PRINCESS   (1300s early)   [K,L6]
Physician/Obstetrician   Italian

ADELMOTE: *See* ADELMOTA OF CARRARA, PRINCESS

ADINE   (12??-13??)   [H2]
Physician   French

ADKINS, DOROTHY CHRISTINA   (1912-)   [W]
Psychologist   American

AECATERINE: *See* CATHERINE OF ALEXANDRIA, SAINT

AELFLEDA, ABBESS   (600s-700s)   [K]
Physician/Surgeon   English

AEMILIA   (300s)   [K]
Physician   French/Roman

AESARA OF LUCANIA   (BC 500s)   [F2]
Philosopher/Mathematician/Author   Greek/Italian

AETHELTHRYTH: *See* ETHELDRIDA, QUEEN

AGAMEDE   (BC 1200 c.)   [Z,K,D1,R]
Physician/Pharmacologist/Botanist   Greek

AGANICE   (BC or early AD)   [R,P5]
Astronomer/Mathematician   Greek

AGASSIZ, ELIZABETH CABOT CARY   (1822-1907)   [Z,I3,O1,R1]
Naturalist/Biologist/Explorer   American

AGENJO, CECILIA RAMON   (1900s)   [E]
Entomologist   Spanish

AGLAONICE   (BC 200 c.)   [Z,W5,R]
Astronomer   Greek

AGNES, COUNTESS OF AIX   (1100s)   [K]
Physician   Spanish

AGNES OF BOHEMIA   (12??-1282)   [K]
Physician   Czechoslovakian

AGNES OF JERUSALEM   (1100s)   [K,B1]
Nurse/Physician   Palestinian

AGNES OF SILESIA   (1200s)   [K]
Physician   German

AGNES OF STRASBOURG Physician	(1300s) German	[H2]
AGNESI, MARIA GAETANA Mathematician	(1718-1799) Italian	[M,N,R,W,B1]
AGNODICE Physician	(BC 300 c.) Greek	[D1,H,Z,S1]
AH MAE WONG Physician	(18??-19??) Chinese	[D1]
AHTEE, LIISA MARJATTA Pharmacologist	(1937-) Finnish	[E]
AJZENBERG-SELOVE, FAY Physicist	(1926-) American	[A,W,P4]

AKELEY, DELIA DENNING: *See* DENNING, DELIA

AKELEY, MARY L. JOBE: *See* JOBE, MARY L.

ALBE, DENISE Neurophysiologist	(1916-) French	[E]
ALBERTSON, MARY A. Botanist	(18??-1914) American	[I3]
ALBIN, MISS Naturalist/Painter	(1700s) English	[O]
ALBRECHT, ROSEMARIE Physician/Otorhinolaryngologist	(1900s) German	[E,L3]
ALBRINK, MARGARET JORALEMON Physician	(1920-) American	[W]
ALCOCK, SARAH Physician/Surgeon	(16??-1665) American	[K]
ALDEN, CYNTHIA WESTOVER Inventor/Linguist	(1858-18??) American	[W5]
ALDRICH, MICHELE L. Geologist/Science Historian	(1942-) American	[A] [*HA*]
ALEXANDER, HATTIE ELIZABETH Bacteriologist/Pediatrician	(1901-1968) American	[N3,O1]
ALEXANDER, MARY LOUISE Geneticist	(1926-) American	[W]
ALI, SAFIEH Physician	(1900s early) Turkish	[D1,W5]
ALLARD, ELIZABETH MAAJ Social Scientist	(1904-) Dutch	[W]

ALLARDYCE, CONSTANCE   (18??-1919)   [I3]
  Geologist   English

ALLEN, DORIS TWITCHELL   (1922-)   [W]
  Microbiologist   American

ALLEN, LOUISA C.: *See* GREGORY, LOUISA CATHERINE ALLEN

ALLEN, MALWINA (INKA) GERSON   (1929-)   [A]
  Chemist   American

ALLEN, MARY BELLE   (1922-)   [W]
  Microbiologist   American

ALLEN, RUTH FLORENCE   (1879-1963)   [R1]
  Plant Pathologist/Cytologist   American

ALLEN, SALLY LYMAN   (1926-)   [W]
  Geneticist   American

ALLIN, ELIZABETH JOSEPHINE   (1905-)   [A,P4]
  Physicist   Canadian

ALLISON, EMMA   (1800s late)   [W5]
  Inventor   American

AL-MALLAH, SAMIRA   (1900s)   [I1]
  Gynecologist   Egyptian

ALMANIA, JACQUELINE FELICIE DE: *See* DE ALMANIA, JACQUELINE
  FELICE

ALMASI, LUCRETIA ROTSCHILD   (1921-)   [W]
  Chemist   Rumanian

ALPER, THELMA G.   (1908-)   [W]
  Psychologist   American

ALPER, TIKVAH   (1909-)   [W]
  Radiobiologist   South African/English

ALSTON-GARNJOST, MARGARET   (1929-)   [A]
  Physicist   American

ALTERMAN, ZIPORA STEPHANIA   (1925-)   [W]
  Mathematician   Israeli

ALVARINO DE LEIRA, ANGELES   (1916-)   [W]
  Biologist/Oceanographer   Spanish/American

AMALIA: *See* HENTSCHEL-GUERNTH, DOROTHEA

AMALOSUNTA   (1400s)   [K]
  Physician   Italian

AMARAL, MARIA LUISA GARCIA Architect/Geographer	(1900s) Mexican	[I8]
AMBRUS, CLARA MARIA BAYER Physician	(1924-) American	[W]
AMELINE Physician	(12??-13??) French	[H2]
AMES, LOUISE BATES Research Psychologist	(1906 c.-) American	[R1,I5,W5]
AMES, MARY L. PULSIFER Botanist	(1845?-1902) American	[I3]
AMLA, INDIRA Physician	(1900s) Indian	[I9]
AMMUNDSEN, ESTHER Physician	(1900s) Danish	[O1]
AMPHICIA Philosopher	(200s) Greek/Roman	[R,P5]
AMYTE: *See* ANICIA		
ANCHEL, MARJORIE WOLFF Chemist	(1910-) American	[W]
ANCKER-JOHNSON, BETSY Physicist/Engineer	(1929-) American	[A,W,O1,K2] [*NE*]
ANDERSEN, DOROTHY HANSINE Pathologist/Pediatrician	(1901-1963) American	[N3]
ANDERSON, CAROL A. Geneticist/Soil Conservationist	(1900s) American	[O1]
ANDERSON, CAROLINE VIRGINIA Physician	(1848-18??) American	[W5]
ANDERSON, ELDA EMMA Health Physicist	(1899-1961) American	[N3]
ANDERSON, ELIZABETH GARRETT Physician	(1836-1917) English/American	[W,Z,H1,O1]
ANDERSON, EVELYN Endocrinologist/Aerospace Physician	(1900s) American	[G]
ANDERSON, JANET Mathematician	(1500s) English	[R5]
ANDERSON, ROSE GUSTAVA Psychologist	(1893-) American	[W]
ANDRE, VALERIE EDMEE Physician/Surgeon/Aviator	(1900s) French	[D1,W5]

ANDREAS-SALOME, LOU Psychoanalyst/Philosopher	(1861-1937) Russian/German	[W5]
ANDREIAN, CABIRIA Mathematician	(1900s) Rumanian	[I8]
ANDROMACHE Physician	(500s) Egyptian	[K]
ANGEL, ANDREA Chemist	(1877-1917?) English	[I3]
ANGIOLINA OF PADUA Obstetrician/Educator	(1700s) Italian	[K]
ANHALT-DESSAU, PRINCESS Mathematician	(1700s) German	[M5,R]
ANICIA Physician	(BC 300 c.) Greek	[K]
ANICIA, JULIA Physician	(472-) Turkish	[K]
ANN MEDICA OF YORK Physician	(1400s) English	[K]
ANNA COMNENA: *See* COMNENA, ANNA		
ANNA OF BOHEMIA Physician	(1200s) Czechoslovakian	[K]
ANNA SOPHIA OF DENMARK, PRINCESS Botanist/Pharmacist	(1500s) Danish	[K]
ANNA SOPHIA OF HESSE Botanist/Natural Scientist	(1600s) German	[K]
ANNE OF DENMARK Alchemist	(1500s-1600s) Danish	[A3]
ANNO, KIMIKO Chemist/Agricultural Researcher	(1900s) Japanese	[O1]
ANSLOW, GLADYS AMELIA Physicist	(1892-) American	[W]
ANTHONY, BERTHA VAN HOUTEN Bacteriologist/Physician	(1900s early) American	[B5]
ANTHUSA Philosopher/Meteorologist	(400s) Roman/Turkish	[R,P5]
ANTIOCHIS OF TARENTUM Physician	(BC 000s) Roman/Italian/Greek	[K]
ANTIOCHIS OF TLOS Physician	(100s) Roman	[K,Z,L6]

ANTIOCHUS Physician	(000s AD) Greek/Roman	[G2,G3]
ANTONIA, DUCHESS OF WURTEMBERG Botanist/Naturalist	(15??-1579) German	[K]
ANTONIA, MAESTRA Physician	(1386-1408) Italian	[H2]
APGAR, B. JEAN Biochemist	(1936-) American	[O1]
APGAR, VIRGINIA Physician/Neonatologist	(1909-1974) American	[C1,B1,L2]
APPLIN, ESTHER RICHARDS Micropaleontologist/Geologist	(1895-1972) American	[R1]
APSLEY, LUCY, LADY Physician/Chemist/Pharmacist	(1620-1675) English	[K]
ARBER, AGNES Biologist	(1879-1960) English	[W,M4,D4]

ARCONVILLE: *See* D'ARCONVILLE, GENEVIEVE CHARLOTTE

ARDINGHELLI, MARIA ANGELA Physicist/Mathematician/Scholar	(1730-1825) Italian	[Z,R]
ARDITI, MICHELE Archaeologist/Scholar	(17??-18??) Italian	[Z]
ARETE OF CYRENE Physicist/Philosopher/Educator	(BC 400 c.) Greek/Libyan	[Z,F2,D4,W5]
ARETHUSA Scholar/Medical Practitioner	(3??-4??) Egyptian/Turkish	[K]
ARGIA Philosopher/Scholar	(BC 300s) Turkish/Egyptian	[R,P5]
ARIA Philosopher	(000s) Roman	[R,P5]
ARIGNOTE OF SAMOS Natural Philosopher/Mathematician	(BC 500s) Greek/Italian	[L6,P5,F2,R]

ARISTOCLEA: *See* THEMISTOCLEA

ARMBRUSTER, MARION Chemist	(1900s early) American	[R1]
ARMFELDT, NATALIA Mathematician	(1800s) Russian	[O]
ARNOLD, MAGDA BLONDIAN Psychologist	(1903-) American	[W]

ARRIA
Philosopher

(000s)   [P5]
Roman

ARTEMISIA
Philosopher

(BC 300s)   [P5]
Turkish/Egyptian

ARTEMISIA OF CARIA
Botanist/Physician/Scholar

(BC 400s-300s)   [K,W5,E2]
Turkish/Persian

ARTIMISIA: *See* ARTEMISIA

ASBOTH, JUDIT TORMA
Engineer

(1900s)   [I8]
Hungarian

ASCLEPIGENIA
Philosopher/Educator

(300s)   [Z,N,R]
Greek/Roman

ASHBY, WINIFRED MAYER
Medical Biologist

(1879-)   [W]
American

ASHLEY, MARY
Astronomer

(1800s-1900s)   [Z,R]
English

ASKINS, BARBARA S.
Inventor

(1900s)   [O]
American

ASKONAS, BRIGITTE ALICE
Immunologist/Biochemist/Biologist

(1923-)   [E,L3]
English   [*FR*]

ASPACIA OF MILETUS: *See* ASPASIA OF MILETUS

ASPASIA
Physician/Author

(100s AD)   [D1,H,Z,S1]
Greek/Roman

ASPASIA OF MILETUS
Scientist/Philosopher

(BC 470-410)   [Z,F4,F3,N]
Greek/Turkish

ASPASIE: *See* ASPASIA

ASSTE, MINUCIA
Physician

(000s-100s)   [G2,G3]
Roman

ASTELL, MARY
Author/Scientist/Educator

(1668-1731)   [F4]
English

ASYLLIA
Physician

(400s)   [K]
North African

ATHENAIS: *See* EUDOCIA

ATRIA
Philosopher

(BC 100s)   [P5]
Roman/Italian

ATWATER, TANYA
Geologist/Geophysicist

(1942-)   [A]
American

AUERBACH, CHARLOTTE
Animal Geneticist/Biologist

(1899-)   [P3,L3,D4]
English/Scottish   [*FR*]

AUSTIN, MARY LELLAH Zoologist	(1896–) American	[W]
AUSTIN, PAULINE MORROW Meteorologist	(1916–) American	[A,O1,P4]
AVRAM, HENRIETTE Computer Systems Analyst	(1900s) American	[O1]
AXIOTHEA Philosopher	(BC 400 c.) Greek	[R,P5]
AYRTON, MATILDA CHAPLIN Physician	(1846–1883) English	[W]
AYRTON, (SARAH) HERTHA MARKS Physicist	(1854–1923) English	[W,B1,Z,I3]

AYRTON, MRS. W.E.: *See* AYRTON, (SARAH) HERTHA MARKS

AZARMIE, SOGHRA Physician/Gynecologist	(1900s) Iranian	[N5]

B

BABCOCK, HARRIET Psychologist	(19??–1952) American	[W]

BACHMAN, MARIA MARTIN: *See* MARTIN, MARIA

BACON, CLARA LATIMER Mathematician	(1866–1948) American	[M8,R1]
BACON–BERCEY, JUNE Meteorologist	(1900s) American	[O] [MI]

BADEN, COUNTESS OF: *See* CATHERINE URSULA OF BADEN

BAETJER, ANNA MEDORA Physiologist/Toxicologist	(1899–) American	[R1,W]
BAI, A.R. KASTURI Zoologist/Agricultural Researcher	(1925–) Indian	[O1]
BAI, BIJUR TARA Chemist/Home Economist	(1900s) Indian	[N5]
BAILAR, BARBARA ANN Mathematician/Statistician	(1935–) American	[A,O1]
BAILEY, CATHERINE HAYES Plant Geneticist/Pomologist	(1921–) American	[A,O1]

BAILEY, ETHEL Botanist/Zoologist	(1890-) American	[O1]
BAILEY, FLORENCE AUGUSTA MERRIAM Ornithologist	(1863-1948) American	[W,N2,O1,L2]
BAILEY, LIBERTY HYDE Horticulturist/Agriculturist	(1800s-1900s) American	[R2]
BAILIE, ANN ECKELS Mathematician	(1900s) American	[G]
BAJEV, ALEXANDRA Scientist	(1900s) Russian	[L3]
BAKER, SARA JOSEPHINE Physician/Public Health Scientist	(1873-1945) American	[W,C1,N1,C2]
BAKHTADZE, KSENIA ERMOLAEVNA Plant Geneticist	(1899-) Russian	[S]
BAKWIN, RUTH MORRIS Physician	(1898-) American	[W]
BALCELLS, MARIAM Mathematician/Physicist	(1864?-1911) Spanish	[I3]
BALELYMA Philosopher/Mathematician	(BC 400s) Greek/Italian	[P5]
BALFOUR, ELIZABETH JEAN Ecologist	(1900s) Scottish	[L3]
BALFOUR, MARGARET IDA Physician/Obstetrician/Gynecologist	(18??-1945) Scottish/Indian	[W,K3,I5]
BALK, CHRISTINA LOCHMAN Geologist	(1907-) American	[W]
BALL, LOUISE CHARLOTTE Oral Surgeon	(1887-1946) American	[W]
BALLOWE, KANCHANA Process Engineer	(1900s) American	[M1] [MI]
BANGA, ILONA Biochemist	(1906-) Hungarian	[W]
BARANGER, ELIZABETH UREY Physicist	(1927-) American	[A]
BARBARA Physician	(13??-14??) German	[J1]
BARDINA, SOFIA Agronomist	(1800s) Russian	[O]

BARDWELL, ELIZABETH M.   (1832?-1899)   [I3]
Astronomer   American

BARI, NINA KARLOVNA   (1901-1961)   [S,M8]
Mathematician   Russian

BARLETT, HELEN BLAIR   (1900s)   [R1]
Mineralogist/Ceramicist   American

BARLOW, ANNE LOUISE   (1925-)   [W2]
Physician   English/American

BARNARD, EDITH ETHEL   (1880-1914)   [I3]
Chemist   American

BARNARD, MARY   (1700s)   [K]
Physician   American

BARNARDINO, CONSUELO   (1900s)   [D1]
Physician/Gynecologist/Educator   Dominican

BARNES, MARGARET   (1900s)   [L3]
Marine Biologist   Scottish

BARNEY, NORA STANTON BLATCH   (1883-1971)   [N3,R1]
Civil Engineer/Architect   American

BARNOTHY, MADELINE FORRO   (1904-)   [W]
Physicist   Hungarian/American

BARNUM, CHARLOTTE CYNTHIA   (1800s)   [S1]
Mathematician   American

BARRERA, ANA M. GALVEZ   (1950-)   [I8]
Anthropologist   Peruvian

BARRERA, OLIVA SABUCO   (1562-1625)   [K,D4,L6,R]
Psychologist/Physician/Philosopher   Spanish

BARRINGER, EMILY DUNNING   (1876-1961)   [W4,K3,I5]
Physician/Surgeon/Gynecologist   American

BARROWS, ISABEL C.   (1800s)   [H3]
Surgeon/Medical Educator   American

BARRY, JAMES MIRANDA (pseudonym): See STUART, MIRANDA

BART, PAULINE   (1900s)   [O]
Sociologist/Psychiatrist   American

BARTON, VOLA PRICE   (1900s early)   [R1]
Physicist   American

BASCOM, FLORENCE   (1862-1945)   [W,F1,N2,O1]
Geologist/Stratigrapher   American

BASS, ELIZABETH   (1900s early)   [K]
Pathologist/Educator   American

BASSA, LAURA: *See* BASSI, LAURE MARIA CATARINA

BASSANI, SIGNORA Inventor	(1800s late) Italian	[Z]
BASSE, MARIE-THERESE Food Technologist	(1900s) Senegalese	[O1]
BASSI, LAURE MARIA CATARINA Physicist/Anatomist/Scientist	(1711-1778) Italian	[W,Z,D1,U1]

BASSI-VERATTI, LAURE MARIA CATARINA: *See* BASSI, LAURE MARIA
  CATARINA

BATCHELDER, ESTHER L. Home Economist	(1897-) American	[W]
BATES, GRACE ELIZABETH Mathematician	(1914-) American	[W]

BATESON, MARGARET MEAD: *See* MEAD, MARGARET

BATH-ZABBIA: *See* ZENOBIA, QUEEN

BATTLE, HELEN IRENE Zoologist	(1903-) Canadian	[W]
BAUCYN, JULIANA Nurse/Medical Worker	(1200s) English	[K]
BAUMGARTEN-TRAMER, FRANZISKA Psychologist	(1900s) Polish/Swiss	[W]
BAUMGARTNER, LEONA Physician	(1902-) American	[W,I5]
BAUTZ, LAURA PAT Astronomer	(1940-) American	[A]
BAYLEY, NANCY Child Psychologist	(1900s early) American	[R1]
BAYNARD, ANNE Mathematician/Astronomer/Physicist	(1672-1697) English	[F4]
BAZANOVA, NAYLYA URAZGULOVNA Physiologist	(1911-) Russian	[S,W,E]
BAZIN, SUZANNE Biochemist	(1912-) French	[W]
BEACH, MARTHA Botanist	(1800s) American	[O]
BEAN, MAURA Food Technologist	(1900s) American	[O1]

BEASELY, JULIE Experimental Psychologist	(1900s) American	[G]
BEATRICE MEDICA OF CANDIA Physician/Scholar	(1300s) Italian	[K]
BEATRICE OF SAVOY Physician	(1200s) French	[K]
BEAUFORT, MARGARET, COUNTESS Medical Practitioner/Scholar	(1443-1509) English	[K]
BEAUJEU, JACQUELINE MARTHE G. Geographer	(1917-) French	[W]

BEAUSOLEIL, BARONESS DE: *See* DU CHATELET, MARTINE DE BIRTEREAU

BEAUVALLET, MARCELLE JEANNE Physiologist	(1905-) French	[W]

BECKE, MARGOT GOEHRING: *See* BECKE-GOEHRING, MARGOT LINE KLARA

BECKE-GOEHRING, MARGOT LINE KLARA Chemist	(1914-) German	[C,W,E]
BECKER, LYDIA Botanist	(1827-1890) English	[I4]
BECKER, LYDIA E. Psychologist	(1800s) English	[I7]
BECKWITH, CORA Zoologist	(18??-19??) American	[R1]
BECKWITH, MARTHA Anthropologist	(1800s) American	[R1]
BECTOZ, CLAUDE DE Scholar/Scientist/Linguist	(15??-1547) French	[F4]
BEDELL, ELIZABETH Physician	(1600s) English	[K]
BEGAK, MARIA LUIZA Cytogeneticist	(1934-) Brazilian	[W]

BEHN, APHARA JOHNSON: *See* BEHN, APHRA

BEHN, APHRA Natural Philosopher/Author	(1640-1687) English	[I4,L4,F4,R]
BEHRE, ELLINOR H. Biologist	(1886-) American	[W]
BEKHTEREVA, NATALYA PETROVANA Physiologist	(1900s) Russian	[E,L3] [SS]

BEKRYASHEVA, ANTONIA: *See* BORISOVA, ANTONIA GEORGIEVNA

BELETSKAYA. I.P. Chemist	(1900s) Russian	[L3] [SS]
BELL, BARBARA Astronomer	(1922-) American	[W]
BELL, JOCELYN: See BURNELL, JOCELYN BELL		
BELOTA Physician	(1300s-1400s) French	[M2,H2,W4]
BELOTA THE JEWESS: See BELOTA		
BELYEA, HELEN R. Geologist	(1913-) Canadian	[A,L3]
BENCE, THALIA Botanist	(1900s) British	[O]
BENDER, LAURETTA Child Psychiatrist/Physician	(1897-) American	[W,I5]
BENEDICT, RUTH FULTON Anthropologist	(1887-1948) American	[W,C1,B1,O1]
BENERITO, RUTH ROGAN Polymer Chemist/Physical Chemist	(1916-) American	[A,O1,W6]
BENGTSON, IDA Bacteriologist	(18??-19??) American	[R1,B2]
BENHAM, RHODA Microbiologist/Medical Mycologist	(1900s early) American	[B5]
BENNETT, ALICE Physician	(1857-1925) American	[K,K3,O1]
BENNETT, DOROTHEA Geneticist	(1929-) American	[W]
BENNETT, ERNA Plant Geneticist/Botanist	(1900s) Irish/American	[O1]
BENNETT, MIRIAM FRANCES Zoologist	(1928-) American	[W]
BENSCHOTEN, ANNA LAVINIA VAN Mathematician	(1866-1927) American	[M8]
BENSON, MARGARET J. Botanist	(18??-1936) English	[W]
BENSTON, MARGARET LOWE Physical Chemist	(1937-) American	[A,Q1]
BERECUNDA, VALERIA Physician	(400s) Roman	[K]

BERENGARIA OF CASTILE, QUEEN   (1100s-1200s)   [K]
  Physician   Spanish

BERGER, KATHARINA BERTHA CHARLOTTE   (1897-)   [W]
  Zoologist   German

BERGQUIST, LOIS MARIE   (1925-)   [W]
  Microbiologist   American

BERGQUIST, PATRICIA ROSE   (1900s)   [L3]
  Scientist   New Zealander

BERKOWITZ, JOAN B.   (1931-)   [A,O1]
  Physical Chemist   American

BERONICE   (BC 000s)   [R,P5]
  Philosopher   Greek/Egyptian

BERTHA OF CONSTANTINOPLE, QUEEN: See COMNENA, BERTHA

BERTHA OF LOMBARDY: See ADELBERGER OF LOMBARDY

BERTHAGYTA, ABBESS   (5??-616 c.)   [K]
  Physician/Educator   English

BERTHILDIS OF CHELLES, ABBESS   (6??-680)   [K]
  Medical Worker/Reformer   French

BERTILE OF CHELLES   (652-702)   [K]
  Physician/Scholar   French

BERTRANDE   (1400s)   [H2]
  Physician   French

BEVIER, ISABEL   (1860-1942)   [N2,L2,R1,V]
  Chemist/Home Economist/Educator   American

BEZNAK, MARGARET   (1914-)   [W]
  Physiologist   Hungarian/Canadian

BIATRIS   (1400s)   [H2]
  Physician   French

BIBRING, GRETE LEHNER   (1899-)   [W]
  Psychiatrist   Austrian/American

BIGELOW, HARRIET   (18??-19??)   [R1]
  Astronomer   American

BIHERON, MLLE.   (1730-??)   [Z,K,L6,R]
  Anatomist   French

BILGER, LEONORA NEUFFER   (1900s)   [O1,W6]
  Chemist   American

BILLIG, FLORENCE GRACE   (1890-1967)   [O]
  Science Educator   American

BILLINGS, KATHERINE FOWLER LUNN: *See* LUNN, KATHERINE FOWLER

BINGEN, SAINT HILDEGARD OF: *See* HILDEGARD OF BINGEN, SAINT

BINGHAM, EULA Toxicologist	(1900s) American	[O]
BINGHAM, MILLICENT Geographer/Nurse	(1880-19??) American	[R1,I5]
BIRCH, CARROLL LAFLEUR Physician	(1896-) American	[W,I5]

BIRGETTA, SAINT: *See* BRIDGET, SAINT, OF SCANDINAVIA

BIRJANDI, PARVIN Clinical Psychologist/Educator	(1900s) Iranian	[N5]
BISCOT, JEANNE Physician	(1601-1664) French	[K]
BISHOP, ANN Chemist	(1900s) English	[E,L3] [*FR*]
BISHOP, HAZEL GLADYS Chemist	(1906-) American	[L2,I5]
BISHOP, ISABELLA BIRD Geographer/Explorer	(1832-1904) English	[S1,Z]
BISHOP, KATHARINE SCOTT Anatomist	(1900s early) American	[R1]
BITTING, KATHERINE E. GOLDEN Microbiologist/Botanist	(18??-19??) American	[Z,R1]
BLACK, HORTENSIA Ornithologist	(18??-19??) American	[R1]
BLACKWELL, ELIZABETH Medicinal Botanist/Obstetrician	(1712-1770) English	[K,L4]
BLACKWELL, ELIZABETH Physician	(1821-1910) English/American	[N2,B1,W,H]
BLACKWELL, EMILY Physician	(1826-1911) American	[N2,L2,O1]
BLAKE, FLORENCE G. Pediatric Nurse/Educator	(1907-) American	[N1]
BLAKE, MARY SAFFORD Physician	(1834-) American	[F1]

BLAKE, SOPHIE JEX: *See* JEX-BLAKE, SOPHIA

BLANCHE, MARIE DE COSTE Physicist/Mathematician/Physician	(1500s) French	[K,R]

BLANCHE OF CASTILE, QUEEN   (1188-1252)   [K]
  Physician   French/Spanish

BLANCHE OF FRANCE AND CASTILE: *See* BLANCHE OF CASTILE, QUEEN

BLATCH, NORA S.: *See* DE FOREST, NORA S. BLATCH

BLEWETT, MYRTLE HILDRED   (1911-)   [A,O1]
  Accelerator Physicist   Canadian/American

BLINOVA, EKATERINA NIKITICHNA   (1906-)   [T,S,W,C,L3]
  Geophysicist/Dynamic Meteorologist Russian   [*SS*]

BLISS, ELEANOR ALBERT   (1899-)   [W,R1,I5]
  Bacteriologist/Pharmacologist   American

BLISS, ELEANORA: *See* KNOPF, ELEANORA FRANCES BLISS

BLODGETT, KATHARINE BURR   (1897-1979)   [W,X,Z,O1]
  Physicist/Physical Chemist   American

BLOMBAEK, M. WETTER   (1925-)   [W]
  Physician/Biochemist   Swedish

BLUKET, NINA ALEKSANDROVNA   (1902-)   [W]
  Botanist   Russian

BLUM, ARLENE   (1946-)   [O]
  Biochemist   American

BLUNT, KATHARINE   (1876-1954)   [R1,I5]
  Chemist/Nutritionist/Educator   American

BOAK, RUTH A.   (1906-)   [W]
  Physician   American

BOAS, MARIE: *See* HALL, MARIA BOAS

BOBINSKI, COUNTESS   (18??-19??)   [Z,R]
  Astronomer   Russian

BOCCHI, DOROTHEA: *See* BUCCA, DOROTEA

BOCHANTSEVA, ZINAIDA PETROVNA   (1907-)   [W]
  Cytologist   Russian

BODLEY, RACHEL LITTLER   (1831-1888)   [N2,K3,D4]
  Botanist/Chemist/Physician   American

BOGDANOFSKY, VERA EVSTAFJEVNA   (18??-1897)   [I3]
  Chemist   Russian

BOIVIN, MARIE ANNE VICTOIRE   (1773-1841)   [K,S1,D1,W4]
  Obstetrician/Physician/Author   French

BOJANOVIC, JELENA   (1918-)   [W]
  Chemist   Yugoslavian

BOKOVA-SECHENOVA, MARIA   (1800s)   [O]
  Ophthalmologist   Russian

BONAPARTE, CAROLINE: See MURAT, CAROLINE BONAPARTE, QUEEN

BONAPARTE, MARIE   (1882-1962)   [O1]
  Psychoanalyst   French

BONAPARTE, MARIE ANNUNCIATA: See MURAT, CAROLINE BONAPARTE,
  QUEEN

BONNAY, MARCHIONESS DU: See DU BONNAY, MARCHIONESS

BONNER, JILL CHRISTINE   (1937-)   [A]
  Physicist   English/American

BONONI, ESTHER   (1800s)   [J2]
  Physician   Italian

BOOLE-STOTT, ALICIA: See STOTT, ALICIA BOOLE

BOOTH, MARY ANN ALLARD   (1843-1922)   [W]
  Microscopist   American

BORG, IRIS Y.   (1928-)   [A,O1]
  Petrologist/Mineralogist/Geologist American

BORING, ALICE M.   (1800s)   [V]
  Geneticist   American

BORISOVA, ANTONIA GEORGIEVNA   (1903-)   [W]
  Botanist   Russian

BORROMEO, CLELIA GRILLO   (1600s-1700s)   [Z,W5,R]
  Physicist/Mathematician/Scholar Italian

BORSTELL, FRAU GENERALIN VON, OF COBLENTZ: See VON BORSTELL,
  FRAU GENERALIN

BOTELHO, STELLA YATES   (1919-)   [W]
  Physiologist   American

BOTSFORD, ANNA: See COMSTOCK, ANNA BOTSFORD

BOURDEL, LEONE   (1907-)   [W]
  Psychologist   French

BOURGEOIS, LOUISE: See BOURGEOISE, LOUYSE

BOURGEOISE, LOUYSE   (1563-1636)   [K,W4,I5,L6]
  Physician/Obstetrician/Surgeon   French

BOURSIER, MADAME   (15??-16??)   [W4]
  Midwife/Obstetrician   French

BOVERI, MARCELLA O'GRADY   (1800s-1900s)   [R1,R]
  Zoologist   American

BOVIN, MME.: *See* BOIVIN, MARIE ANNE VICTOIRE

BOWEN, SUSAN Zoologist	(18??-1886) American	[R1,R]
BOWLES, CATHERINE Surgeon	(1700s) English	[K,L6]
BOYD, ELLA F. Geologist	(1800s-1900s) American	[Z]

BOYD, HARRIET A.: *See* HAWES, HARRIET A. BOYD

BOYD, LOUISE ARNER Geographer/Scientific Explorer	(1887-) American	[W,R1,I5,H3]
BOYD, MARY E. Astronomer	(1800s-1900s) American	[Z]
BRADFORD, JANET MARY Zoologist/Oceanographer	(1900s) New Zealander	[I8]
BRAHE, SOPHIA Astronomer	(1500s late) Danish	[H,Z,U1,R]
BRANDEGEE, MARY Botanist	(1800s) American	[R1]
BRANHAM, SARA Bacteriologist	(1888-) American	[B5,I5,R1]
BRANT, LAURA Physicist	(1800s-1900s) American	[R1]
BRATHCHER, TWILA Invertebrate Zoologist	(1900s) American	[O1]
BRATKOWSKA-SENIOW, BARBARA Physician	(1923-) Polish	[W]
BRAUN, EMMA LUCY Botanist/Conservationist	(1889-1971) American	[N3]
BREDIHANA, EVGENIJA ALEKSANDROVNA Mathematician	(1922-1974) Russian	[M8]
BREED, MARY BIDWELL Chemist	(18??-19??) American	[R1,R2]
BREGMAN, ELSIE O. Industrial Psychologist	(1900s early) American	[R1]
BRELA OF BOHEMIA Physician	(700s) Czechoslovakian	[K]
BRELA OF BOHEMIA Physician	(1400s) Czechoslovakian	[K]

BRENCHLEY, WINIFRED ELSIE   (1883-1953)   [W]
  Botanist   English

BRES, MADELEINE   (1800s)   [B1]
  Physician/Surgeon   French

BRETEUIL, EMILIE DE, MARQUISE DU CHATELET: *See* CHATELET,
  GABRIELLE-EMILIE DU

BREYER, MARIA GERDINA BRANDWIJK   (1899-)   [W]
  Biochemist   Dutch/South African

BRIDGET, SAINT, OF IRELAND   (453-525)   [K,W4]
  Physician   Irish

BRIDGET, SAINT, OF SCANDINAVIA   (1304-1373)   [K,W4]
  Physician   Swedish

BRIERE, NICOLE-REINE ETABLE DE LA   (1723-1788)   [N4]
  Astronomer   French

BRIGHTWEN, MRS. ELIZA ELDER   (1830-1906)   [I3]
  Biologist   Scottish

BRISCOE, ANNE M.   (1918-)   [A]
  Biochemist   American

BRITTON, ELIZABETH GERTRUDE KNIGHT (1858-1934)   [N2,L2,S1,Z]
  Bryologist/Botanist   American

BROADHURST, JEAN   (1900s early)   [R1]
  Biologist   American

BROCK, SYLVIA   (1900s)   [O]
  Chemist   American

BRODY, SYLVIA   (1914-)   [W]
  Psychologist   American

BRONGERSMA, MARGARETHA SANDERS   (1905-)   [W]
  Oceanographer   Dutch

BRONNER, AUGUSTA FOX   (1881-1966)   [N3,R1]
  Clinical Psychologist   American

BROOKS, HARRIET   (18??-19??)   [R1]
  Physicist   American

BROOKS, MATILDA MOLDENHAUER   (1900s)   [A,O1,I5]
  Physiologist/Biologist/Toxicologist American

BROOMALL, ANNA E.   (1847-1931)   [O1,K3,I5]
  Obstetrician/Physician   American

BROPHY, DOROTHY HALL: *See* HALL, DOROTHY

BROSSEAU, KATE   (18??-1938)   [W]
  Psychologist   American

BROWN, ALICE Astronomer	(1800s-1900s) English	[Z]
BROWN, CHARLOTTE Physician	(18??-1904) American	[O1]
BROWN, ELIZABETH Astronomer	(18??-1899) American	[I3]
BROWN, ELLEN Physician	(1912-) American	[W]
BROWN, JEANETTE E. Chemist	(1900s) American	[M1] [MI]
BROWN, NELLIE Plant Pathologist	(18??-1956) American	[R1,R2]
BROWN, RACHEL FULLER Biochemist	(1898-) American	[P,Y,I5,D4]
BROWNE, ETHEL: See HARVEY, ETHEL BROWNE		
BRUCE, CATHERINE WOLFE Astronomer	(1816-1900) American	[I3,R]
BRUCE, MARY, LADY Microscopist/Bacteriologist	(18??-19??) English	[O1,B5]
BRUCKNER, FRAU DR. Physician/Orthopedicist	(1700s-1800s) German	[K]
BRUES, ALICE MOSSIE Physical Anthropologist	(1913-) American	[W]
BRUNETTA Physician	(1400s late) Italian	[J1]
BRUNFELS, FRAU Physician	(1500s) Swiss	[K]
BRYAN, ELIZABETH LETSON Zoologist/Conchologist	(1875?-1919) American	[I3]
BRYAN, MARGARET Astronomer/Educator/Author	(17??-18??) English	[L4,R]
BRYAN, MARY Plant Pathologist	(1900s early) American	[R1,R2]
BRYANT, LOUISE STEVENS Physician/Statistician	(18??-19??) American	[R1]
BRYANT, SOPHIE WILLOCK Mathematician/Statistician	(18??-1922) American	[M8,R]

BUCCA, DOROTEA   (1400-1436)   [K,Z,L6,R]
Physician/Philosopher/Educator   Italian

BUCCHI, DOROTHEA: See BUCCA, DOROTEA

BUCKLAND, MRS. WILLIAM   (1800s)   [Z]
Geologist   English

BUDENBACH, MARY H.   (1900s)   [01]
Mathematician/Cryptologist   American

BUELL, MARY VAN RENSSELAER   (1893-)   [W]
Biochemist   American

BULBRING, EDITH   (1900s)   [E,L3]
Pharmacologist   English   [FR]

BULL, NINA   (1880-)   [W]
Research Psychologist   American

BUNCE, ELIZABETH THOMPSON   (1915-)   [A,01]
Geophysicist/Oceanographer   American

BUNTING, MARY INGRAHAM   (1910-)   [A,W1,01,B5]
Microbiologist/Educator   American   [NB]

BUNZEL, RUTH L.   (1898-)   [W,R1]
Anthropologist   American

BUONSIGNORE, MADALENA   (1300s)   [K]
Physician   Italian

BURBIDGE, (ELEANOR) MARGARET PEACHEY (c. 1925-)   [A,01,D4,E2]
Astronomer   English/American   [NS,FR]

BURGESS, MARY AYRES   (1885-1953)   [M8]
Mathematician/Statistician/Educator American

BURKS, MARTHA A.   (1900s)   [D3]
Computer Scientist   American   [HA]

BURLIN, NATALIE CURTIS   (1875-1921)   [L2]
Anthropologist/Ethnologist   American

BURNELL, JOCELYN BELL   (1900s)   [01,P7]
Radio Astronomer/Astrophysicist   English

BURNS, ELEANOR   (1800s-1900s)   [R1]
Physicist   American/Turkish

BURNS, LOUISA   (1869-1958)   [W]
Osteopathic Physician   American

BURTON, BEVERLY S.   (18??-1904)   [I3]
Chemist   American

BURY, ELIZABETH   (1644-??)   [K,F4]
Anatomist/Physician/Mathematician   English

BUSH, KATHARINE JEANNETTE   (1855-1937)   [W,Z,S1,R1]
  Marine Zoologist   American

BUSSEY, JOANNA   (1900s early)   [R1]
  Physicist   American

BUTLER, MARGARET K.   (1924-)   [W,O1]
  Computer Scientist/Mathematician American

BUTTELINI, MARCHESA   (1700s)   [K]
  Physician   Italian

BUVINIC, MAYRA   (1900s)   [O1]
  Social Psychologist   Chilean/American

BYERS, NINA   (1930-)   [A,O1]
  Physicist   American

BYO   (BC 400s)   [P5]
  Philosopher/Mathematician   Greek/Italian

BYRD, EMMA   (1800s-1900s)   [R1,R]
  Astronomer   American

BYRON, ADA AUGUSTA: *See* LOVELACE, ADA BYRON

C

CADE, RUTH ANN   (1937-)   [O1]
  Statistician/Computer Scientist American

CAERELLA: *See* CAERELLIA

CAERELLIA   (BC 000s)   [P5]
  Philosopher/Author/Educator   Greek/Roman

CAETANI-BOVATELLI, DONNA ERSILIA   (1800s-1900s)   [Z]
  Archaeologist   Italian

CAHOON, MARY ODILE, SISTER   (1929-)   [A,O1]
  Cell Physiologist/Biologist   American

CALDERONE, MARY S.   (1904-)   [K2]
  Physician/Public Health Educator American

CALDERONE, NOVELLA   (1300s)   [K,R]
  Physician   Italian

CALDICOTT, HELEN   (1900s)   [O]
  Pediatrician/Physician/Educator Australian

CALDWELL, MARY E.   (1900s early)   [R1]
  Bacteriologist   American

CALDWELL, MARY L. Biochemist	(1890-1972) American	[O1,R1,W6]
CALENDA, COSTANZA Physician/Educator	(13??-14??) Italian	[H2,W4]
CALENDA, LAURA Physician/Educator	(1400s late) Italian	[K]
CALENDA, LAUREA CONSTANTIA Physician/Educator	(1400s early) Italian	[K]
CALKINS, MARY WHITON Psychologist	(1863-1930) American	[N2,L2,O1,V]
CALL, EMMA L. Physician	(1800s late) American	[D1,K3]
CALLOWAY, DORIS HOWES Nutritionist	(1923-) American	[W]
CALVERT, ADELIA SMITH Zoologist	(1800s-1900s) American	[R1]
CAMBRIERE, CLARICE Physician	(1300s early) French	[K,L6]
CANNON, ANNIE JUMP Astronomer	(1863-1941) American	[D,X,Z,W,B1] [HA]
CAPEN, BESSIE Chemist	(1800s late) American	[R1]
CAPO, MARY ANN Nuclear Engineer	(1900s) American	[O1]
CARLSON, ELIZABETH Mathematician	(1896-) American	[W]
CARLSON, LUCILE Geographer	(1904-) American	[W]
CAROLINE OF BRANDENBURG ANSPACH Mathematician/Physicist/Scholar	(1682-1737) German/English	[M5,D5,F4,R]

CAROLINE WILHELMINA DOROTHEA OF BRANDENBURG-ANSPACH: *See*
CAROLINE OF BRANDENBURG ANSPACH

CAROTHERS, E. ELEANOR Geneticist/Zoologist	(1882-) American	[R1,V,A1,S2]
CARPEGNA, COUNTESS, OF ROME Natural Scientist/Physician	(1600s) Italian	[K,R]
CARPENTER, ESTHER Zoologist	(1903-) American	[W]

CARPENTER, MIRIAM: *See* STRONG, MIRIAM CARPENTER

CARR, EMMA PERRY   (1880-1972)   [W,O1,N3,R1]
  Chemist/Educator   American

CARROLL-RUSK, EVELYN TERESA: *See* RUSK, EVELYN TERESA CARROLL

CARSON, RACHEL LOUISE   (1907-1964)   [W,N3,O1,H]
  Ecologist/Marine Biologist   American

CARSTEN, MARY E.   (1922-)   [W]
  Biochemist/Physiologist   American

CARTER, EDNA   (1800s)   [R1]
  Physicist   American

CARTER, ELIZABETH   (1717-1806)   [L4,D4,R]
  Astronomer/Physicist/Scholar   English

CARTER, MARY EDDIE   (1925-)   [A,O1]
  Fiber Chemist/Organic Chemist   American

CARTESIENNE, LA: *See* DUPRE, MARIAE

CARTWRIGHT, MARY LUCY, DAME   (1900-)   [W,L3,P3]
  Mathematician   English   [*FR*]

CARUS, MARY HEGELER   (1861-1936)   [R1]
  Mathematician   American

CARVAJALES Y CAMINO, LAURA M. DE   (18??-)   [D1]
  Physician   Cuban

CARVALHO, DOMITILA DE   (1900s)   [D1]
  Physician   Portuguese

CARVILL, MAUD   (18??-1944)   [O1]
  Ophthalmologist   American

CASE, ERMINE COWLES   (1871-1953)   [V,I5]
  Geologist/Paleontologist   American

CASE, MARY S.   (1800s-1900s)   [R1]
  Psychologist   American   [*HA*]

CASEIRO, MARJORIE C.   (1900s)   [O1,W6]
  Physical Organic Chemist   American

CASSANDRA FIDELIS   (1465-??)   [Z,K,R3,F4]
  Scientist/Physician/Scholar   Italian

CASTELLANI, MARIA   (1900s)   [W]
  Mathematician   Italian/American

CASTLE, CORA SUTTON   (18??-19??)   [R1]
  Psychologist/Statistician   American

CATANI, GIUSEPPINA   (18??-19??)   [Z,L6,R]
  Pathologist   Italian

CATERINA, MADONNA: See MADONNA CATERINA

CATHARINA: See CATHERINE OF ALEXANDRIA, SAINT

CATHARINA MEDICA DE CRACOVIE: See CATHERINE MEDICA OF CRACOW

CATHERINA   (1400s)   [H2]
  Physician   Italian

CATHERINE MEDICA OF CRACOW   (1300s)   [K,L6]
  Physician   Polish

CATHERINE OF ALEXANDRIA, SAINT   (2??-3??)   [P5,E2,R]
  Philosopher/Mathematician/Scientist Egyptian

CATHERINE OF BOLOGNA, SAINT   (1413-1463)   [K,E2]
  Physician   Italian

CATHERINE OF GENOA, SAINT   (1447-1510)   [K,F2,E2]
  Physician   Italian

CATHERINE OF SIENA, SAINT   (1347-1380)   [K,E2,B6]
  Physician   Italian

CATHERINE THE GREAT: See CATHERINE THE SECOND, QUEEN

CATHERINE THE SECOND, QUEEN   (1729-1796)   [K,F4,B6,R]
  Educator/Medical Reformer   German/Russian

CATHERINE URSULA OF BADEN   (1600s)   [K]
  Medical Practitioner/Scholar   German

CAUCHOIS, YVETTE   (1900s)   [C]
  Chemist/X-ray Spectroscopist   French

CAULLEY, MARY M.   (1800s)   [O]
  Botanist   American

CAUQUIL, GERMAINE ANNE   (1897-)   [W]
  Chemist   French

CAUSEY, CALISTA ELIOT   (1900s early)   [R1]
  Bacteriologist   American

CAUSEY, NELL BEVEL   (1910-)   [W]
  Invertebrate Zoologist   American

CAVENDISH, MARGARET, DUCHESS   (1624-1674)   [K,H,L4,F4]
  Natural Philosopher/Author   English

CEAUSESCU, ELENA   (1900s)   [I8,L3]
  Scientist/Engineer   Rumanian

CECELIA OF OXFORD   (1300s)   [K,W4]
  Surgeon/Physician   English

CELLIER, ELIZABETH   (1600s)   [K,W4]
  Midwife/Medical Statistician   English

CESNIECE-FREUDENFELDE, ZELMA   (1892-1929)   [F3]
  Physician   Latvian

CHAIX, PAULETTE AUDEMARD   (1904-)   [C]
  Biochemist   French

CHAKRAVARTI, DEBI MUKERJI   (1924-)   [W]
  Chemist   Indian

CHALUBINSKA, AMIELA   (1902-)   [C]
  Geographer   Polish

CHAMBERS, ANNETTE   (1900s)   [G]
  Guidance Project Engineer   American

CHANG, ANNIE C.Y.   (1900s)   [O]
  Genetic Engineer   American

CHANG, MARGUERITE SHUE-WEN   (1900s)   [O1]
  Research Chemist/Inventor   American

CHANIN, MARGARET   (1917-)   [O]
  Dentist   American   [HA]

CHANTAL, MME. DE: *See* DE CHANTAL, MME.

CHAPELLE, MARIE LOUISE: *See* LA CHAPELLE, MARIE LOUISE DUGES

CHARTZ, MARCELLINE   (1900s)   [G]
  Computer Scientist   American

CHASE, MARY AGNES MEARA   (1869-1963)   [N3,R,R1,A1]
  Botanist   American

CHASTELET, GABRIELLE-EMILIE: *See* CHATELET, GABRIELLE-EMILIE DU

CHATELET, GABRIELLE-EMILIE DU   (1706-1749)   [H,M,N,Z,B1]
  Mathematician/Physicist   French

CHATELET-LONOMT, GABRIELLE-EMILIE LE TONNELIER DE BRETEUIL,
  MARQUISE DU: *See* CHATELET, GABRIELLE-EMILIE DU

CHATHAM, ALICE   (1900s)   [G,H3]
  Design Engineer   American

CHATTERJEE, ASHIMA MUKHERJEE   (1900s)   [W,I6,I9]
  Chemist   Indian

CHAUCER, MRS., DUCHESS OF SUFFOLK   (14??-1475)   [K]
  Physician   English

CHAWLA, S.   (1927-)   [W]
  Physician   Indian

CHELLIER-FUMAT, DOROTHEE Physician	(1800s-1900s) Algerian	[D1,R]
CHEN, OLIVIA L. Environmental Engineer	(1900s) American	[M1] [*MI*]
CHIANG KAI-SHEK, MADAME Sociologist/Politician	(1898-) Chinese	[Q1]
CHILIA, ELVIRA REY Physician	(1900s) Cuban	[D1]
CHILONIS Natural Philosopher/Mathematician	(BC 400s) Greek	[P5]
CHILTON, MARY DELL MATCHETT Biochemist/Agricultural Chemist	(1939-) American	[A] [*NS*]
CHINCHON, COUNTESS OF Medical Innovator	(1599-1641) Spanish/Peruvian	[Z,K,L6]
CHING, TE MAY TSOU Physiologist	(1923-) Chinese/American	[W]
CHINN, MAY E. Physician	(1896-) American	[O1] [*MI*]
CHINNAPPA, LUCIA NARAMANIC V. Physician	(1900s early) Indian	[D1]
CHINNATAMBY, SIVA Gynecologist/Obstetrician	(1900s) Sri Lankan/Ceylonese	[O1]

CHISHOLM, GRACE: See YOUNG, GRACE CHISHOLM

CHISHOLM-YOUNG, GRACE: See YOUNG, GRACE CHISHOLM

CHMIELEWSKA, IRENA Biochemist/Biologist	(1905-) Polish	[C,E,L3]

CHMIELEWSKA, IRENE: See CHMIELEWSKA, IRENA

CHRISTINA, QUEEN OF SWEDEN Mathematician/Scientist/Scholar	(1626-1689) Swedish	[Z,K,M5,T1]
CHRISTINA OF HESSE Mathematician/Scientist	(1578-1658) German	[K,B1]

CHRISTINE DE PISAN: See PISAN, CHRISTINE DE

CHRISTINE OF SWEDEN, QUEEN: See CHRISTINA, QUEEN OF SWEDEN

CHUTE, HETTIE MORSE Botanist	(1900s early) American	[R1]

CIBRARIO, MARIA: See CINQUINI, MARIA DEI CONTI CIBRARIO

CIMINI, MARIA DOLORES Clinical Psychologist	(1900s) American	[D3] [*HA*]

CINCHON, COUNTESS OF: *See* CHINCHON, COUNTESS OF

CINQUINI, MARIA DEI CONTI CIBRARIO   (1906-)   [C,W,M9]
  Mathematician   Italian

CINQUINI-CIBRARIO, MARIA: *See* CINQUINI, MARIA DEI CONTI CIBRARIO

CIORANESCU-NENITZESCU, ECATERINA   (1909-)   [C]
  Organic Chemist   Rumanian

CLAGHORN, KATE HOLLODAY   (1800s-1900s)   [S1]
  Industrial Statistician   American

CLAPP, CORNELIA MARIA   (1849-1934)   [N2,L2,R1,Z]
  Marine Biologist/Zoologist   American

CLARA OF ASSISI, SAINT   (1200s)   [K]
  Physician   Czech/Italian

CLARICE OF ROUEN: *See* CLARISSE OF ROTOMAGO

CLARISSE OF ROTOMAGO   (12??-13??)   [K,H2,L6]
  Physician   French

CLARISSE OF ROUEN: *See* CLARISSE OF ROTOMAGO

CLARK, ARABELLA   (1700s-1800s)   [O]
  Botanist   American

CLARK, BERTHA   (1800s-1900s)   [R1]
  Physicist/Educator   American

CLARK, CORA   (1800s)   [R1]
  Zoologist   American

CLARK, EUGENIE   (1922-)   [W,O1,I5]
  Ichthyologist/Marine Zoologist   American

CLARK, JANET HOWELL   (1900s early)   [R1]
  Physiologist   American

CLARK, YVONNE   (1929-)   [O1]
  Mechanical Engineer   American

CLARKE, CORA HUIDEKOPER   (1851-1916)   [Z,R1,I3]
  Botanist/Entomologist   American

CLARKE, EDITH   (1883-1959)   [N3,O1,E1]
  Electrical Power Systems Engineer   American

CLARKE, ELIZABETH L.   (1900s)   [R1]
  Agricultural Scientist   American

CLARKE, NANCY TALBOT   (1825-1901)   [W4,I5]
  Physiologist/Physician   American

CLARKE, PATRICIA HANNAH   (1919-)   [E,L3]
  Microbial Biochemist   English   [FR]

CLAUDIA FELICITAS, QUEEN: See FELICITAS, CLAUDIA

CLAYPOLE, AGNES: See MOODY, AGNES CLAYPOLE

CLAYPOLE, EDITH JANE   (18??-1915)   [Z,I3,R1]
  Pathologist/Biologist   American

CLAYTON, BARBARA   (1922-)   [O]
  Chemical Pathologist/Educator   English

CLAYTON, FRANCES ELIZABETH   (1922-)   [W]
  Geneticist   American

CLEA   (100 c.)   [R,P5]
  Philosopher/Scholar   Greek

CLEAECHMA   (BC 400s)   [P5]
  Philosopher/Mathematician   Greek

CLEAVE, MARY   (1900s)   [O]
  Phycologist   American   [AS]

CLEMENT, JACQUELINE   (1916-)   [W]
  Biochemist   French

CLEMENT, MARGARET   (1508-1570)   [F4]
  Scholar/Scientist/Linguist   English

CLEMENTS, EDITH SCHWARTZ   (18??-19??)   [R1]
  Botanist/Plant Ecologist   American

CLEOBULINA   (BC 600s-500s)   [R,P5]
  Philosopher/Physician/Author   Greek

CLEOBULINE: See CLEOBULINA

CLEOPATRA   (000s-100s)   [K,Z,B1,L6]
  Physician/Gynecologist/Educator   Greek/Roman

CLEOPATRA   (000s-100s)   [K,A4,R]
  Cosmetic Chemist   Roman/Egyptian

CLEOPATRA THE ALCHEMIST   (100s)   [C5,C8,C9,R]
  Alchemist/Physicist/Inventor   Egyptian

CLEOPATRA THE COPT: See CLEOPATRA THE ALCHEMIST

CLEOPATRE: See CLEOPATRA

CLERKE, AGNES MARY   (1842-1907)   [Z,S1,I3,I5]
  Astronomer   English/Irish

CLERKE, ELLEN M.   (1800s-1900s)   [Z,R]
  Astronomer   English

CLIFFORD, ANN, LADY Scientist/Alchemist/Scholar	(1500s-1600s) English	[K]
CLOTHILDE OF BURGANDY Physician	(400s-500s) French	[K]
COBB, JEWEL PLUMMER Cell Physiologist/Educator	(1924-) American	[A] [NB,MI]
COBB, MARGARET Psychologist	(18??-19??) American	[R1]
COBB, ROSALIE M. KARAPETOFF Chemist	(1900s early) American	[R1]
COBBE, ANNE PHILIPPA Mathematician	(1920-1971) English	[M8]
COBBE, FRANCES POWER Social Scientist	(1822-1904) Irish/English	[I4]
COBBE, MARGARET Midwife/Obstetrician	(1400s) English	[K]
CODERE, HELEN FRANCES Anthropologist	(1917-) American	[W]
COHN, MILDRED Biophysicist/Biochemist	(1913-) American	[A,O1,W6] [NS]
COLDEN, JANE Botanist	(1724-1766) American	[N2,R1,V]
COLE, ISABELLA J. Mathematician	(1900s) American	[M1] [MI]
COLE, LUELLA: See PRESSEY, LUELLA COLE		
COLE, REBECCA Physician	(1800s) American	[D1] [MI]
COLINET, MARIE: See VON HILDEN, MARIE COLINET		
COLLINS, MARY Psychologist	(1900s) Scottish	[L3]
COLSON, ELIZABETH FLORENCE Anthropologist	(1917-) American	[A,O1] [NS]
COLWELL, RITA R. Microbiologist	(1934-) American	[A,F]
COMBES, FRANCES Obstetrician/Medical Practitioner	(1700s) American	[W4]
COMNENA, ANNA Physician/Mathematician/Scholar	(1083-1148) Turkish/Byzantine	[K,B1,U1,D4]

COMNENA, BERTHA Physician	(1100s) Hungarian/Byzantine	[K,B1]

COMNENA, IRENE, QUEEN: See IRENE, QUEEN

COMSTOCK, ANNA BOTSFORD Entomologist/Zoologist/Botanist	(1854-1930) American	[W,N2,L2,R1]
COMYNS-LEWER, ETHEL Ornithologist	(1800s-1900s) English	[S1]
CONE, CLARIBEL Pathologist	(18??-1929) American	[D1,K3]
CONNOR, JEAN Medical Scientist	(1900s early) Australian	[D1]
CONVERSE, JEANNE Physician	(1300s early) French	[K,L6]
CONWAY, ELSIE Botanist	(1900s) Scottish	[L3]
CONWELL, ESTHER MARLEY Physicist/Engineer	(1922-) American	[A,W,O1] [NE]
COOK, ALICE CARTER Botanist	(18??-19??) American	[R1]
COOK, MARGUERITE Mathematician/Statistician	(1900-1965) American	[M8]
COOKSIN, ISABEL CLINTON Paleobotanist	(1893-) Australian	[W]
COOPER, ELIZABETH MORGAN Mathematician	(1890?-1967) American	[M8]
COPELAND, LENNIE PHOEBE Mathematician	(1881-1951) American	[M8]

CORANO, HELENA LUCRETIA: See CORNERO, ELLENA LUCRETIA

CORI, GERTY THERESA RADNITZ Biochemist	(1896-1957) Czech/American	[D,L,W,Y,C1] [NL,NS]

CORNARO, HELENA LUCRETIA: See CORNERO, ELLENA LUCRETIA

CORNERO, ELLENA LUCRETIA Mathematician/Scientist/Physician	(1646-1684) Italian	[K,I4,F4,R]
CORREIA, ELISA Physician	(1800s-1900s) Portuguese	[D1]
CORREL, HELEN B. Aquatic Biologist	(1907-) American	[O1]

CORTESE, ISABELLA   (15??-1561)   [K]
  Chemist/Alchemist/Physician   Italian

COSTA BLANCHE, MARIE DE: See BLANCHE, MARIE DE COSTE

COSTON, MARTHA J.   (1800s)   [R]
  Inventor   American

COUDRAY, ANGELIQUE DU: See DU COUDRAY, ANGELIQUE MARGUERITE

COUDREAU, OCTAVIE, MADAME   (1800s)   [Z,U1]
  Naturalist/Cartographer/Explorer   French

COUSIN, GERMAINE   (1900s)   [C]
  Biologist   French

COWLEY, ANNE PYNE   (1938-)   [A,O1]
  Astronomer/Stellar Spectroscopist   American

COX, CATHARINE: See MILES, CATHARINE COX

COX, GERTRUDE MARY   (19??-1978)   [O1]
  Statistician   American   [NS]

COX, RACHEL DUNAWAY   (1904-)   [W]
  Psychologist   American

COXE, MATILDA: See STEVENSON, MATILDA COXE EVANS

CRAIGHILL, REBECCA: See LANCEFIELD, REBECCA CRAIGHILL

CRAM, ELOISE BLAINE   (1896-1957)   [R1]
  Parisitologist/Zoologist   American

CRAMER, CATHERINE GERTRUDE   (1655-1746)   [K]
  Midwife/Obstetrician   Dutch

CRANE, JOCELYN   (1909-)   [Y,R1,I5]
  Zoologist   American

CRANNELL, CAROL JO ARGUS   (1938-)   [A]
  Astrophysicist   American

CRANWELL, LUCY M.   (1900s)   [L3]
  Scientist   New Zealander

CRAWFORD, JEAN VEGHTE   (1919-)   [W]
  Chemist   American

CREIGHTON, HARRIET   (1900s early)   [R1]
  Botanist   American

CREMER, ERIKA   (1900-)   [C,W]
  Physical Chemist   Austrian

CROSBY, ELIZABETH CAROLINE   (1888-)   [W,S2,R1,A1]
  Anatomist   American

CROTTY, GERTRUDE: *See* DAVENPORT, GERTRUDE CROTTY

CRUTCHFIELD, MITSCH Physician	(1900s) American	[M1] [*MI*]
CRUZ, JUANA INEZ DE LA Scholar/Author/Philosopher	(1651-1695) Mexican	[F4]
CRUZ, ZENAIDA G. Veterinarian	(1900s) Philippine	[L3]
CULLIS, WINIFRED CLARA Physiologist	(1875-1956) English	[R1,I5,I7]
CULLUM, JANE KEHOE Applied Mathematician	(1938-) American	[A]
CUMMINGS, CLARA EATON Cryptogamic Botanist	(1855-1906) American	[Z,I3]
CUMMINGS, LOUISE DUFFIELD Mathematician	(1870-1947) Canadian/American	[M7,M8]
CUNEGUNDE Physician	(1200s) Polish	[K]
CUNEGUNDE Physician	(900s-1000s) German	[K]
CUNITZ, MARIA Astronomer/Author	(1610-1664) German/Italian	[H,B1,S1,Z]
CUNNINGHAM, SUSAN Astronomer/Mathematician	(18??-19??) American	[Z,R1,A]
CURBY, NORMA Structural Design Engineer	(1900s) American	[O] [*MI*]
CURIE, MARIE SKLODOWSKA Chemist/Physicist	(1867-1931) Polish/French	[H,L,W,Z,C1] [*NL*]
CURRAN, MARY Botanist	(1800s late) American	[O]
CURTIS, KATHLEEN M. Scientist	(1900s) New Zealander	[L3]
CUSHMAN, FLORENCE Astronomer	(1800s-1900s) American	[Z]
CUST, AILEEN Veterinary Surgeon	(1900s early) British	[B1]
CUTTER, ELIZABETH GRAHAM Botanist	(1900s) Scottish	[L3]

D

DACIER, MADAME: *See* LEFEVRE, ANNE

DACK, GAIL Pathologist	(1900s early) American	[B2]
DAI, MINH THI Chemical Engineer	(1900s) American	[M1] [MI]
DAMO Natural Philosopher/Mathematician	(BC 500s) Greek/Italian	[R,P5]
DANIEL, ANNIE Physician	(18??-1944) American	[O1]
DANIEL, LOUISE JANE Biochemist	(1912-) American	[W]
DANIELLO, ANTONIA Physician/Educator	(13??-14??) Italian	[K]
DANIELS, AMY Chemist/Home Economist/Psychologist	(1900s early) American	[R1,V]
DANTE, THEODORA Mathematician/Educator	(1500s) Italian	[F4,R]
D'ARCONVILLE, GENEVIEVE CHARLOTTE Anatomist/Chemist/Natural Scientist	(1720-1805) French	[K,B1,D4,L6]
DASTIDAR, SUJATA D. Biomedical Scientist	(1900s) Indian	[I9]
D'AUXERRE, JEANNE Surgeon	(1300s) French	[H2]
DAVENPORT, GERTRUDE CROTTY Zoologist	(1800s) American	[R1,V]
DAVIDSON, ADA D. Geologist	(18??-19??) American	[Z,R1]
DAVIDSON, BETTY Biochemist	(1933-) American	[A] [HA]
DAVIS, AUDREY KENNON Physiologist	(1920-) American	[W]
DAVIS, GRACE Physicist	(1800s-1900s) American	[R1]
DAVIS, MARGARET BRYAN Paleoecologist	(1931-) American	[A] [NS]

DAVIS, RUTH MARGARET   (1928-)   [A,O1]
Computer Scientist/Mathematician   American   [NE]

DAWSON, MERNA   (1900s)   [G]
Analytical Chemist   American

DAY, MARY   (18??-19??)   [R1]
Botanist   American

DE ALMANIA, JACQUELINE FELICIE   (1300s)   [M2]
Physician   German/French

DEANE, HELEN WENDLER   (1917-)   [W]
Anatomist   American

DE BEAUSOLEIL, MARTINE: See DU CHATELET, MARTINE DE BIRTEREAU

DE BIHERON, MLLE.: See BIHERON, MLLE.

DEBORAH OF JUDEA   (BC 1300 c.)   [K,F3]
Physician   Judean

DE BREAUTE, ELEONORE-NEIL-SUZANNE   (1786-1867)   [W]
Physician   French

DE BRETEUIL, EMILIE, MARQUISE DU CHATELET: See CHATELET,
   GABRIELLE-EMILIE DU

DE BROUCKERE, LUCIA   (1904-)   [C]
Physical Chemist   Belgian

DECANDOLLE, ANNE CASIMIR   (1836-1918)   [I3]
Botanist   Swiss

DE CASTRA, ANNA   (1600s)   [K]
Philosopher/Scholar   Spanish

DE CHAILLY, JEANNE   (1400s)   [H2]
Physician   French

DE CHANTAL, MME.   (1572-1641)   [K]
Midwife/Obstetrician   French

DE FERRE, YVETTE   (1915-)   [C]
Botanist   French

DE FOREST, NORA S. BLATCH: See BARNEY, NORA STANTON BLATCH

DE FORLI, MADAME: See SFORZA, CATHERINE

DE FOSCHUA, ULRICHA   (1300s)   [K]
Oculist   German

DE GORZANO, LEONETTA   (1300s)   [K]
Physician   Italian

DE GROOT, JEANNE LAMPL   (1895–)   [W]
Psychiatrist   Dutch

DE GY, MARIE   (13??–14??)   [H2]
Physician   French

DE HILDEN, MARIE: *See* VON HILDEN, MARIE COLINET

DEJERINE–KLUMPKE, AUGUSTA   (1889–1927)   [W,R]
Neurologist   French

DE LAGUNA, FREDERICA ANNIS   (1906–)   [A,W,O1]
Anthropologist   American   [*NS*]

DE LALANDE, MME. LEFRANCAISE: *See* LALANDE, MARIE LEFRANCAIS DE

DE LA MARCHE, MARGUERITE DU TERTRE   (1638–1706)   [W4,K,L6]
Obstetrician/Educator/Author   French

DE LA MOTTE, MADAME   (1600s)   [K]
Midwife/Obstetrician/Educator   French

DE LANGE, CORNELIA CATHARINA   (1871–1950)   [W,D1,I5]
Physician/Pediatrician   Dutch

DELANO, JANE ARMINDA   (1862–1919)   [B1,N2]
Nurse   American

DE LA SABLIERE, MARGUERITE: *See* SABLIERE, MARGUERITE DE LA

DELAUNEY, MARGUERITE DE STAEL   (1693–1750)   [B1,K,R]
Anatomist   French

DE LEBRIX, FRANCOISE   (1500s)   [K]
Physician   Spanish

DEL MUNDO, FE   (1900s)   [D1]
Physician   Philippine

DE MEDICI, CATHERINE: *See* MEDICI, CATHERINE DE

DE MELUN, MLLE.   (16??–1679)   [K]
Nurse/Physician   French

DE MEURON–LANDOLT, MONIQUE   (1900s)   [I6]
Biochemist   French/English

DE MONTANEIS, STEPHANIE   (1200s)   [H2]
Physician   French

DEMUD   (1300s)   [K]
Physician   German

DENNING, DELIA   (1800s–1900s)   [R1]
Geographer   American

DENNIS, OLIVE WETZEL Safety Engineer	(1885-1957) American	[W,R1,I5]
DE NOCHERA, MARIA TERESA MORA Public Health Physician	(1900s early) American	[D1] [MI]
DE NOLDE, HELENE ALDEGONDE Physician	(1600s-1700s) German	[K]
DENSMORE, FRANCES THERESA Anthropologist/Ethnomusicologist	(1867-1957) American	[N3,R1]

DE PARTHENAY, CATHERINE: See PARTHENAY, CATHERINE DE

DE PISAN, CHRISTINE: See PISAN, CHRISTINE DE

DE ROMANA, FRANCESCA: See DE ROMANA, FRANCOISE

DE ROMANA, FRANCOISE Surgeon	(1300s) Italian	[K,Z,H2,L6]
DERSCHEID-DELCOURT, MARIE Physician/Medical Historian	(18??-19??) Belgian	[K,D1]
DER WOLFF, FRAULEIN Surgeon	(1300s) German	[K]
DE SALINS, GUIGNONNE Physician	(1400s) French	[K]
DE SEVIGNE, MADAME Physician	(1629-1696) French	[K]

DE SILVA, YA MEI KIN: See YA MEI KIN

DE STAEL DELAUNEY, MME.: See DELAUNEY, MARGUERITE DE STAEL

DE STAEL HOLSTEIN, MME.: See NECKER, ANNE GERMAINE

D'ESTE, ISABELLA: See ESTE, ISABELLA D'

DES WOLFFES, FRAULEIN Physician/Surgeon	(13??-14??) German	[H2]
DETMERS, FREDA Botanist	(18??-19??) American	[R1]
DEUTSCH, HELENE Psychologist/Psychoanalyst	(1884-1982) Polish/Austrian	[O1,D4]
DE VALOIS, MADAME Physician	(1200s) French	[K]
DEWEY, JANE Physicist/Spectroscopist	(1900s early) American	[R1]

DE WITT, LYDIA MARIA ADAMS   (1859-1928)   [N2,B2,R1]
  Anatomist/Pathologist/Physician   American

DE WOLFE, BARBARA BLANCHARD   (1912-)   [W]
  Zoologist   American

DE YPRA, MARGUERITE: See MARGARET OF YPRES

DIANA OF POITIERS   (1400s-1500s)   [R3]
  Natural Scientist/Physician/Artist French

DIAZ, ELOIZA   (18??-)   [D1]
  Physician   Chilean

DIBLAN, MAKBULE   (1900s)   [D1]
  Physician   Turkish

DI CANDIA, BEATRICE   (12??-13??)   [H2]
  Physician   Italian

DICK, GLADYS ROWENA HENRY   (1881-1963)   [N3,O1,R1]
  Microbiologist/Physician   American

DICKENS, HELEN OCTAVIA   (1900s)   [O1]
  Obstetrician/Gynecologist/Surgeon American   [MI]

DIETRICH, JUSTINA: See SIEGEMUNDIN, JUSTINE DITTRICHIN

DIETRICH, (KONKORDIE) AMALIE NELLE   (1821-1891)   [W,Z,I5]
  Botanist/Naturalist   German/Australian

DIEULAFOY, JEANNE PAULE MAGRE   (1851-1916)   [Z,I5,R]
  Archaeologist   French

DIMOCK, SUSAN   (1847-1875)   [N2,B1,D1]
  Surgeon/Physician   American

DINER, HELEN: See ECKSTEIN-DIENER, BERTHA

DI NOVELLA, MARIA   (1200s)   [K]
  Mathematician/Educator   Italian

DIOTIMA   (BC 400s)   [F2,Z,F4,P5]
  Scholar/Natural Scientist/Educator Greek

DIOTYMA: See DIOTIMA

DIX, DOROTHEA LYNDE   (1802-1887)   [W,W4]
  Nurse/Mental Health Reformer   American

DOBREANU-ENESCU, VIORICA   (1924-)   [W]
  Physician   Rumanian

DOKHMAN, GENRIETTA ISAAKOVNA   (1897-)   [W]
  Phytocenologist/Geobotanist   Russian

DOLLEY, SARAH H. ADAMSON   (1829-1909)   [O1,S1,K3]
  Physician   American

DOLLEY, SARAH R.E.: *See* DOLLEY, SARAH R. ADAMSON

DOMBROVSKAYA, YULIYA FOMINICHNA Pediatrician	(1891-) Russian	[S,W]
DOMNA, JULIA Philosopher/Educator	(1??-217) Syrian/Roman	[G3,F4,R,P5]
DOMNINA Physician	(100s-200s) Roman/Asian	[G2]
DONAJ, CECILIA KRIEGER Mathematician	(19??-1974) Canadian	[M8]
DONALD, MARY JANE Geologist	(18??-19??) American	[S1]
DONNE, MARIA DALLE Physician/Surgeon/Physicist	(1778-1842) Italian	[Z,K,D1,H,R]

DONNE, MARIA DELLE: *See* DONNE, MARIA DALLE

DORABIALSKA, ALICE DOMENICA Chemist/Radiochemist	(1897-) Polish	[W,C]
DORETY, ANGELA, SISTER Botanist	(18??-19??) American	[R1]
DOUBLEDAY, NELTJE B. DE GRAFF Naturalist	(1865-1918) American	[N2]
DOUVIN, ELIZABETH Psychologist	(1926-) American	[Q1]
DOWNEY, JUNE ETTA Psychologist	(1875-1932) American	[N2,L2,R1]
DOWNS, CORA Bacteriologist/Virologist	(1900s) American	[O1,B5]
DOWNS, CORNELIA MITCHELL Microbiologist	(1892-) American	[W]
DRANT, PATRICIA HART Dermatologist	(1895-1955) American	[W]
DRAPER, MARY ANNA PALMER Astrophysicist	(18??-1914) American	[I3]
DREBENEVA-UKHOVA, VARVARA PAVLOVNA Entomologist	(1903-) Russian	[W]
DRESSELHAUS, MILDRED S. REIF Physicist/Electrical Engineer	(1930-) American	[A,O1,K2,C3] [NS,NE]
DU BOIS, CORA Anthropologist	(1903-) American	[R1,W]

DU BONNAY, MARCHIONESS   (1700s)   [K]
  Botanist/Herbalist   French

DUBREIL-JACOTIN, MARIE-LOUISE   (1905-1972)   [C,M8]
  Mathematician   French

DU CHATELET, GABRIELLE-EMILIE (MARQUISE): *See* CHATELET,
  GABRIELLE-EMILIE DU

DU CHATELET, MARTINE DE BIRTEREAU   (1602-1642)   [W,Z,H,I5,R]
  Mineralogist/Mining Engineer   French

DU COUDRAY, ANGELIQUE MARGUERITE   (1712-1789)   [K,B1,W4,I4]
  Obstetrician/Educator   French

DU COUDRAY, LOUISE LEBOURSIER   (1700s)   [K]
  Obstetrician/Educator   French

DUFFY, ELIZABETH   (1904-)   [W]
  Psychologist   American

DUGES, MARIE-JONET   (1730-1797)   [K,W4]
  Obstetrician/Midwife   French

DUGES, MARIE LOUISE: *See* LA CHAPELLE, MARIE LOUISE DUGES

DUIGNAN-WOODS, EILEEN   (1900s)   [O1]
  Project Engineer   American

DU LUYS, GUILLEMETTE   (1400s late)   [H2]
  Surgeon   French

DUMEE, JEANNE   (16??-1706)   [W,Z,I5,N4]
  Astronomer/Author   French

DUNBAR, ALICE DAVIS   (18??-19??)   [R1]
  Chemist   American

DUNBAR, (HELEN) FLANDERS   (1902-)   [W,N3]
  Psychiatrist   American

DUNHAM, KATHERINE   (1910-)   [L2]
  Anthropologist/Ethnologist   American

DUNN, LOUISE BRISBIN   (18??-1902)   [I3]
  Botanist   American

DUNNING, WILHELMINA FRANCES   (1904-)   [W]
  Biologist   American

DU PIERRY, MME.   (1600s-1700s)   [Z,R]
  Astronomer/Mathematician/Author   French

DUPRE, MARIAE   (16??-1675)   [F4,R]
  Philosopher/Scholar/Scientist   French

DUROCHER, MARIE JOSEFINA MATILDE   (1809-1895)   [D1,I5]
  Obstetrician/Physician   French/Brazilian

DU SAULT, LUCILLE ANNE   (1900s)   [W]
  Radiological Physicist   American

DUSEL-BACON, CYNTHIA   (1946-)   [A,D3]
  Geologist/Metamorphic Petrologist American   [*HA*]

DYE, MARIE   (1891-)   [W,I5]
  Nutrition Research Worker   American

DYER, HELEN M.   (1900s)   [O1,R1,W6]
  Biochemist/Oncologist   American

E

EADY, DOROTHY   (1904-1981)   [H3,D4]
  Archaeologist   English/Egyptian

EARLE, SYLVIA   (1935-)   [O1,H3,D4]
  Marine Biologist/Ecologist   American

EASLEY, ANNIE   (1932-)   [U]
  Computer Scientist   American   [*MI*]

EASTMAN, ALICE   (1800s-1900s)   [Z]
  Botanist   American

EASTWOOD, ALICE   (1859-1953)   [W,N3,R1,A1]
  Botanist   American

EAVES, ELSIE   (1898-)   [O1,R1,I5]
  Civil Engineer   American

EBERLEIN, PATRICIA JAMES   (1925-)   [A]
  Computer Scientist   American

EBERS, EDITH HEIRICH   (1894-)   [W]
  Geologist   German

ECATERINA: *See* CATHARINE OF ALEXANDRIA, SAINT

ECATERINE THE MARTYR: *See* CATHERINE OF ALEXANDRIA, SAINT

ECCELLO OF LUCANIA   (BC 400s)   [P5]
  Natural Philosopher/Mathematician Greek/Italian

ECHECRATIA THE PHILIASIAN   (BC 400s)   [P5]
  Philosopher/Mathematician   Greek/Italian

ECKERSON, SOPHIA H.   (1800s-1900s)   [R1,A1,B2]
  Botanist/Plant Physiologist   American

ECKERT, MARION   (1899-1969)   [R1]
  Geographer   American

ECKSTEIN-DIENER, BERTHA Sociologist	(1900s) German	[O1]
ECKSTORM, FANNIE PEARSON HARDY Ornithologist/Naturalist	(1865-1946) American	[N2,L2]
EDDY, BERNICE ELAINE Microbiologist/Viral Oncologist	(1903-) American	[A,O1]
EDDY, IMOGEN W. Mathematician	(18??-1904) American	[I3]
EDDY, MARY PIERSON Physician	(1800s-1900s) Syrian	[D1]
EDGEWORTH, MARIA Engineering Educator/Author	(17??-18??) English	[T4]
EDINGER, TILLY Vertebrate Paleontologist	(1897-) German/American	[W,N3,R1] [HA]
EDSON, FANNY CARTER Micropaleontologist/Geologist	(1887-1952) American	[R1]
EDWARDS, AMELIA ANN BLANFORD Archaeologist/Explorer	(1831-1892) English	[Z,I3]
EDWARDS, CECILE HOOVER Nutritionist	(1926-) American	[W]
EDWARDS, MARIE Psychologist	(1926?-) American	[Q1]
EGLUI, ELLEN Inventor	(1800s) American	[O] [MI]
EICHELBERGER, LILLIAN Biochemist	(1897-) American	[W]
EIGENMANN, ROSA SMITH Ichthyologist/Zoologist	(1858-1947) American	[N2,R1,Z,V]
EIMMART, MARIE CLAIRE Astronomer	(1676-1717) German	[N4,R]
ELDERTON, ETHEL MARY Mathematician/Statistician	(1878-1954) British	[M8]
ELEANOR OF AQUITAINE, QUEEN Physician/Scholar	(1122-1204) French	[K]
ELEANORA, DUCHESS OF MANTUA Obstetrician/Physician	(1600s) Italian	[K]
ELEANORA, DUCHESS OF TROPPAU Physician/Pharmacist/Nutritionist	(15??-16??) German	[K]

ELEPHANTIS: *See* PHILISTA

ELION, GERTRUDE BELLE Pharmacologist/Biochemist	(1918-) American	[A,O1,W6]
ELIOT, MARTHA M. Medical Scientist/Physician	(1891-1978) American	[R1,K3]

ELISABETH DE HONGRIE: *See* ELIZABETH OF HUNGARY, SAINT

ELIZABETH Physician	(1200s) Czechoslovakian	[K]
ELIZABETH Physician	(1300s) Polish/Hungarian	[K]
ELIZABETH, COUNTESS OF KENT Pharmacist/Physician/Author	(1500s-1600s) English	[K,L6]

ELIZABETH FREDERICA OF BOHEMIA: *See* ELIZABETH OF BOHEMIA,
PRINCESS

ELIZABETH OF ARAGON Physician	(1271-1336) Spanish/Portuguese	[K]
ELIZABETH OF BOHEMIA, PRINCESS Mathematician/Scientist/Physician	(1618-1680) German/Czech	[Z,K,M5,T1]
ELIZABETH OF BRANDENBURG, PRINCESS Physician	(1550-) German	[K]
ELIZABETH OF HUNGARY, SAINT Physician	(1207-1230) Hungarian	[K,L6]
ELIZABETH OF PORTUGAL, QUEEN Physician	(1400s) Portuguese	[K]
ELIZABETH OF SCHONAU Physician	(1129-1165) German	[W4]
ELLIOTT, CHARLOTTE Plant Pathologist	(1883-1974) American	[R1,R2]
ELLIS, ARVILLA J. Botanist	(18??-1889) American	[I3]
ELLIS, CONSTANCE Physician	(1900s early) Australian	[J2]
ELLIS, FLORENCE HAWLEY Anthropologist	(1906-) American	[W]
ELLISOR, ALVA CHRISTINE Micropaleontologist/Geologist	(1892-1964) American	[R1]

ELPES: *See* HELPES

EL SAADAWI, NAWAL Physician/Psychiatrist	(1930-) Egyptian	[O1]

EL SADEEK, WAFAA Archaeologist	(1900s) Egyptian	[O]
ELVIUS, AINA Astronomer	(1900s) Swedish	[L3]
ELY, ACHSAH M. Mathematician	(1848-1904) American	[I3]
EMERSON, ELLEN RUSSELL Anthropologist/Ethnologist	(1837-1907) American	[L2]
EMERSON, GLADYS ANDERSON Biochemist	(1903-1984) American	[P,W,Y,O1]
ENG, HU KING Physician	(18??-19??) Chinese	[K3]
ENGELBRECHT, MILDRED AMANDA Bacteriologist	(1899-) American	[W]
ENGERASIE Physician	(BC or early AD) Greek	[L6]
EPSTEIN, CYNTHIA FUCHS Sociologist	(1900s) American	[O1]
ERDMANN, RHODA Geneticist	(1800s) American	[V]
ERDMUTHE, SOPHIE Medical Practitioner/Scholar	(1644-1675) German	[K]
ERMOLIEVA, ZINAIDA VISSARIONOVNA Microbiologist	(1898-) Russian	[S,W]
ERXLEBEN, DOROTHEA CHRISTIANE Physician/Scientist	(1715-1762) German	[W,B1,D1,O1]
ESAU, KATHERINE Botanist	(1898-) American	[A,W,O1,R1] [NS]
ESTE, ISABELLA D' Archaeologist	(1474-1539) Italian	[Z,I5,R3]
ESTON, VERONICA RAPP Radiobiologist	(1918-) Brazilian	[W]
ESTRELA, MARIE AUGUSTA GENEROSO Physician	(1800s) Brazilian	[D1]
ESTRIN, THELMA A. Electrical/Biomedical Engineer	(1924-) American	[A,O1]

ETHELBERGA, ABBESS: *See* BERTHAGYTA, ABBESS

ETHELDREDA, SAINT: *See* ETHELDRIDA, QUEEN

ETHELDRIDA, QUEEN Physician/Educator	(630 c.-679) English	[K,E2]
EUDOCIA Philosopher/Scholar/Scientist	(1400s) Byzantine/Turkish	[P5,R]
EUDOCIA (ATHENAIS) Astronomer/Mathematician/Scholar	(396-460) Greek/Turkish/Roman	[F3,K,E2,R]

EUDOXIA, EMPRESS: See EUDOCIA (ATHENAIS)

EUGERASIA Physician	(100s) Roman	[K]

EUMETIS: See CLEOBULINA

EUPHEMIA OF WHERWELL, ABBESS Physician	(1100s-1200s) English	[K]
EURYDICE Philosopher	(100 c.) Greek/Egyptian	[R,P5]
EURYDICE OF ILLYRIUM Scholar	(BC or ealy AD) Greek/Yugoslavian	[P5]
EVANS, ALICE CATHERINE Bacteriologist/Microbiologist	(1881-1975) American	[N3,O1,R1]
EVANS, MARJORIE WOODARD Chemical Physicist	(1921-) American	[W]
EVANS, VIRGINIA JOHN Biologist	(1913-) American	[W]
EVENS, MARTHA WALTON Computer Scientist	(1935-) American	[A]
EVERARD, MS. Chemist/Pharmacist	(1600s late) English	[K]
EVERETT, ALICE Astronomer	(1800s-1900s) English	[Z,R]

F

FABER, SANDRA MOORE Astronomer	(1944-) American	[A] [NS]
FABIOLA Physician/Surgeon/Nurse	(3??-399 AD) Roman	[D1,B1,Z,K]

FABRI, CORNELIA   (1869-)   [M8,R]
  Mathematician/Physician   French/Italian

FABRICIUS, MARIE   (1600s)   [K]
  Surgeon   Swiss

FAILEY, HOYLANDE D. YOUNG   (1903-)   [A,O1]
  Nuclear Chemist   American

FAIRFAX, MARY: *See* SOMERVILLE, MARY FAIRFAX GREIG

FANNIA   (000s)   [P5]
  Philosopher   Roman

FARNSWORTH, ALICE   (1900s early)   [R1]
  Astronomer   American

FARQUHAR, MARILYN GIST   (1928-)   [W]
  Cell Biologist/Pathologist   American   [*NS*]

FARR, WANDA KIRKBRIDE   (1895-)   [W,X,Z,I5]
  Plant Physiologist/Biochemist   American

FARRAR, LILLIAN K.P.   (1800s-1900s)   [D1,K3]
  Radiologist/Gynecologist/Surgeon   American

FAUSTINA   (400s)   [K]
  Scholar/Medical Practitioner   Roman

FAVILLA   (100s)   [K]
  Physician   Roman

FAYE, MME.   (1800s-1900s)   [Z]
  Astronomer   French

FEARN, ANNE WALTER   (1865-1939)   [W,N2,I5]
  Physician/Surgeon   American

FEDELE, CASSANDRA: *See* CASSANDRA FIDELIS

FEGAN, CLAUDIA DAVIS   (1900s)   [O]
  Physician   American   [*MI*]

FELDMAN, JACQUELINE   (1900s)   [I6]
  Physicist   French

FELICIE, JACOBA   (1280 c.-13??)   [H,Z,H2,W4]
  Physician   French

FELICIE, JACOBINE: *See* FELICIE, JACOBA

FELICITAS, CLAUDIA   (1640-1705)   [K]
  Physician/Surgeon/Scholar   Austrian

FELL, ELIZA   (1800s)   [O]
  Botanist   American

FELL, HONOR BRIDGET, DAME Physiologist	(1900–) English	[E,D4,L3] [FR]
FELL, SARAH ANN Botanist	(1800s) American	[O]
FENNEL, DOROTHY I. Mold Microbiologist	(1900s) American	[O1]
FENSELAU, CATHERINE Chemist/Pharmacologist	(1939–) American	[A]
FENWICK, FLORENCE Chemist	(1900s early) American	[R1]
FEODOROWNA, MARIA Physician/Educator	(17??–1828) Russian	[K]
FERGUSON, MARGARET CLAY Botanist	(1863–1951) American	[N3,R1,V,A1]
FERNALD, GRACE Psychologist	(18??–19??) American	[R1]
FERNALD, MABEL Psychologist	(18??–1952) American	[R1]
FERNANDES, ROSETTE MERCEDES B. Botanist	(1916–) Portuguese	[W]

FERRAND, JACQUELINE LELONG: See LELONG, JACQUELINE FERRAND

FERRAR, AGNES Nurse/Medical Worker	(1200s) English	[K]

FERREE, GERTRUDE RAND: See RAND, MARIE GERTRUDE

FERRERO, GINE LOMBROSO Physician/Psychologist	(1872–1944) Italian	[I5]
FERRETTI, ZAFFIRA Physician	(1300s) Italian	[K]
FERRY, EDNA LOUISE Physiological Chemist	(18??–1920) American	[R1]
FESHBACH, NORMA DEITCH Psychologist	(1926–) American	[W]

FIDELI, CASSANDRA: See CASSANDRA FIDELIS

FIDELLE, CASSANDRA: See CASSANDRA FIDELIS

FIELD, JOANNA Psychologist	(1900–) English	[Q1]
FIELDE, ADELE MARION Entomologist/Biologist	(1839–1916) American	[R1,I3]

FIELDS, EWAUGH FINNEY Mathematician/Educator	(1900s) American	[0] [MI]
FIESER, MARY Chemist	(1900s) American	[01,W6]
FIFKOVLA, EVA Neuroanatomist	(1932-) Czechoslovakian	[W]
FIGNER, VERA Physician	(1800s) Russian	[0]
FINK, KAY FERGUSON Biochemist	(1917-) American	[W]
FINKEL, MIRIAM POSNER Biologist	(1916-) American	[W]
FINKELSTEIN, BEATRICE Aerospace Nutritionist	(1912-) American	[A,G]
FISCHER, CHARLOTTE FROESE Mathematician/Computer Scientist	(1929-) Canadian/American	[A,01]
FISCHER, IRENE KAMINKA Geodesist/Cartographer/Engineer	(1907-) American	[A] [NE]
FISCHER-HJALMARS, INGA MARGRETE Physicist/Chemist	(1918-) Swedish	[W,L3]
FISH, MARIE POLAND Ichthyologist	(1921-) American	[W,I5]
FISHER, ANNE L. Physician	(1950-) American	[01] [AS]
FISHER, ELIZABETH F. Geologist	(1800s) American	[R1]
FITCH, ANNE LOUISE MACKINNON Mathematician	(18??-1940) American	[M8,R]
FITZGERALD, MABEL PUREFOY Physiologist	(1872-) English	[01]
FITZROY, NANCY DELOYE Mechanical Engineer	(1927-) American	[A,01]
FLAMEL, PERRENELLE Alchemist	(13??-1413) French	[A3,R]
FLAMMARION, CAMILLE Astronomer	(18??-19??) French	[Z,R]
FLEMING, AMALIA C., LADY Bacteriologist	(1909?-) Greek/English	[Q1]

FLEMING, WILLIAMINA PATON STEVENS   (1857-1911)   [W,O1,N2,C2]
Astronomer   Scottish/American

FLETCHER, ALICE CUNNINGHAM   (1838-1923)   [L2,B1,D4,Z]
Anthropologist/Ethnologist   American

FLETCHER, ANN   (1900s)   [O1]
Engineer   American

FLETCHER, SHIRLEY   (1900s)   [O]
Process Engineer   British

FLOCK, EUNICE VERNA   (1904-)   [W]
Biochemist   American

FLOREY, MARY ETHEL   (1900s early)   [D1]
Medical Researcher   Australian/English

FLORIAN   (1300s)   [H2]
Physician   French

FLOYD, THEODORA A.   (1896-)   [N1]
Nurse   American

FLUGGE-LOTZ, IRMGARD   (1903-1974)   [N3,O1]
Aeronautical Engineer/Mathematician German/American

FLUME, JIMMIE   (1900s)   [G]
Immunologist   American   [HA]

FOLLETT, MARY PARKER   (1868-1933)   [W,N2]
Management Scientist/Psychologist   American

FOOT, EUNICE   (1800s)   [F1]
Physicist   American

FOOT, KATHERINE   (1852-1944)   [Z,R1,S2,A1]
Geneticist/Zoologist/Cell Biologist American

FOQUET, MARIE, VICOMTESSE DE VAUX   (1600s)   [K]
Medical Author/Educator   French

FORBES-RESHA, JUDITH   (1900s)   [M1]
Engineer   American   [MI]

FORLI, COUNTESS OF: See SFORZA, CATHERINE

FORREST, IRENE STEPHANIE NEUBERG   (1908-)   [W]
Biochemist   American

FORTUNE, MARGARET MEAD: See MEAD, MARGARET

FOSDICK, NELLIE   (18??-1917)   [I3]
Botanist   American

FOSSEY, DIAN   (1932-1985)   [O]
Primatologist/Animal Behaviorist   American

FOSSLER, MARY   (18??-19??)   [R1]
  Chemist   American

FOSTER, MARGARET D.   (18??-1971)   [R1]
  Chemist/Geologist/Mineralogist   American

FOSTER, MARY LOUISE   (1900s early)   [R1]
  Industrial Chemist   American

FOUQUET, MARIE, VICOMTESSE: See FOQUET, MARIE, VICOMTESSE DE
  VAUX

FOWLER, LYDIA FOLGER   (1822-1879)   [N2,L2,O1]
  Physician   American

FOWLER-BILLINGS, KATHARINE   (1902-)   [W,I5]
  Geologist   American

FOX, MATTIE RAE SPIVEY   (1923-)   [W]
  Biochemist   American

FOX, PHYLLIS   (1923-)   [A]
  Computer Scientist   American

FOX, RUTH   (1895-)   [W]
  Psychiatrist   American

FRANCES OF BRITTANY   (1400s)   [K]
  Physician   French

FRANCESCA   (1200s)   [H2]
  Physician   Italian

FRANCINI, ELEANORA   (1904-)   [C]
  Botanist   Italian

FRANCOISE   (1400s)   [K]
  Surgeon/Gynecologist/Physician   Italian

FRANKENHAEUSER, MARIANN VON W.   (1925-)   [W]
  Experimental Psychologist Swedish

FRANKLIN, CHRISTINE: See LADD-FRANKLIN, CHRISTINE

FRANKLIN, ROSALIND (ELSIE)   (1920-1958)   [O1,D4]
  Crystallographer/Biophysicist   English

FRANTZ, VIRGINIA KNEELAND   (1896-1967)   [N3]
  Surgical Pathologist/Educator   American

FRANZ, JUDITH ROSENBAUM   (1930-)   [A]
  Physicist   American

FREDGA, KERSTIN   (1900s)   [L3]
  Geophysicist   Swedish

FREEMAN, RUTH BENSEN   (1906-)   [W]
  Nurse   American

FREHAFER, MABEL Physicist	(1800s-1900s) American	[R1]
FREI, TERESA Physician	(1700s-1800s) German	[Z]
FREIDLINA, RAKHIL' KHATSKELEVNA Organic Chemist	(1906-) Russian	[S,T,W,C,L3] [SS]
FRENKEL-BRUNSWIK, ELSE Psychologist	(18??-19??) German/American	[R1]
FREUD, ANNA Psychologist/Psychoanalyst	(1895-) Austrian/American	[O1,D4]
FREUND, IDA Chemist	(18??-1914) English	[I3]
FRIEDL, ERNESTINE Anthropologist	(1900s) American	[O] [NB]
FRIEDMAN, JOYCE BARBARA Computer Scientist	(1928-) American	[A]
FRIEND, CHARLOTTE Medical Microbiologist/Oncologist	(1921-) American	[O1,C3] [NS]
FRINGS, MABLE RUTH SMITH Sensory Physiologist	(1912-) American	[W]
FRITZ, MADELEINE ALBERTA Paleontologist	(1900s) Canadian	[A,L3]
FROMM, ERIKA Psychologist	(1910-) American	[W]
FROST, ROSA F. Process Engineer Specialist	(1900s) American	[M1] [MI]
FULFORD, MARGARET HANNAH Botanist	(1904-) American	[W]
FULHAME, ELIZABETH Chemist/Author	(17??-18??) English	[C5,P6]
FULLER, MARGARET Nurse/Author	(1810-1850) American	[I4]
FULTON, MARY Physician/Medical Educator	(1800s-1900s) American	[O1]
FULTON, RUTH: See BENEDICT, RUTH FULTON		
FURBISH, KATE Botanist/Artist	(1834-1931) American	[N2,L2,O1]

FURNESS, CAROLINE ELLEN Astronomer	(1869-1936) American	[R1,W]
FUSS, MARGARITA Midwife/Obstetrician	(15??-1626) German	[K]

G

GABE, DINA RUFINOVA Plant Geneticist/Geomicrobiologist	(1912-) Russian	[C]
GADEGBEKU, TONI Chemist	(1900s) American	[O] [MI]
GAGE, SUSANNA S. PHELPS Embryologist/Zoologist/Anatomist	(1857-1915) American	[Z,R1,I3,A1]
GAIGE, HELEN THOMPSON Zoologist	(1800s-1900s) American	[R1]
GAILLARD, MARY K. Physicist	(1900s) American	[O]
GALINDO, BEATRIX Physician/Philosopher/Scholar	(1473-1535) Spanish	[K,D4]
GAMBLE, ELEANOR A.M. Psychologist	(1900s early) American	[R1]

GANDERSHEIM OF BAVARIA: See HROSVITHA OF GANDERSHEIM

GANTT, ELISABETH Biologist/Plant Physiologist	(1934-) American	[A,O1]

GAPOSCHKIN, CECILIA: See PAYNE-GAPOSCHKIN, CECILIA HELENA

GARCIA, ELIZABETH Chemical Engineer	(1900s) American	[M1] [MI]
GARDNER, HILDA FLOREY Pathologist	(1900s) Australian	[D1]
GARDNER, JULIA ANNA Stratigraphic Paleontologist	(1882-1960) American	[F1,N3,R1]

GARRETT, ELIZABETH: See ANDERSON, ELIZABETH GARRETT

GARRETT, SUE ANDERSON Scientist	(1900s) American	[O]
GATES, FANNY COOK Physicist	(1872-1931) American	[R1,I3,R2,R]

GAY, HELEN Biologist	(1918–) American	[W]
GEERTZ, HILDRED Social Anthropologist	(1900s) American	[O1]
GEIRINGER, HILDA Applied Mathematician/Statistician	(1893–1973) Austrian/American	[N3,M8]
GEMINAE (MOTHER) Philosopher	(200s) Roman	[R,P5]
GEMINAE (DAUGHTER) Philosopher	(200s) Roman	[R,P5]
GENTHE, MARTHA KRUG Geographer	(18??–19??) American	[R1]
GENTRY, RUTH Mathematician	(1862–1917) American	[M8,R1,R]
GENUNG, ELIZABETH F. Bacteriologist	(18??–1975) American	[R1]
GEORG, LUCILLE KATHARINE Microbiologist	(1912–) American	[W]
GERMAIN, SOPHIE Mathematician/Physicist	(1776–1831) French	[M,N,W,Z,U1]
GERRY, ELOISE Botanist/Forest Scientist	(18??–19??) American	[R1]
GERTRUDE Surgeon	(12??–13??) French	[H2]
GETZOWA, SOPHIE Pathologist	(1900s) Israeli	[D1]
GEY, MARGARET Virologist/Oncologist	(1900s early) American	[R1]
GHAFARUNISSA, DR. Biomedical Scientist	(1900s) Indian	[I9]
GHIELIETTA: See GHILIETTA		
GHILIETTA Physician	(11??–12??) Italian	[H2,L6]
GIANNINI, MARGARET JOAN Physician/Pediatrician	(1921–) American	[A,O1]
GIBBS, ERMA LEONHARDT Medical Scientist	(1904–) American	[W]

GIBLETT, ELOISE ROSALIE
  Hematologist
(1921-)
American
[A,W]
        [NS]

GIBLIN, LOUISE
  Chemist
(1900s early)
American
[R1]

GIBSON, ELEANOR JACK
  Psychologist
(1910-)
American
[O]
        [NS]

GIBSON, MARGARET DUNLOP
  Archaeologist
(1843-1920)
English
[Z,I5,T2]

GILBERT, RUTH
  Bacteriologist
(18??-19??)
American
[R1]

GILBRETH, LILLIAN EVELYN MOLLER
  Management Engineer/Psychologist
(1878-1972)
American
[K1,E1,X,Z]

GILCHRIST, MAUDE
  Botanist/Educator
(18??-19??)
American
[R1]

GILIANI, ALESSANDRA
  Anatomist
(1307 c.-1326)
Italian
[K,H,Z,H2,R]

GILL, JOCELYN RUTH
  Astronomer
(1916-1984)
American
[W,O1]

GILLAIN, MARIE ANNE VICTOIRE: *See* BOIVIN, MARIE ANNE VICTOIRE

GILMAN, CHARLOTTE PERKINS
  Sociologist
(1860-1935)
American
[G4,H3]

GILMAN, ELIZABETH
  Chemist
(1900s early)
American
[R1]

GILROY, HELEN
  Physicist
(1800s-1900s)
American
[R1]

GISELLE
  Physician
(600s)
French
[K]

GIURGEA, MARGARETA ALEXANDRU V.
  Physicist
(1915-)
Rumanian
[W]

GLASGOW, MAUDE
  Physician
(1868-1955)
American
[K3,I5,Q1]

GLASS, JEWELL JEANNETTE
  Geologist
(1888-1966)
American
[R1]

GLEASON, JOSEPHINE
  Psychologist
(1892-)
American
[R1]

GLEASON, KATE
  Mechanical Engineer/Inventor
(18??-1933)
American
[O1,E1,R1]

GLENNON, NAN
  Mechanical Engineer
(1900s)
American
[G]

GLOUCESTER, DUCHESS OF Physician	(1400s) English	[K]
GLUECK, ELEANOR TOUROFF Research Criminologist/Sociologist	(1898-1972) American	[W,N3,L2]

GLUECKSOHN-WAELSCH, SALOME: *See* WAELSCH, SALOME GLUECKSOHN

GOCHOLASHVILI, MARIYA MIKIEVNA Plant Physiologist	(1904-) Russian	[W]

GOEPPERT, MARIA: *See* MAYER, MARIA GOEPPERT

GOEPPERT-MAYER, MARIA: *See* MAYER, MARIA GOEPPERT

GOKDOGEN, NUZHET Astronomer/Educator	(1900s) Turkish	[B1,N5]
GOKSU-OGELMAN, YETER Physicist	(1900s) Turkish	[O]
GOLD, LORNE W. Glaciologist/Engineering Physicist	(1928-) Canadian	[A,L3]

GOLDEN, KATHERINE: *See* BITTING, KATHERINE E. GOLDEN

GOLDFRANK, ESTHER S. Anthropologist	(1900s early) American	[R1]
GOLDHABER, GERTRUDE SCHARFF Physicist	(1911-) American	[A,W,O1,P4] [*NS*]
GOLDHABER, SULAMITH Physicist	(1923-1965) American	[W]
GOLDMAN, HETTY Archaeologist	(1900s) American	[O1]
GOLDMAN, RACHEL Scientist	(1900s) Israeli	[O]
GOLDRING, WINIFRED Paleobotanist/Paleontologist	(1888-1971) American	[N3,F1,R1]
GOLDSCHMIDT, LEONTINE Biochemist	(1913-) American	[W]
GOLDSMITH, GRACE ARABELL Internist/Nutritionist	(1904-1975) American	[W,N3]
GOLDTHWAITE, NELLIE Chemist	(1900s early) American	[R1]
GOLINEVICH, ELENA MIKHAILOVNA Microbiologist	(1901-) Russian	[W]
GOLOVINA, ANASTASIA Physician	(18??-1932) Bulgarian	[D1,I5]

GONZALEZ, ELMA Cell Biologist	(1942-) American	[A,M1] [MI]
GONZALEZ, NANCIE LOUDON Anthropologist	(1900s) American	[O1]
GOOD, MARY LOWE Chemist	(1931-) American	[A,O1,W6] [NB]
GOODALL, JANE Ethologist/Primatologist	(1934-) English/Kenyan	[H,O1,D4]
GOODENOUGH, FLORENCE LAURA Developmental Psychologist	(1886-1959) American	[N3,R1,A1]
GOODMAN, MARY ELLEN HOHEISEL Anthropologist	(1911-) American	[W]
GOODRICH, ANNIE WARBURTON Nurse/Educator	(1866-1954) American	[N3,N1,O1]
GORDON, RUTH VIDA Structural Engineer	(1900s) American	[O1]

GORZANO, LEONETTA DE: See LEONETTA MEDICA OF TURIN

GOULD, ALICE BACHE Scientist	(1800s-1900s) American	[M1] [MI]
GOULDING, ANNA Physician	(1800s) American	[O]
GOWAN, SISTER M. OLIVIA Nurse	(1888-) American	[N1]
GRAHAM, FRANCES KEELER Psychologist	(1918-) American	[W]
GRAHAM, HELEN TREDWAY Biochemist/Pharmacologist	(1900s early) American	[R1]
GRAHAM, RUTH MOORE Cytologist	(1917-) American	[W]
GRANDJEAN, ETTIENNE P. Physiologist	(1914-) Swiss	[C]
GRAY, MARIA EMMA Botanist	(1786?-1876) English	[I3]
GREEN, ARDA A. Biochemist	(19??-1958) American	[O1,W6]
GREENE, CATHERINE LITTLEFIELD Inventor	(1731-1794?) American	[Z,H,U1,I5]
GREENE, EVA HIRDLER Mining Engineer	(1884-1982) American	[O]

GREER, SANDRA CHARLENE Physical Chemist	(1945-) American	[A,F]
GREGORY, EMILY L. Botanist	(18??-1897) American	[R1,I3]
GREGORY, EMILY RAY Biologist	(18??-19??) American	[R1]
GREGORY, LOUISA CATHERINE ALLEN Home Economist	(1848-1920) American	[F1]
GREIG, MARGARET ELIZABETH Pharmacologist	(1907-) Canadian/American	[W]
GREISHEIMER, ESTHER MAUD Physiologist	(1891-) American	[W]
GREY, JANE, LADY Philosopher/Scholar/Scientist	(1537-1554) English	[F4,E2]
GRIERSON, CECILIA Physician/Obstetrician/Educator	(18??-) Argentinian	[D1]
GRIERSON, CONSTANTIA Scholar/Mathematician/Philosopher	(1706-1733) Irish	[F4]
GRIFFIN, HARRIET MADELINE Mathematician/Educator	(1903-) American	[W]
GRIFFITHS, MARY Physicist/Biophysicist	(1800s) American	[R1]
GRIFFITHS, MRS. Biologist/Algologist	(1768?-1858) English	[I3]
GRINNELL, ELIZABETH Naturalist	(1800s-1900s) American	[S1]
GRUBB, GERD Mathematician	(1800s) Danish	[O]
GRUNBERG-MANAGO, MARIANNE Cell Biologist/Molecular Biologist	(1900s) French	[L3]
GUARNA, REBECCA DE Physician/Educator	(1200s-1300s) Italian	[K,Z,W4,L6]
GUARNA, SENTIA Physician/Educator	(1400s) Italian	[K]
GUERNSEY, JANET BROWN Physicist	(1913-) American	[A]
GUILD, ELIZABETH (BETSY) Biological Acoustician/Psychologist	(1900s) American	[G]
GUILLAMETTE DE LUYS Surgeon	(1400s) French	[H2]

GUION, CONNIE   (1883-)   [K3,O1,W5]
  Physician/Medical Educator/Surgeon   American

GULLETT, LUCY E.   (1900s early)   [D1]
  Physician   Australian

GUNTER, ERNA   (1896-)   [W]
  Anthropologist   American

GUTHRIE, JANET   (1900s)   [O]
  Physicist   American

GUTHRIE, MARY JANE   (1895-)   [R1,A1,S2]
  Zoologist/Cytologist   American

GUTTMAN, HELENE AUGUSTA NATHAN   (1930-)   [A,W]
  Microbiologist   American

GUTTMAN, RITA   (1912-1983)   [A,O1]
  Biophysicist/Neurophysiologist   American

H

HAAS, MARY ROSAMOND   (1900s)   [O1]
  Anthropologist/Linguist   American   [NS]

HAAS, VIOLET BUSHWICK   (1926-)   [A]
  Electrical Engineer   American

HAGOOD, MARGARET LOYD JARMAN   (1907-1963)   [N3]
  Statistician/Sociologist   American

HAHN, DOROTHY ANNA   (1876-1950)   [N2]
  Organic Chemist   American

HAINAULT, COUNTESS OF   (1200s)   [K]
  Physician   French

HALBERG, JULIA   (1954-)   [O1]
  Chronobiologist   American

HALDIMAN, JANE: See MARCET, JANE HALDIMAN

HALKET, ANNA MURRAY, LADY: See HALKETT, ANNE, LADY

HALKETT, ANNE, LADY   (1622-1699)   [K,L6,F4]
  Physician/Surgeon/Author/Scholar   Scottish/English

HALL, DOLLIE RADLER   (1900s early)   [R1]
  Micropaleontologist/Geologist   American

HALL, DOROTHY   (1900s early)   [R1]
  Chemist   American

HALL, EDITH H.
Archaeologist
(1800s–1900s)   [Z]
American

HALL, JULIA BRAINERD
Chemist/Engineer
(1859–)   [E1,V1]
American

HALL, MARIA BOAS
Science Historian
(1900s)   [O]
English/American

HALLIDAY, NELLIE
Biologist
(1900s early)   [R1]
American

HALLOWELL, SUSAN MARIA
Botanist
(1835–1911)   [R1,I3,R]
American

HALPIR, SALOMEE ANNE: *See* RUSIECKA, SALOMEA

HAMILL, FRANCES
Mathematician
(1923–1956)   [M8]
British

HAMILTON, ALICE
Physician/Toxicologist/Educator
(1869–1970)   [P,K1,X,Z,H]
American

HAMLIN, ALICE
Psychologist
(18??–19??)   [R1]
American

HAMMER, MARIE SIGNE
Naturalist
(1907–)   [W]
Danish

HAMMOND, DOROTHY BRAMSON
Anthropologist
(1900s early)   [R1]
American

HANSEN, LUISA FERNANDEZ
Physicist
(1900s)   [A,O1]
Chilean/American

HANSEN, HAZEL D.
Archaeologist
(1899–1962)   [R1]
American

HAOYS OF PARIS
Physician
(12??–13??)   [K,H2]
French

HARCOURT, HARRIET EUSEBIA
Scholar/Linguist/Scientist
(1705–1745)   [F4]
English

HARDCASTLE, FRANCES
Mathematician
(1866–1941)   [M8,R]
British

HARDESTY, MARY
Reproductive Biology Researcher
(1900s early)   [B2]
American

HARDY, MIRIAM PAULS
Audiologist
(1912–)   [W]
American

HARMON, ELISE F.
Electrical Engineer/Inventor
(1900s)   [O1]
American

HARPER, MARILYN HILL
Anesthesiologist/Physician
(1938–)   [O]
American   *[MI]*

HARRIS, ANITA Geologist	(1900s) American	[O]
HARRISON, ANNA JANE Physical Chemist	(1912-) American	[A,O1] [NB]
HARRISON, JANE ELLEN Archaeologist	(1850-1928) English	[Z,S1,D4]
HARRISON-ROSS, PHYLLIS ANN Pediatrician/Psychiatrist	(1936-) American	[W1] [MI]
HART, HELEN Plant Pathologist	(1900-1971) American	[R1]
HARTT, CONSTANCE ENDICOTT Plant Physiologist	(1900-) American	[W]
HARVEY, ETHEL BROWNE Cell Biologist/Embryologist	(1885-1965) American	[N3,R1,A1]
HARWOOD, FANNY Dental Surgeon/Physician	(1889-1973) British	[B1,O1]
HARWOOD, MARGARET Astronomer	(1885-) American	[O1,N4]
HASKINS, ALICE Botanist	(1900s early) American	[R1]
HASKOVA, VERA Scientist	(1900s) Czechoslovakian	[L3]
HASLE, GRETHE R. Marine Botanist	(1900s) Norwegian	[L3]
HASLETT, CAROLINE, DAME Electrical Engineer	(1895-1957) English	[I5,I7,P3]
HASSE, CLARA Plant Pathologist	(1900s early) American	[R1,R2]
HASTINGS, ALICIA E. Physician	(1900s) American	[O] [MI]
HATHAWAY, MILLICENT LOUISE Nutritionist/Physiological Chemist	(1898-) American	[W,B2]
HATSHEPSUT, QUEEN Scholar/Philosopher/Physician	(BC 1530 c.-1479 c.) Egyptian	[K,F2]
HAWES, HARRIET A. BOYD Archaeologist	(1871-) American	[Z,R1,I5]
HAWKES, JACQUETTA HOPKINS Archaeologist	(1910-) English	[Q1]

HAY, ELIZABETH DEXTER Anatomist	(1927–) American	[A] *[NS]*
HAYES, DORA KRUSE Biophysicist/Biochemist	(1931–) American	[A,O1]
HAYES, ELLEN AMANDA Applied Mathematician/Astronomer	(1851–1930) American	[M7,M8,R1,R]
HAYMAKER, EVELYN ANDERSON: *See* ANDERSON, EVELYN		
HAYNER, LUCY Physicist	(1900s early) American	[R1]
HAYNES, LINDEN C. SMITH Zoologist/Physiologist	(1900s) American	[O] *[MI]*
HAYS, MARGARET Textile Physicist	(1900s early) American	[R1]
HAYWARD, EVANS VAUGHAN Physicist	(1922–) American	[A,F]
HAYWOOD, CHARLOTTE Zoologist	(1900s early) American	[R1]
HAZEN, ELIZABETH LEE Microbiologist/Mycologist	(1885–1975) American	[N3]
HAZLETT, OLIVE C. Mathematician	(1890–1974) American	[R1,A1,S2]
HEALY, AUGUSTA BRONNER: *See* BRONNER, AUGUSTA FOX		
HEARST, PHOEBE APPERSON Anthropologist	(1800s late) American	[R1,R2]
HEBDEN, KATHERINE Physician/Surgeon/Pharmacist	(1600s) American	[W4,K]
HEBEL, MEDICIENNE Physician	(1300s late) German	[K,H2]
HEDGES, FLORENCE Botanist	(1900s early) American	[R1]
HEDGPETH, MARY Computer Scientist	(1900s) American	[G]
HEDWIG, QUEEN OF SILESIA Physician	(1174–1243) Polish/German	[K,B6]
HEDWIG, SAINT: *See* HEDWIG, QUEEN OF SILESIA		
HEDWIG, WILHELMINA, PRINCESS Naturalist/Medical Practitioner	(1681–) German	[K]

HEGELER, MARY: *See* CARUS, MARY HEGELER

HEIDBREDER, EDNA   (1890–)   [W]
  Psychologist   American

HEIKEL, ROSINA   (1800s–1900s)   [D1]
  Physician   Finnish

HEILBRONN–WIKSTROM, EDITH   (1925–)   [W]
  Biochemist   Swedish

HEIM–VOGTLIN, MARIE   (1845–1916)   [B1,D1,I5]
  Physician   Swiss

HEISING–GOODMAN, CAROLINE   (1900s)   [O]
  Nuclear Engineer   American

HELENA, EMPRESS   (300s)   [D5]
  Archaeologist   Roman

HELL, MME. HOMMAIRE DE: *See* HOMMAIRE DE HELL, MME.

HELLWIG, CHRISTINA REGINA   (1600s)   [K]
  Physician/Pharmacist   German

HELMHOLTZ, ANNA   (18??–1899)   [I3]
  Scientist   German

HELOISA: *See* HELOISE

HELOISE   (1101–1164)   [K,Z,B1,W4]
  Physician/Mathematician/Scholar French

HELOYS, DAME, OF PARIS   (12??–13??)   [K,H2]
  Physician   French

HELPES   (500s)   [F4]
  Scholar/Scientist/Author   Italian

HENIN, FRANCOISE GABRIELLE   (1934–)   [W]
  Physicist   Belgian

HENLE, GERTRUDE SZPINGIER   (1912–)   [A,W]
  Virologist   American   [NS]

HENNEL, CORA BARBARA   (18??–1947)   [M8]
  Mathematician   American

HENRY, GLADYS: *See* DICK, GLADYS ROWENA HENRY

HENTSCHEL–GUERNTH, DOROTHEA   (1749–1813)   [K,B1]
  Nutritionist/Physician/Author   German

HEREFORD, COUNTESS   (1100s)   [K]
  Physician   French

HERFORTH, LIESELOTT   (1900s)   [E,L3]
  Radiation Physicist   German

HERRAD, ABBESS OF HOHENBURG: *See* HERRADE OF LANDSBERG

HERRADE OF LANDSBERG   (11??-1195)   [K,W4,Z,R]
  Scientist/Author/Educator/Scholar   German/French

HERRICK, SOPHIE   (1800s)   [R1]
  Entomologist   American

HERSCHEL, CAROLINE LUCRETIA   (1750-1848)   [I,N,W,H,B1]
  Astronomer   German/English

HERSEND: *See* HERSENDE OF CHAMPAGNE

HERSENDE, ABBESS OF FONTEVRAULT   (1100s)   [K]
  Physician   French

HERSENDE OF CHAMPAGNE   (1200s)   [K,H2]
  Physician   French

HERSENDE OF THE ORDER OF SAINT COSMO: *See* HERSENDE OF CHAMPAGNE

HERSKOVITS, FRANCES SHAPIRO   (1900s early)   [R1]
  Anthropologist   American

HERVORDEN, ABBESS OF: *See* ELIZABETH OF BOHEMIA, PRINCESS

HERZENBERG, CAROLINE S. LITTLEJOHN   (1932-)   [A,W2,W3,I2]
  Physicist/Educator/Author   American

HERZENBERG, LEONORE   (1900s)   [O]
  Immunologist   American

HESSE, CHRISTINA OF: *See* CHRISTINA OF HESSE

HESSE, FRAU   (1800s late)   [B5]
  Microbiologist   Dutch

HESSEN PHILLIPSTHAL, PRINCESS OF: *See* HEDWIG, WILHELMINA, PRINCES

HESTIAEA   (4??-5??)   [P5]
  Mathematician/Philosopher   Greek

HEUREAUX, MERCEDES A.   (1900s early)   [D1]
  Physician   Dominican

HEVELIUS, ELIZABETH KOOPMAN   (1600s-1700s)   [Z,N4,R]
  Astronomer   Polish

HEWITT, DOROTHY   (1900s early)   [R1]
  Biologist   American

HIBBARD, HOPE   (1893-)   [R1,A1,S2]
  Zoologist   American

HICKS, BEATRICE ALICE   (1919-)   [A,O1,I5]
  Electrical Engineer   American

HIGHT, CATHERINE GERTRUDE: *See* CRAMER, CATHERINE GERTRUDE

HIGHTOWER, RUBY USHER   (1880?-1959)   [M8]
  Mathematician   American

HILDA OF WHITBY, ABBESS   (614-680)   [K,Z,U1]
  Physician/Educator/Surgeon   English

HILDEGARD OF BINGEN, SAINT   (1098-1179)   [K,Z,W,H,B1]
  Physician/Biologist/Scholar   German

HILDEGARDE OF BINGEN: *See* HILDEGARD OF BINGEN, SAINT

HILDEGURDIS, ABBESS: *See* HILDEGARD OF BINGEN, SAINT

HILDEN, MARIE VON: *See* VON HILDEN, MARIE COLINET

HILDRETH, GERTRUDE   (1900s early)   [R1]
  Psychologist   American

HILL, DOROTHY   (1900s)   [L3]
  Geologist   English/Australian   [*FR*]

HILL, JUSTINE HAMILTON   (1893-)   [R1,I5]
  Bacteriologist   American

HIMMS-HAGEN, JEAN   (1933-)   [A]
  Biochemist   Canadian

HINCKLEY, MARY H.   (1800s-1900s)   [Z]
  Biologist   American

HINES, MARION   (1889-)   [W,R1]
  Neuroanatomist   American

HINKLE, BEATRICE   (1900s early)   [R1]
  Psychoanalyst   American

HINMAN, ALICE HAMLIN: *See* HAMLIN, ALICE

HINRICHS, MARIE AGNES   (1892-)   [W,B2]
  Physiologist/Zoologist   American

HINSON, LOIS E.   (1926-)   [O1]
  Veterinarian   American

HIPPARCHIA OF MARONEIA   (BC 200s)   [Z,G2,G3,F4]
  Philosopher/Author   Greek/Syrian/Turkish

HIPPARCHIA THE MARONITE: *See* HIPPARCHIA OF MARONEIA

HIPPIA: *See* HYPATIA

HIPPO   (BC 500s)   [R,P5]
  Natural Philosopher/Astrologer   Greek

HIRSCHBOECK, KATHERINE   (1900s)   [O]
  Geoscientist/Botanist   American

HOBBS, LUCY B.   (1833-1910)   [B1,O1]
  Dentist/Dental Surgeon   American

HOBY, LADY Surgeon/Physician	(1571-) English	[K]
HODGKIN, DOROTHY MARY CROWFOOT Chemist/Crystallographer	(1910-) English	[L,Q,W,C1] [NL,FR
HODGSON, ELIZA AMY Scientist	(1900s) New Zealander	[L3]
HOFFLEIT, ELLEN DORRUT Astronomer	(1907-) American	[W]
HOGG, HELEN BATTLES SAWYER Astronomer	(1905-) Canadian	[W,Y,L3,I5]

HOHENBURG, ABBESS OF: See HERRADE OF LANDSBERG

HOKE, CALM MORRISON Chemist/Metallurgist	(1887-1952) American	[R1]
HOL, JACOBA BRIGITTA LOUISA Geographer	(1886-) Dutch	[W]
HOLDEN, RUTH Botanist	(18??-1917) American	[I3]
HOLDER, MRS. Surgeon	(1600s) English	[K]
HOLLANDER, NINA Biochemist	(1927-) American	[W]
HOLLEY, MARY A. Botanist/Naturalist	(1700s-1800s) American	[O]
HOLLINGWORTH, LETA ANNA STETTER Educational Psychologist	(1886-1939) American	[N2,C2,D4,V]
HOLLINSHEAD, ARIEL CAHILL Physician/Viral Oncologist	(1929-) American	[A,O1]
HOLLISTER, GLORIA Zoologist/Explorer	(1900s early) American	[B1,R1]
HOLMAN, MOLLIE ELIZABETH Scientist	(1900s) Australian	[L3]
HOLMES, MARY E. Geologist	(18??-19??) American	[F1,R1]
HOLMES, VERENA Mechanical Engineer	(1900s early) British	[B1]

HOLSTEIN, MADAME DE STAEL: See NECKER, ANNE GERMAINE

HOLTER, HARRIETT Sociologist	(1900s) Norwegian	[L3]

HOLTON, NINA   (18??-1908)   [I3]
  Botanist   American

HOMMAIRE DE HELL, MME.   (1819-)   [Z,R]
  Geologist/Explorer   French

HOOBLER, ICIE MACY: *See* MACY-HOOBLER, ICIE GERTRUDE

HOOKER, HENRIETTA   (18??-19??)   [R1]
  Botanist   American

HOOKER, MRS. HENSLOW   (18??-1874)   [I3]
  Botanist   English

HOON, PIERRA: *See* VEIJJABU, PIERRA HOON

HOOPER, LUCY   (1800s)   [O]
  Botanist   American

HOPPER, GRACE MURRAY   (1906-)   [A,C1,M,D4]
  Mathematician/Computer Scientist   American   [*NE*]

HORACKOVA, EVA HEYROVSKA   (1923-)   [W]
  Psychologist   Czechoslovakian

HORENBURG, ANNA ELIZABETH VON: *See* VON HORENBURG, ANNA ELIZABETH

HORENBURGIN, ANNA ELIZABETH: *See* VON HORENBURG, ANNA ELIZABETH

HORNER, MATINA   (1940-)   [O1]
  Experimental Psychologist   American

HORNEY, KAREN DANIELSSEN   (1885-1952)   [W,N3,L2,O1]
  Psychiatrist/Psychoanalyst   German/American

HORNING, MARJORIE G.   (1917-)   [A,O1]
  Pharmacologist/Biochemist   American

HORSTMANN, DOROTHY MILLICENT   (1911-)   [A,W,O1]
  Epidemiologist/Pediatrician   American   [*NS*]

HORSFORD, CORNELIA   (1800s)   [S1]
  Archaeologist   American

HORTON, MILDRED MCAFEE: *See* MCAFEE, MILDRED

HOUTZ, SARA JANE   (1913-)   [W]
  Exercise Physiologist/Kinesiologist   American

HOWARD, ALMA   (1913-)   [W]
  Biologist   Canadian/English

HOWARD, RUTH   (1900s early)   [R1]
  Psychologist   American   [*MI*]

HOWARD-LOCK, HELEN ELAINE   (1938-)   [A,O1]
  Engineering Physicist   Canadian

HOWE, MRS. Inventor	(1800s) American	[U1]
HOWES, ETHEL D. PUFFER Psychologist	(1872-) American	[R1,A1,S2]

HROSVITHA OF BRAUNSCHWEIG: See HROSVITHA OF GANDERSHEIM

HROSVITHA OF GANDERSHEIM Physician/Scientist/Mathematician	(935-1000) German	[Z,K]

HROSWITHA: See HROSVITHA

HSIEH, HILDA Physicist	(1900s) Chinese	[O]
HU, FUNAN Dermatologist	(1919-) Chinese/American	[W]
HUBBARD, RUTH Biochemist/Biologist/Sociologist	(1924-) American	[A,O1]
HUBER, AIMEE Naturalist	(1800s) Swiss	[Z]
HUDSON, HILDA PHOEBE Mathematician	(1881-1965) British	[M8,R]
HUETER, MME. Physician	(1800s) German	[L6]
HUFF, MRS. WILLIAM BASHFORD Physicist	(1884?-1913) American	[I3]
HUGGINS, MARGARET LINDSAY, LADY Astronomer	(18??-1915) Irish/English	[Z,I3,N4,R]

HUGHES, SALLY: See HUGHES-SCHRADER, SALLY

HUGHES-SCHRADER, SALLY Zoologist	(1895-) American	[W,R1,A1,S2]
HUGONAY, VILMA Physician	(1800s-1900s) Hungarian	[D1]
HUMMEL, KATHARINE PATTEE Biologist	(1904-) American	[W]
HUNSCHER, HELEN ALVINA Nutritionist/Educator	(1904-) American	[W]
HUNT, HARRIOT K. Physician	(1805-1875) American	[W4,K3,I5]
HUNTER, GERTRUDE T. Pediatrician	(1900s) American	[K2] [MI]

HURD-MEAD, KATE CAMPBELL　　　　(1867-1941)　　　　[N2,B1,D1]
　Physician/Science Historian　　American

HURDON, ELIZABETH　　　　　　　　(1868-1941)　　　　[O1,K3,I5]
　Gynecological Pathologist/Physician English/Canadian

HURSTON, ZORA NEALE　　　　　　　(1907-1960)　　　　[N3,R1,I5]
　Anthropologist/Author　　　　American　　　　　　　[MI]

HUTCHINSON, ANNE　　　　　　　　　(1700s)　　　　　[O1]
　Medical General Practitioner　American

HUTCHINSON, LUCY: See APSLEY, LUCY, LADY

HUTCHINSON, MARGARET H.　　　　　(1900s)　　　　　[O1]
　Chemical Engineer　　　　　　American

HUTCHISON, DORRIS JEANNETTE　　(1918-)　　　　[W]
　Microbiologist　　　　　　　　American

HUTTON, MRS.　　　　　　　　　　　(1700s)　　　　　[K]
　Botanist/Pharmacist/Physician　English

HUXLEY, HENRIETTA HEATHORN　　　(18??-1914?)　　　[Z,I3]
　Scientist　　　　　　　　　　　English

HYDE, IDA HENRIETTA　　　　　　　(1857-1945)　　　　[O1,N2,R1,Z]
　Physiologist　　　　　　　　　American

HYMAN, LIBBIE HENRIETTA　　　　　(1888-1969)　　　　[X,Z,W,B1]
　Invertebrate Zoologist　　　American　　　　　　　[NS]

HYPATIA　　　　　　　　　　　　　(370-415)　　　　　[H,I,M,N,C1]
　Physicist/Inventor/Mathematician　Egyptian/Greek

HYSPECKA, LUDMILA　　　　　　　　(1900s)　　　　　[L3]
　Scientist　　　　　　　　　　　Czechoslovakian

I

IBERIN, VERONICA　　　　　　　　(1600s)　　　　　[K]
　Midwife/Obstetrician/Author　German

ILG, FRANCES　　　　　　　　　　(1900s early)　　[R1]
　Research Psychologist　　　　American

INCARNATA, MARIA　　　　　　　　(1300s)　　　　　[Z,K]
　Surgeon　　　　　　　　　　　Italian

INGELS, MARGARET　　　　　　　　(1900s early)　　[R1]
　Mechanical Engineer　　　　　American

INGLIS, ELSIE Physician	(18??-1917) Scottish	[D1]
IONESCU-SOLOMON, IRINA Chemist	(1916-) Rumanian	[W]
IRENE, QUEEN Physician	(1000s-1100s) Turkish	[K]
IRWIN, MARIAN: See OSTERHOUT, MARIAN IRWIN		
ISAACA, SUSAN Child Psychologist	(1885-1948) English	[D4]
ISABEL Medical Practitioner/Physician	(12??-1269) French	[K]
ISABELLE Physician	(1400s early) French	[H2]
ISABIAU OF PARIS Physician	(1200s-1300s) French	[K]
ISAIE, TOMASIA DE MATTEO DE CASTRO Surgeon	(1300s) Italian	[K]
ISIS Alchemist/Physician/Educator	(000s) Egyptian	[A4]
ISLAMBOOLI, MISS Physician	(18??-19??) Syrian	[K3]
IUSOPOVA, SARADZHAN MIKHAILOVNA Geochemist	(1910-) Russian	[S,W]
IWANOWSKA, WILHELMINA Astrophysicist/Astronomer	(1905-) Polish	[C,E,L3]

J

JACARUSO, KAREN M. Biologist/Educator	(1900s) American	[D3]	[HA]
JACKSON, DAPHNE F. Physicist	(1936-) English	[E]	
JACKSON, DEBORAH JEAN Physicist	(1900s) American	[O]	[MI]
JACKSON, JACQUELYNE JOHNSON Medical Sociologist	(1900s) American	[O1]	[MI]

JACKSON, MARGARET   (1900s)   [G,H3]
  Environmental Physiologist   American

JACKSON, MERCY BISBEE   (1800s)   [O]
  Physician   American

JACKSON, SHIRLEY ANN   (1946-)   [O1]
  Theoretical Physicist   American   [MI]

JACOBA FELICIE: See FELICIE, JACOBA

JACOBI, MARY CORINNA PUTNAM   (1834-1906)   [N2,L2,O1,Z]
  Pediatrician/Neurologist/Physician   American

JACOBINA FELICIE: See FELICIE, JACOBA

JACOBINA MEDICA OF BOLOGNA   (12??-13??)   [K,H2,L6]
  Physician   Italian

JACOBINA OF FLORENCE   (1300s)   [K]
  Physician   Italian

JACOBINE MEDICA: See JACOBINA MEDICA OF BOLOGNA

JACOBS, ALETTA HENRIETTE   (1849-1929)   [W,B1,D1,I5]
  Physician   Dutch

JACOBS, PATRICIA ANN   (1934-)   [W,L3]
  Biologist/Anatomist   British/Scottish

JACOBSEN, CLARA   (1900s early)   [B2]
  Physiologist/Physician   American

JACOPA   (1400s late)   [H2]
  Physician   Italian

JACOPA OF PASSAU   (1400s)   [K]
  Physician   German

JACOTIN, MARIE-LOUISE DUBREIL: See DUBREIL-JACOTIN, MARIE-
  LOUISE

JACOX, MARILYN ESTHER   (1929-)   [W,O1]
  Physical Chemist   American

JACQUARD, MADAME   (17??-18??)   [U1]
  Inventor   French

JAHN, ELSE   (1913-)   [W]
  Biologist   Austrian

JAKOWSKA, SOPHIE   (1922-)   [W]
  Biologist   American

JAMESON, ANNA BROWNELL MURPHY   (1794-1860)   [Z,I5]
  Archaeologist   Irish

JAMESON, DOROTHEA Neuroscientist/Psychologist	(1920-) American	[A] [*NS*]
JANOVSKAJA, SOF'JA ALEKSANDROVNA Mathematician/Logician	(1896-1966) Russian	[M8]
JANSEN, MME. Astronomer	(1800s-1900s) French	[Z,R]
JEANES, ALLENE ROSALIND Carbohydrate Chemist	(1906-) American	[W,O1,W6]
JEFFERSON, MILDRED FAY Physician	(1900s early) American	[D1] [*MI*]
JEHANETTE Physician	(1400s) French	[H2]
JEHANNETTE OF PARIS Physician	(1200s-1300s) French	[K]
JERNOW, JANE Chemist	(1900s) American	[W]
JEX-BLAKE, SOPHIA Physician	(1840-1912) Scottish/English	[B1,H,H1,D1]
JEZKOVA, ZDENKA Immunologist/Bacteriologist	(1921-) Czechoslovakian	[W]
JEZOWSKA-TRZEBIATOWSKA, BOGUSLAWA Chemist/Physicist	(1900s) Polish	[E,L3]
JOAN Medical Practitioner	(13??-14??) English	[H2]
JOANNA Physician	(1300s) French	[M2,H2]
JOBE, MARY L. Geographer/Botanist/Educator	(1886-19??) American	[R1,W5]

JOHANNA: *See* JOANNA

JOHANNA MEDICA Physician	(1200s) Polish	[K,L6]
JOHANSSON, INGEBRIGT Mathematician	(1904-) Norwegian	[C,L3]
JOHN, DOROTHY B. Mathematician	(1900s) American	[G] [*MI*]

JOHNSON, ANNA: *See* WHEELER, ANNA JOHNSON PELL

| JOHNSON, BARBARA CRAWFORD
Aerospace Engineer | (1900s)
American | [O1] |

JOHNSON, DOROTHY DURFEE MONTGOMERY Physicist	(1909-) American	[W]
JOHNSON, HILDEGARDE BINDE Geographer	(1908-) American	[W]
JOHNSON, KATHERINE Physicist	(1918-) American	[U] [MI]
JOHNSON, KRISTEN Medical Physicist	(1900s) American	[O1]
JOHNSON, LAURA Botanist	(1700s-1800s) American	[O]
JOHNSON, LOUISA Botanist	(1800s) American	[O]
JOHNSON, VIRGINIA ESHELMAN Psychologist/Sex Researcher	(1925-) American	[W,C1,W1,O1]

JOHNSON-MASTERS, VIRGINIA: *See* JOHNSON, VIRGINIA ESHELMAN

JOHNSON-PELL-WHEELER, ANNA: *See* WHEELER, ANNA JOHNSON PELL

JOLIOT-CURIE, IRENE Physical Chemist/Physicist	(1897-1956) French	[L,D,W,H,C1] [NL]
JOLY, SEBASTIANA Microbiologist	(1920-) Brazilian	[W]
JONAS, ANNA I. Petrologist/Geologist	(1881-1974) American	[F1,R1]
JONES, AMANDA THEODOSIA Inventor	(1835-1914) American	[N2,L2]

JONES, CHRISTINE: *See* JONES-FORMAN, CHRISTINE

JONES, EVA ELIZABETH Comparative Pathologist	(1898-) American	[W]
JONES, MARGARET Botanist/Pharmacist/Midwife	(16??-1648) American	[K]
JONES, MARY COVER Child Psychologist	(1900s early) American	[R1]
JONES, MARY ELLEN Biochemist/Nutritionist	(1922-) American	[A] [NS]
JONES, RENA TALLEY Microbiologist	(1937-) American	[A] [MI]
JONES, VELDA CYNTHIS Civil/Environmental Engineer	(1900s) American	[M1] [MI]

JONES-FORMAN, CHRISTINE Astrophysicist/X-ray Astronomer	(1949-) American	[A,O1]
JOO, P. KIM Seed Physiologist	(1900s) American	[M1] [*MI*]
JORDAN, LOUISE Micropaleontologist/Geologist	(1908-1966) American	[R1,I5]
JORGENSEN-KROGH, MARIE Physiologist	(1800s-1900s) Danish	[D1]
JOSHEE, ANANDIBAI YUMNA Physician	(1856-1887) Indian	[O1,D1,I5]
JOSLIN, LULU Physicist	(1800s-1900s) American	[R1]
JOSSELYN, IRENE MILLIKEN Psychiatrist	(1904-) American	[W]
JOTEYKO, JOSEPHINE Physician	(1800s-1900s) Polish	[D1]
JUHN, MARY Reproductive Endocrinologist	(1900s early) American	[B2]
JUILLARD, JACQUELINE Chemical Engineer	(1900s) Swiss	[O1]
JULIA ANICIA: *See* ANICIA, JULIA		
JUS, KAROLINA FRYST Physician	(1914-) Polish	[W]
JUSTIN, MARGARET Home Economist/Nutritionist	(18??-19??) American	[R1]

K

KABLICK, JOSEPHINE Botanist/Paleontologist	(1787-) Czechoslovakian	[Z,I5]
KACZOROWSKA, ZOFIA Geographer/Climatologist	(1902-) Polish	[C]
KAEISER, MARGARET Botanist	(1912-) American	[W]
KAHN, IDA Physician	(18??-19??) American/Chinese	[D1,K3]

KAILA, ARMI KAARINA   (1920-)   [W]
  Agricultural Chemist   Finnish

KALAPOTHAKES, MARY: *See* KALAPOTHAKIS, MINNIE

KALAPOTHAKIS, MINNIE   (18??-19??)   [D1,K]
  Physician   Greek

KALTENBEINER, VICTORINE   (1700s)   [K]
  Physician/Midwife/Educator   Swiss

KANKUS, ROBERTA A.   (1953-)   [O1]
  Nuclear Engineer   American

KANTER, ROSABETH MOSS   (1900s)   [Q1]
  Sociologist   American

KAPLAN, JOAN C.   (1900s)   [O]
  Medical Scientist   American   [*HA*]

KAPUR, PROMILA   (1900s)   [I9]
  Sociologist   Indian

KARLE, ISABELLA LUGOSKI   (1921-)   [A,O1,K2,C3]
  Crystallographer/Physical Chemist   American   [*NS*]

KARLIK, BERTA   (1904-)   [C,L3]
  Physicist   Austrian

KARP, CAROL RUTH   (1926-1972)   [M8]
  Mathematician/Logician   American

KARPOWICZ, LUDMILA   (1903-)   [C]
  Botanist/Ecologist   Polish

KASCHEWAROW, MME.: *See* KASHEVAROVA-RUDNEVA, VARVARA

KASHEVAROVA-RUDNEVA, VARVARA   (1800s)   [Z]
  Physician   Russian

KASSA OF BOHEMIA: *See* BRELA OF BOHEMIA

KATAKURA, MOTOKO   (1900s)   [I1]
  Anthropologist   Japanese

KATSURADA, YOSHI   (1900s)   [O1]
  Mathematician   Japanese

KAUFMAN, JOYCE J.   (1929-)   [A,O1,W6]
  Biochemist/Psychopharmacologist   American

KEDAR, JASSA   (1900s)   [O]
  Scientist   Israeli

KEDEN, ORA   (1900s)   [O]
  Scientist   Israeli

KEEN, ANGELINA MYRA Paleontologist	(1905-) American	[W]
KEEN, CHARLOTTE ELIZABETH Marine Geophysicist	(1943-) Canadian	[A,L3]
KEESOM, MISS Low Temperature Physicist	(1900s early) Dutch	[O]
KEIL, ELIZABETH MARGARETA Midwife/Obstetrician/Author	(16??-1699) German	[K]
KEITH, MARCIA Physicist	(1800s-1900s) American	[R1,V]
KELDYSH, LUDMILLA VSEROLODOVNA Mathematician	(1904-) Russian	[S,W,B1]
KELLEMS, VIVIEN Engineer	(1896-) American	[I5]
KELLER, EVELYN FOX Physicist/Mathematical Biologist	(1936-) American	[A,O2]
KELLER, FLORENCE Physician	(1800s-1900s) New Zealander	[O1]
KELLER, SUZANNE Sociologist	(1900s) American	[O1]
KELLEY, LOUISE Chemist	(1900s early) American	[R1]
KELLY, LENA Chemist	(1900s early) American	[R1]
KELSEY, FRANCES OLDHAM Physician/Pharmacologist	(1914-) Canadian/American	[A,O1]

KEMPNER, LYDIA RABINOVITCH: See RABINOWITSCH-KEMPNER, LYDIA

KENDALL, CLARIBEL Mathematician	(1889-1965) American	[M8]
KENDRICK, PEARL Medical Scientist	(1900s early) American	[R1]
KENNEDY, CORNELIA Agricultural Biochemist	(18??-) American	[R1]
KENNEDY, SUZANNE Veterinarian/Zoologist	(1953-) American	[A,O1]
KENNY, ELIZABETH (SISTER KENNY) Nurse/Physiotherapist	(1886-1952) Australian	[W,C1,G4,H3]

KENT, COUNTESS OF: See ELIZABETH, COUNTESS OF KENT

KENT, GRACE Clinical Psychologist	(1900s early) American	[R1]
KENWIX, MARGARET Herbalist/Pharmacist	(1500s) English	[K]
KENYON, KATHLEEN Agricultural Archaeologist	(1900s) British	[O1,T3]
KERLING, LOUISE Biologist	(1900-) Dutch	[C]
KHUSU, AMILIYA PAVLOVNA Mathematician	(1922-) Russian	[W]
KIELAN-JAWOROWSKA, ZOFIA Paleontologist/Biologist	(1925-) Polish	[W,L3]
KIELY, HELEN U. Chemist	(1900s early) American	[R1]
KIES, MARY Inventor	(17??-18??) American	[Z,H,W5]
KIMBER, ABAGAIL Botanist	(1800s) American	[O]
KING, ALICE: *See* CHATHAM, ALICE		
KING, GLADYS FLORENCE SMITH Biologist	(1917-) American	[W]
KING, HELEN DEAN Geneticist/Zoologist/Embryologist	(1869-) American	[R1,V,A1,S2]
KING, JESSIE L. Zoologist	(1900s early) American	[R1]
KINGSLEY, LOUISE Geologist	(1800s-1900s) American	[F1]
KINGSLEY, MARY HENRIETTA Botanist/Ethnologist/Explorer	(1862-1900) English	[Z,S1,I3,U1]
KIN-YIEN HSU Physician	(18??-19??) Chinese	[D1]
KIRCH, MARIA MARGERITE WINCKELMANN Astronomer/Author	(1620-1720) German	[D,W,Z,H,I5]
KIRKBRIDE, MARY Bacteriologist	(18??-19??) American	[R1]
KISTIAKOWSKY, VERA Elementary Particle Physicist	(1928-) American	[A,O1]
KLADIVKO, EILEEN Geoscientist/Soil Physicist	(1900s) American	[O]

KLAPPER, MARGARET STRANGE (1914–) [W]
Physician American

KLEIMAN, ANNA (1800s) [O]
Physician Russian

KLEIMAN, DEVRA (1942–) [A]
Zoologist/Ethologist American

KLEIN, MELANIE REIZES (1882–1960) [O1,D4]
Child Psychoanalyst Austrian/American

KLEOPATRA: See CLEOPATRA THE ALCHEMIST

KLIBURSKY, MARIA VOGL (1900s) [I8]
Geologist Hungarian

KLINE, VIRGINIA HARRIET (1910–1959) [R1]
Micropaleontologist/Geologist American

KLOSKOWSKA, ANTONINA (1919–) [W]
Sociologist Polish

KLUCKHOHN, FLORENCE ROCKWOOD (1905–) [W]
Educator American

KULMPKE, AUGUSTA (1800s) [Z]
Physician American/French

KLUMPKE, DERJINE (1900s early) [K3]
Research Physician French

KLUMPKE, DOROTHEA (1861–1942) [Z,N4,R1,M8]
Astronomer/Applied Mathematician American/French

KLUMPKE-ROBERTS, DOROTHEA: See KLUMPKE, DOROTHEA

KNIGHT, ELIZABETH: See BRITTON, ELIZABETH GERTRUDE KNIGHT

KNIGHT, MARGARET E. (1838–1914) [N2,L2,G4,Z]
Inventor American

KNOCK, FRANCES ENGELMANN (1921–) [W]
Chemist/Surgeon American

KNOPF, ELEANORA FRANCES BLISS (1883–1974) [W,N3,R1,F1]
Geologist/Structural Petrologist American

KOBLIKOVA, JITKA (1900s) [L3]
Scientist Czechoslovakian

KOCH, MARIE LOUISE (1899–) [W]
Medical Microbiologist American

KOCHANOVSKA, ADELA (1900s) [E,L3]
Solid State Engineer Czechoslovakian

KOCHINA, PELAGEYA YAKOVLEVNA (1899-) [S,T,W,C,L3]
Hydrodynamicist/Physicist   Russian   [SS]

KOHTS, MME.   (1900s early) [T3]
Animal Behaviorist   Russian

KOLLER, NOEMIE BENCZER   (1933-)   [A]
Physicist   American

KOLTAY, BORBALA GYARMATI   (1900s)   [I8]
Physicist   Hungarian

KOMAROVSKY, MIRRA   (1900s)   [O1]
Sociologist   Russian/American

KOOPMAN, ELIZABETH: See HEVELIUS, ELIZABETH KOOPMAN

KOPEC, MARIA   (1919-)   [E,L3]
Radiobiologist   Polish

KOPROWSKA, IRENE GRASBERG   (1917-)   [W]
Physician   American

KORN, DORIS ELFRIEDE   (1904-)   [W]
Mineralogist   German

KORSHUNOVA, OLGA STEPANOVNA (1909-)   [W]
Microbiologist   Russian

KORSINI, NATALIA   (1800s)   [O]
Physician   Russian

KORVINA-KRUKOVSKI, SOPHIE: See KOVALEVSKY, SOFIA VASILIYEVNA

KOSHLAND, MARIAN ELLIOTT   (1921-)   [A]
Immunologist   American   [NS,NB]

KOVALEVSKAYA, SOFYA VASILEVNA KORVIN-KRUKOVSKAYA: See
KOVALEVSKY, SOFIA VASILIYEVNA

KOVALEVSKI, SONYA: See KOVALEVSKY, SOFIA VASILIYEVNA

KOVALEVSKI, SOPHIE: See KOVALEVSKY, SOFIA VASILIYEVNA

KOVALEVSKY, SOFIA VASILIYEVNA (1850-1891) [D,M,N,W,B1]
Mathematician   Russian/Swedish

KOVALEVSKY, SONYA CORVIN-KURTOVSKY: See KOVALEVSKY, SOFIA
VASILIYEVNA

KOVALEVSKY, SOPHIE KROUKOVSKY: See KOVALEVSKY, SOFIA VASILIYEVNA

KOVRIGINA, MARIA DMITRIEVNA (1900s)   [D1]
Physician   Russian

KRASNOW, FRANCES   (1894-)   [W]
Biochemist   American

KRAUS, IDA RAGINA   (1900s early) [B2]
Physiological Chemist   American

KRIEGER-DONAJ, CECILIA: *See* DONAJ, CECILIA KRIEGER

KRUKOVSKY, SONYA: *See* KOVALEVSKY, SOFIA VASILIYEVNA

KRUPSKAYA, NADEZHDA Mathematician	(1800s-1900s) Russian	[O]
KRYNICKA-DROZDOWICZ, EWA Nuclear Physicist	(1900s) Polish	[O]
KUJALOVA, VERA Biologist	(1925-) Czechoslovakian	[W]
KULEY, MUFIDE Physician	(1900s) Turkish	[I1]

L

LACEY, ELLA PHILLIPS Medical Educator	(1900s) American	[O] 	[MI]
LA CHAPELLE, MARIE LOUISE DUGES Obstetrician/Physician	(1769-1821) French	[K,W,D1,W4]	
LA CHOPILLARDE, MARGUERITE Surgeon	(1300s) French	[H2]	

LADD, CHRISTINE: *See* LADD-FRANKLIN, CHRISTINE

LADD-FRANKLIN, CHRISTINE Psychologist/Mathematician/Logician	(1847-1930) American	[W,N2,B1,L2]

LA FLESCHE, SUSAN: *See* PICOTTE, SUSAN LAFLESCHE

LAIRD, ANNA KANE Biologist	(1922-) American	[W]
LAIRD, ELIZABETH REBECCA Physicist	(1874-) Canadian/American	[R1,W]
LAIS Physician	(BC 300s) Greek	[K,L6]
LALANDE, MARIE LEFRANCAIS DE Astronomer/Mathematician	(1760-1832) French	[Z,M5,R]
LAMBIN, SUZANNE Microbiologist	(1902-) French	[W]
LAMBORN, HELEN MORNINGSTAR Paleontologist	(1800s-1900s) American	[F1]
LAMME, BERTHA Electrical Engineer	(1869-1943) American	[E1,R]

LAMONTE, FRANCESCA RAYMOND   (1900s)   [W]
  Ichthyologist   American

LANCEFIELD, REBECCA CRAIGHILL   (1895-)   [A,O1,B5]
  Bacteriologist/Microbiologist   American   [NS]

LANGDON, FANNIE E.   (1800s-1900s)   [Z]
  Zoologist   American

LANGDON, LADEMA M.   (1900s early)   [R1]
  Botanist   American

LANGE, LINDA B.   (1900s early)   [R1]
  Bacteriologist   American

LANGFORD, GRACE   (1800s-1900s)   [R1]
  Physicist   American

LANKESTER, MRS.   (18??-1900)   [I3]
  Botanist   English

LARRIEU, MARIE JOSETTE BOUBEE   (1926-)   [W]
  Physician   French

LARSON, GERALDINE   (1930-)   [O1]
  Botanist/Forester   American

LA SABLIERE, MARGUERITE DE: See SABLIERE, MARGUERITE DE LA

LAS HUELGAS, ABBESS OF   (1100s)   [K]
  Physician   Spanish

LASTHENIA OF ARCADIA   (BC 400 c.)   [Z,R,P5]
  Philosopher/Scientist/Mathematician Greek

LATHROP, KATHERINE AUSTIN   (1915-)   [W]
  Radiobiologist   American

LATTIRI, ZUBEIDA   (1900s)   [I1]
  Engineer   Tunisian

LATYSHEVA, KLAVDIYA YAKOLEVNA   (1897-1956)   [M8]
  Mathematician   Russian

LAUCHIS, BETTIE E.   (1900s)   [O1]
  Botanist/Horticulturist   American

LAVINDER, MARY   (1776-1845)   [W4]
  Pediatrician/Midwife   American

LAVOISIER, MARIE ANNE PIERRETTE   (1758-1836)   [L5,A2,I5,Z]
  Chemist   French

LAVOISIER DE RUMFORD, MARIE ANNE PIERRETTE PAULZE: See
  LAVOISIER, MARIE ANNE PIERRETTE

LAW, ANNIE E.   (18??-1889)   [I3]
  Zoologist/Conchologist   Maltese/English

LAWRENCE, BARBARA Zoologist	(1909-) American	[W]
LAZARENKO, NATALIA IOASAFOVNA Inventor	(1911-) Russian	[S]
LEACH, CAROLYN Endocrinologist/Physiologist	(1940-) American	[A]
LEACOCK, ELEANOR BURKE Anthropologist	(1922-) American	[W]
LEAKEY, MARY Anthropologist/Archaeologist	(1904-) English/Kenyan	[O1,H3,D4]
LEAVITT, HENRIETTA SWAN Astronomer	(1868-1921) American	[D,W,O1,N2] [*HA*]

LEBOURSIER, MADAME DUCOUDRAY: *See* DU COUDRAY, ANGELIQUE
MARGUERITE

LE BRETON, ELAINE Physiologist/Cell Biologist	(1897-) French	[C]
LECKBAND, SUSANNE M. Agricultural Engineer	(1900s) American	[O1]
LECLERCQ, SUZANNE CELINE Paleobotanist	(1901-) Belgian	[C]
LEE, LUCY Poultry Research Chemist	(1931-) American	[D1]
LEE, REBECCA Physician	(1800s) American	[D1,O1] [*MI*]
LEE, ROSE HUM Sociologist	(1904-1964) American	[N3]
LEFEBRE, MME. Chemist/Inventor	(1800s) French	[Z]
LEFEVRE, ANNE Scholar/Linguist	(1654-1720) French	[Z,F4,R,P5]

LEFRANCAIS, MME.: *See* LALANDE, MARIE LEFRANCAIS DE

LEGEY, LA DOCTORESSE Physician/Anthropologist	(1900s early) Moroccan	[K]
LEHMANN, INGE Geodesist/Seismologist/Geologist	(1888-) Danish	[O1,P7,L3]
LEHR, MARGUERITE Mathematician	(1898-) American	[W]
LEKCZYNSKA, JADWIGA Agricultural/Forestry Scientist	(1900s) Polish	[L3]

LELAND, EVA F.   (18??-19??)   [Z,R]
  Astronomer   American

LELONG, JACQUELINE FERRAND   (1918-   )   [C,W,O1,M9]
  Mathematician   French

LELONG-FERRAND, JACQUELINE: *See* LELONG, JACQUELINE FERRAND

LEMARCHAND-BERAUD, THERESE MARIE   (1928-   )   [W]
  Chemist   Swiss

LEMMON, SARAH A. PLUMMER   (1800s-1900s)   [Z]
  Botanist   American

LEMONE, MARGARET ANNE   (1900s)   [A,O1,P2]
  Meteorologist   American

LEONETTA MEDICA OF TURIN   (1300s)   [K,H2,L6]
  Physician   Italian

LEONTARIUM: *See* LEONTIUM

LEONTIKIN: *See* LEONTIUM

LEONTIUM   (BC 300 c.)   [Z,F4,R,P5]
  Natural Philosopher/Philosopher   Greek

LEOPARDA   (200s-300s)   [Z,K,S1,L6]
  Physician/Gynecologist   Roman/Italian

LEOPOLD, ESTELLA BERGERE   (1927-   )   [A,O1]
  Botanist/Paleontologist/Geologist   American   [NS]

LEPAUTE, HORTENSE   (1723-1788)   [Z,M5,D4,R]
  Astronomer/Mathematician/Physicist   French

LEPAUTE, MME. JEAN ANDRE: *See* BRIERE, NICOLE-REINE ETABLE DE LA

LEPESHINSKAIA, OLGA BORISOVNA   (1871-??)   [S,W]
  Biologist   Russian

LEPIN, LYDIA KARLOVNA   (1891-   )   [S,W]
  Physical Chemist   Russian

LEPINSKY, MELANIE   (18??-19??)   [K,Z]
  Physician/Medical Historian   Polish/French

LEPORIN-ERXLEBEN, DOROTHEA CHRISTINA: *See* ERXLEBEN, DOROTHEA
  CHRISTIANE

LERMONTOVA, JULIA   (1800s)   [R]
  Chemist   Russian

LERNER, EMMA   (1906-   )   [O]
  Mathematician   American

LESLEY, SUSAN INCHES   (1823-1904)   [I3]
  Geologist   American

L'ESPERANCE, ELISE DEPEW STRANG   (1878?-1959)   [W,N3,I5]
  Pathologist/Research Physician   American

LETHAS, MADAME: See FLAMEL, PERRENELLE

LEVI-MONTALCINI, RITA   (1909-)   [A,O1]
  Neurobiologist/Neurologist   American/Italian   [NS]

LEVY, JERRE MARIE   (1938-)   [A]
  Neuropsychologist/Biopsychologist   American

LEWES, VIVIAN BYNAM   (1852-1915)   [I3]
  Chemist   English

LEWIS, AGNES SMITH   (1843-1926)   [W,Z,I5,T2]
  Archaeologist   Scottish/British

LEWIS, FLORENCE PARTHENIA   (1877-1964)   [M8,R1]
  Mathematician/Astronomer   American

LEWIS, GRACEANNA   (1800s)   [R1,R2]
  Ornithologist   American

LEWIS, ISABEL MARTIN   (18??-19??)   [R1]
  Computer Scientist   American

LEWIS, JESSICA HELEN   (1917-)   [W]
  Physician   American

LEWIS, LENA ARMSTRONG   (1910-)   [W]
  Physiologist   American

LEWIS, MARGARET REED   (1881-)   [R1,A1,I5]
  Embryologist/Anatomist/Physiologist American

LEWIS, MRS. WARREN H.   (1881-)   [S2]
  Anatomist   American

LIBBY, LEONA WOODS MARSHALL   (1919-)   [A,W,O1]
  Physicist   American

LIBERMANN, PAULETTE   (1900s)   [E,M9]
  Mathematician   French

LIBUSSA OF BOHEMIA   (700s)   [K]
  Physician   Czechoslovakian

LICHTENSTEIN, PEARL RUBENSTEIN   (1917-)   [W]
  Astronomer   American

LIEPINIA, LYDIA: See LEPIN, LYDIA KARLOVNA

LINCOLN, ALMIRA HART: See PHELPS, ALMIRA HART LINCOLN

LINCOLN, EDITH MAAS   (19??-1977)   [O1]
  Pediatrician/Medical Researcher   American

LINDAHL-KIESSLING, KERSTIN   (1900s)   [E,L3]
Zoologist/Animal Physiologist   Swedish

LINDNER, KATALIA SZOTYORI   (1920-)   [W]
Chemist   Hungarian

LINDSAY, MISS B.   (18??-1917)   [I3]
Biologist   English

LIPINSKA, MELANIE: *See* LEPINSKY, MELANIE

LITRICIN, OLGA   (1918-)   [W]
Ophthalmologist   Yugoslavian

LITTLEJOHN, CAROLINE STUART: *See* HERZENBERG, CAROLINE STUART
    LITTLEJOHN

LITVINOVA, ELIZAVETA FEDOREVNA   (1800s)   [R]
Mathematician   Russian

LITZINGER, MARIE   (1899-1952)   [W,M7,M8]
Mathematician   American

LIUBATOVICH, OLGA   (1800s)   [O]
Physician   Russian

LJOTCHITCH-MILOCHEVITCH, DRAGA   (18??-1927)   [D1,I5]
Physician   Yugoslavian

LLOYD, RACHEL   (1800s)   [R1]
Chemist   American

LOCATELLI, PIERA   (1900s)   [D1]
Pathologist   Italian

LOCHMANN, CHRISTINA   (1900s early)   [R1]
Chemist   American

LOCKETT, MARY FAURIEL   (1911-)   [W]
Pharmacologist   English/Australian

LOCUSTA   (000s AD)   [B6]
Physician   Roman

LOEBLICH, HELEN NINA TAPPAN   (1917-)   [W]
Paleontologist   American

LOEWE, LOTTE LUISE FRIEDERICKE   (1900-)   [W]
Chemist   German

LOGAN, MYRA ADELE   (1908-1977)   [P,O1]
Anatomist/Physician/Surgeon   American   [*MI*]

LOGSDON, MAYME IRWIN   (1881-1967)   [M8]
Mathematician   American

LOLLINI, CLELIA   (1800s-1900s)   [D1]
Physician   Italian/Libyan

LONG, RUBY PAULINE KING Physiologist	(1914-) American	[W]
LONGSHORE, HANNAH E. MYERS Physician/Anatomist	(1819-1901) American	[W,N2,L2,K2]
LONGSTAFF, MRS. GEORGE BLUNDELL Geologist	(1800s-1900s) American	[S1]
LONSDALE, KATHLEEN YARDLEY Physicist/Crystallographer	(1903-1971) Irish/English	[W,B1,I7,Q] [FR]
LOPEZ, RITA LOBATO VELHO Physician	(1866-) Brazilian	[D1,I5]
LOSA, ISABELLA Physician	(1473-1546) Spanish	[K,R]
LOSER, MARGARET SIBYLLA VON: *See* VON LOSER, MARGARET SIBYLLA		
LOSTROH, ARDIS JUNE Biologist	(1925-) American	[W]
LOUDON, JANE Botanist	(18??-1858) English	[I3,W5]
LOUGHLIN, WINIFRED CATHERINE Physician	(1900s) American	[O] [HA]
LOUISE OF SAVOY Scholar	(1500s) French	[K,R3]
LOVELACE, ADA AUGUSTA BYRON, LADY Computer Scientist/Mathematician	(1815-1852) English	[I,M,I4,M5]
LOVELACE, COUNTESS OF: *See* LOVELACE, ADA AUGUSTA BYRON, LADY		
LOW, BARBARA WHARTON Biochemist	(1920-) American	[W]
LOWATER, FRANCES Physicist	(1800s-1900s) American	[R1]
LOZIER, CLEMENCE SOPHIA HARNED Physician	(1813-1888) American	[W,N2,L2,K3]
LUCHINS, EDITH HIRSCH Mathematician	(1921-) American	[A,O1]
LUCIA, SAINT Ophthalmologist	(700s) Italian	[K]
LUCID, SHANNON W. Biochemist	(1943-) American	[O1] [AS]
LUCY, ALICE, LADY Physician	(1600s) English	[K]

LUISI, PAULINA Physician	(1900s) Uruguayan	[D1]
LULBURENEN, MADAME Physician	(1500s) French	[K]
LUND, EBBA Virologist	(1923-) Danish	[W]
LUNN, KATHERINE FOWLER Geologist	(1800s-1900s) American	[F1]
LUOMALA, KATHARINE Anthropologist	(1907-) American	[W]
LUSE, SARAH AMANDA Anatomist	(1918-) American	[W]
LUTZ, ELIZABETH Mathematician	(1914-) French	[C]
LUXOSE, MARY POONEN Physician/Surgeon	(1900s) Indian	[I9]
LYELL, MRS. Geologist	(1800s) English	[Z]
LYNDS, BEVERLY TURNER Astronomer	(1929-) American	[A,O1]
LYON, MARY Chemist/Science Educator	(1797-1849) American	[R1,R]
LYON, MARY FRANCES Geneticist/Radiobiologist	(1900s) English	[E,L3] [FR]

M

MAATHAI, WANGARI Biologist/Forestry Scientist	(1900s) Kenyan	[O]
MACALPINE, IDA Psychiatrist	(1899-1974) German	[B1]
MACDONALD, ELEANOR J. Cancer Epidemiologist	(1909-) American	[W,O1]
MACDOUGALL, MARY Zoologist	(1900s early) American	[R1]
MACE, HANNA Astronomer	(1800s) American	[Z,R]

MACGILL, ELIZABETH MURIEL GREGORY: *See* MACGILL, ELSIE GREGORY

MACGILL, ELSIE GREGORY Aeronautical Engineer	(1905-) Canadian	[A,O1]
MACGILLAVRY, CAROLINA HENRIETTE Crystallographer/Chemist	(1904-) Dutch	[C,W]
MACHA, QUEEN Physician	(BC 600 c.) Irish	[K]
MACINTYRE, SHEILA SCOTT Mathematician	(1910-1960) Scottish	[M7,M8]
MACK, PAULINE BEERY Chemist/Educator	(1891-1974) American	[W,O1,I5,W6]

MACKINNON-FITCH, ANNE LOUISE: *See* FITCH, ANNE LOUISE MACKINNON

MACKLIN, MADGE THURLOW Geneticist/Physician	(1893-1962) American	[N3]
MACKOWSKY, MARIE THERESE Mineralogist	(1913-) German	[W]
MACLEOD, ANNA MACGILLIVRAY Biologist	(1900s) Scottish	[L3]
MACLEOD, GRACE Nutritionist	(1800s) American	[R1]
MACLIN, ARLENE Physicist	(1900s) American	[O] [MI]
MACMURCHY, HELEN Physician	(1862-1953) Canadian	[D1,K3,I5]
MACNAMARA, JEAN Bacteriologist/Physician	(1900s early) Australian	[H3]
MACRINA Physician	(300s) Italian	[K]
MACY-HOOBLER, ICIE GERTRUDE Biochemist/Physiological Chemist	(1892-) American	[W,O1,R1,W6]
MADDISON, ISABEL Mathematician/Educator	(18??-1950) English/American	[M7,M8,R1,R
MADONNA CATERINA, MEDICA Physician	(1300s) Italian	[K]
MAGANA, MARIA Electrical Engineer	(1900s) American	[M1] [MI]
MAGNAC-VALETTE, DENYSE JULIETTE Physicist	(1924-) French	[W]

MAGNILLA Philosopher	(100s-200s) Roman Empire	[G2]
MAHOUT, COUNTESS OF ARTOIS Physician/Scholar	(12??-1329) French	[K]
MAIA Physician	(BC) Greek	[L6]
MAKEMSON, MAUD WORCESTER Astronomer	(1891-) American	[W,R1,I5]
MALAHLELE, MARY SUSAN Physician	(1900s) South African	[D1] [MI]
MALING, HARRIET FLORENCE MYLANDER Pharmacologist	(1919-) American	[W]
MALLORY, EDITH BRANDT Psychologist	(1901-) American	[W]
MALTBY, MARGARET ELIZA Physicist	(1860-1944) American	[N2,O1,J,H]
MALTRANERSA, ADELMOTA Physician	(1200s) Italian	[H2]
MAMMANA, CONSTANTIA Midwife/Obstetrician	(12??-1308) Italian	[K]
MAN, EVELYN BROWER Biochemist	(1904-) American	[W]
MANCE, JEAN Physician	(1606-1673) French/Canadian	[K]
MANCINI, ANNE MARIA Physician	(1600s) Italian	[K]
MANDL, INES Biochemist	(1917-) American	[W]
MANICATILDE, ELENA Physician	(1800s-1900s) Rumanian	[D1]
MANN, HELEN Computer Scientist	(1900s) American	[G]
MANNING, MRS. A.H. Inventor	(1800s) American	[Z]
MANOOCHEHRIAN, MEHRANGUIZ Psychologist/Philosopher/Lawyer	(1900s) Iranian	[N5]

MANTINEA, PRIESTESS OF: *See* DIOTIMA, PRIESTESS OF MANTINEIA

MANTON, IRENE Botanist	(1900s) English	[E,L3] [FR]

MANTON, SIDNIE   (1902-1979)   [D4]
  Zoologist   English   [FR]

MANTUA, MARCHIONESS DE: See ESTE, ISABELLA D'

MANZOLINI, ANNA: See MORANDI-MANZOLINI, ANNA

MANZOLINE, ANNE: See MORANDI-MANZOLINI, ANNA

MARCELLA   (300s?)   [D1,K]
  Physician   Roman

MARCELLO-MOCENIGO, LOREDANA   (1500s late)   [F2]
  Medicinal Botanist/Pharmacologist   Italian

MARCET, JANE HALDIMAN   (1769-1858)   [W,C5,I5,C7]
  Chemist/Author/Botanist/Physician   Swiss/English

MARCH, BERYL ELIZABETH   (1920-)   [A,L3]
  Poultry Nutrition Scientist   Canadian

MARCHIONNA-TIBILETTI, CESARINA   (1920-)   [W]
  Mathematician   Italian

MARGARET OF BOURGOGNE, QUEEN OF SICILY: See MARGUERITE OF
  BOURGOGNE, QUEEN

MARGARET OF GERMANY   (1200s)   [K]
  Physician   German

MARGARET OF THE NETHERLANDS   (1400s)   [K]
  Physician   Dutch

MARGARET OF YPRES   (12??-13??)   [M2,H2]
  Physician   French

MARGARET, QUEEN   (1200s)   [K]
  Physician   German

MARGARET, QUEEN OF SCOTLAND   (1100s)   [K]
  Physician   Scottish

MARGARETA   (100s)   [K]
  Physician/Surgeon   Roman

MARGARITA   (1100s)   [Z]
  Physician   Italian

MARGUERITE OF BOURGOGNE, QUEEN   (12??-13??)   [K]
  Physician   French/Italian

MARGUERITE OF NAPLES   (1300s-1400s)   [K,W4,H2,L6]
  Ophthalmologist/Physician   Italian/German

MARGUERITE OF YPRA: See MARGARET OF YPRES

MARGULIS, LYNN   (1938-)   [A]
  Cell Biologist   American   [NS]

MARIA FEODOROWNA, QUEEN   (17??-1828)   [K]
  Physician/Educator   Russian

MARIA INCARNATA: See INCARNATA, MARIA

MARIA KOPT   (300 c.?)   [A4,H4,B6]
  Alchemist   Egyptian

MARIA OF ALEXANDRIA: See MARIA THE JEWESS

MARIA PROPHETESS: See MARIA THE JEWESS

MARIA PROPHETISSA: See MARIA THE JEWESS

MARIA THE COPT: See MARIA KOPT

MARIA THE EGYPTIAN: See MARIA KOPT

MARIA THE JEWESS   (000s?)   [C5,C8,C9,R]
  Alchemist/Inventor/Author/Educator Egyptian/Syrian

MARIE, DAME, OF PARIS   (12??-13??)   [K,H2]
  Physician   French

MARIE DE MEDICIS: See MEDICIS, MARIE DE

MARIE LA JUIVE: See MARIA THE JEWESS

MARILLAC, LOUISE   (1591-1671)   [K]
  Nurse/Surgeon/Pharmacist   French

MARLATT, ABBY LILLIAN   (1869-1943)   [N2,L2,R1]
  Home Economist/Educator   American

MARQUET, SIMONE   (1922-)   [C]
  Mathematician/Statistician   French

MARRETT, CORA BAGLEY   (1900s)   [O]
  Sociologist   American   [MI]

MARRIOTT, ALICE LEE   (1910-)   [I5]
  Ethnologist   American

MARSDEN, KATE   (18??-19??)   [O]
  Explorer/Nurse   English

MARSHALL, LEONA WOODS: See LIBBY, LEONA WOODS MARSHALL

MARSHALL, SHEINA MACALISTER (1896-)   [W]
  Marine Biologist   Scottish

MARTERTERA, AEMILIA HILARIA: See AEMILIA

MARTHA, SISTER   (1751-1824)   [K]
  Surgeon   French

MARTIN, ARLENE PATRICIA   (1926-)   [W]
  Biochemist   American

MARTIN, EMILIE NORTON Mathematician	(1869-1936) American	[M8]
MARTIN, LILLIEN JANE Psychologist	(1851-1943) American	[W,N2,L2,R1]
MARTIN, MARIA Naturalist/Nature Painter	(1796-1863) American	[F1,N2]
MARTIN, VIVIAN S. Geographer	(18??-1897) English?	[I3]
MARTINEAU, HARRIET Sociologist/Social Scientist	(1802-1876) English	[I4,R]
MARVIN, URSULA BAILEY Mineralogist/Meteoriticist	(1921-) American	[A,O1]

MARY THE COPT: *See* MARIA KOPT

MARY THE JEWESS: *See* MARIA THE JEWESS

MARY THE PROPHETESS: *See* MARIA THE JEWESS

MASEVICH, ALLA G.: *See* MASSEVITCH, ALLA GENRIKHOVNA

MASKEWITZ, BETTY F. Mathematician/Computer Scientist	(1900s) American	[O1]
MASSEVITCH, ALLA GENRIKHOVNA Astrophysicist	(1918-) Russian	[W,H3]
MASTELLARI, MARIE Physician	(17??-18??) Italian	[L6]
MASTERS, SYBILLA Inventor	(16??-1720) American	[H,N2]

MASTERS-JOHNSON, VIRGINIA: *See* JOHNSON, VIRGINIA ESHELMAN

MATEYKO, GLADYS MARY Biologist	(1921-) American	[W]
MATHER, SARAH Inventor	(1800s) American	[Z,W5]
MATHEWS, JESSICA TUCHMAN Biochemist	(1900s) American	[O]
MATHIAS, MILDRED ESTHER Botanist	(1906-) American	[W]
MATHILDA OF QUEDLINBURG, ABBESS Physician	(900s) German	[K]
MATIKASHVILI, NINA Veterinary Surgeon/Protozoologist	(1900s) Russian	[B1]

MATILDA, QUEEN   (10??-1118)   [K]
   Physician   Scottish/English

MATTEO, THOMASIA DE   (1100s)   [Z]
   Surgeon/Physician   Italian

MATTHEWS, ALVA T.   (1900s)   [O1]
   Engineer/Applied Mathematician   American

MAUD, QUEEN   (800s-900s)   [K]
   Physician   German

MAUD, QUEEN: *See also* MATILDA, QUEEN

MAUNDER, ANNIE SCOTT DILL RUSSELL   (1868-1947)   [W]
   Astronomer   British

MAURY, ANTONIA CAETANA   (1866-1952)   [N3,O1,S1,Z]
   Astronomer   American

MAURY, CARLOTTA JOAQUINA   (1874-1938)   [W,F1,R1,I5]
   Paleontologist/Geologist   American

MAYER, MARIA GOEPPERT   (1906-1972)   [B,L,L1,B1]
   Physicist   German/American   [*NL,NS*]

MAYOR, HEATHER DONALD   (1930-   )   [W]
   Medical Scientist   American

MCAFEE, MILDRED   (1899-   )   [R1]
   Sociologist   American

MCAFEE, NAOMI J.   (1900s)   [O1]
   Quality Control Engineer   American

MCCAMMON, HELEN   (1900s)   [F]
   Ecologist   American

MCCLINTOCK, BARBARA   (1902-   )   [A,O1,R1,A1]
   Geneticist/Botanist   American   [*NL,NS*]

MCCORMICK, KATHERINE DEXTER   (1800s)   [M1]
   Scientist   American   [*MI*]

MCCOY, ELIZABETH   (1903-   )   [W,O1,R1,B5]
   Soil Microbiologist   American

MCDONALD, JANET   (1905-   )   [W]
   Mathematician   American

MCDONALD, MARGARET RITCHIE   (1910-   )   [W]
   Biochemist   American

MCDOWELL, LOUISE   (18??-19??)   [R1]
   Physicist   American

MCDOWELL, MARGARET ANN, SISTER   (1912-   )   [W]
   Biologist   American

MCGEE, ANITA NEWCOMB Physician/Surgeon	(1864-) American	[K3,R1,I5]
MCGEER, EDITH GRAEF Chemist	(1923-) American/Canadian	[W]
MCGRATH, LOUISE Chemist	(1900s early) American	[R1]
MCHALE, KATHRYN Psychologist	(1890-1956) American	[W,I5]
MCKINLEY, SUZANNE Organic Chemist	(1936-) American	[O]
MCKINNON, EMILY H.S. Physician	(1800s-1900s) New Zealander	[D1]
MCLAREN, ANNE LAURA Geneticist/Developmental Biologist	(1927-) English/Scottish	[E,L3] [FR]
MCLEAN, HELEN VINCENT Psychoanalyst	(1894-) American	[W]
MCNALLY, MARGARET Engineer	(1900s early) American	[I5]
MCNEAL, CATHERINE J. Chemist	(1900s) American	[O]
MCSHERRY, DIANA HARTRIDGE Biophysicist/Computer Scientist	(1900s) American	[A]
MCVEIGH, IDA Biologist	(1905-) American	[W]
MCWHINNIE, MARY ALICE Biologist/Animal Physiologist	(1922-) American	[A,O1]

MEAD, KATE CAMPBELL HURD: *See* HURD-MEAD, KATE CAMPBELL

MEAD, MARGARET Cultural Anthropologist	(1901-1979) American	[G1,C1,X,Z] [NS]

MEAD, SYLVIA EARLE: *See* EARLE, SYLVIA

MEARS, ELEANOR COWIE LOUDON Gynecologist	(1917-) British	[W]
MEARS, MARTHA Obstetrician/Gynecologist/Author	(1700s) English	[K]
MECHTHILD OF HACKECDORN Physician	(1212-1282) German	[K]

MECHTHILD OF HACKECDORN AND MAGDEBURG: *See* MECHTHILD OF
HACKECDORN

MEDAGLIA, DIAMANTE
Mathematician/Author/Educator
(1700s)   [Z,U1]
Italian

MEDES, GRACE
Chemist
(19??-1969)   [O1,W6]
American

MEDICI, CATHERINE DE
Physician/Astronomer
(1519-1589)   [K,T1,R]
Italian

MEDICIS, MARIE DE
Alchemist
(1573-1642)   [A3,B6]
French

MEDVEDEVA, NINA BORISOVNA
Pathophysiologist
(1899-)   [W]
Russian

MEEK, LOIS HAYDEN
Research Psychologist
(1900s early)   [R1]
American

MEINEL, MARJORIE PETTIT
Astronomer
(1922-)   [A,O1]
American

MEITNER, LISE
Physicist
(1878-1968)   [Y,W,I,R,Q]
Austrian/Swedish

MELCHIOR, JACKLYN BUTLER
Biochemist
(1918-)   [A,W]
American

MELISSA
Natural Philosopher/Mathematician
(BC 400s)   [R,P5]
Greek

MELITINE
Physician
(000s-100s)   [G2,G3]
Roman

MELLEN, IDA
Veterinarian/Ichthyologist
(1900s early)   [R1]
American

MELNICK, MATILDA BENYESH
Virologist
(1926-)   [W]
American

MENDENHALL, DOROTHY REED
Research Physician
(1874-1964)   [N3,O1,K3]
American

MENDOZA-GUAZON, MARIA PAZ
Pathologist/Bacteriologist
(1800s-1900s)   [O1]
Philippine

MENTON, MAUD
Biochemist
(1900s early)   [B2]
American

MENTUHETEP, QUEEN
Scholar/Physician
(BC 2300 c.)   [K]
Egyptian

MERCURIADA
Surgeon/Educator
(1200s-1300s)   [K,Z,W4]
Italian

MERCURIADE: *See* MERCURIADA

MERIAN, DOROTHEA
Naturalist/Artist
(16??-17??)   [Z,H3]
German

MERIAN, HELENA   (16??-17??)   [Z,H3]
  Naturalist/Artist   German

MERIAN, MARIA SIBYLLA   (1647-1717)   [W,Z,K,I5,R]
  Entomologist/Botanist/Explorer   German/Dutch/Swiss

MERIT PTAH: *See* PTAH, MERIT

MERITT, LUCY TAXIS SHOE   (1906-)   [W]
  Archaeologist   American

MERNISSI, FATIMA   (1900s)   [I1]
  Sociologist   Moroccan

MERRELL, MARGARET   (1900s early)   [R1]
  Biostatistician   American

MERRIAM, FLORENCE: *See* BAILEY, FLORENCE AUGUSTA MERRIAM

MERRILL, HELEN ABBOT   (1864-1949)   [M7,M8]
  Mathematician   American

MESHKE, EDNA DOROTHY   (1906-)   [W]
  Textile Scientist   American

MESTORF, JOHANNA   (1829?-1909)   [I3]
  Archaeologist   German

METCALF, BETSEY   (1700s)   [Z]
  Inventor   American

METCHNIKOFF, MME.   (18??-19??)   [K3,R]
  Research Physician   French

METRADORA: *See* METRODORA

METRODORA   (100s)   [Z,K,L6,E3]
  Physician/Gynecologist/Author   Greek/Roman

METZGER, HELENE   (1889-1944 c.)   [D4]
  Chemist/Science Historian   French

MEURDRAC, MARIA   (1600s)   [K,C5,C6,W6]
  Chemist   French/German

MEURDRAC, MARIE: *See* MEURDRAC, MARIA

MEURODACIA   (100s)   [K]
  Physician/Midwife/Obstetrician   Roman

MEYER, EDITHNA PAULA CHARTKOFF   (1903-)   [I5]
  Engineer   American

MEYER, LUISE: *See* MEYER-SCHUTZMEISTER, LUISE

MEYER-SCHUTZMEISTER, LUISE   (1915-1981)   [A]
  Physicist   American

MICHELET, MME. JULES Biologist/Naturalist	(18??-1899) French	[I3,R]
MIDDLEHURST, BARBARA MARY Astronomer	(1915-) American	[W]
MIELCZAREK, EUGENIE V. Physicist	(1931-) American	[A,F]
MIGDALSKA, BARBARA CHOJNACKA Physician	(1928-) Polish	[W]
MILDMAY, GRACE SHERRINGTON Physician/Scholar/Alchemist	(1552-1620) English	[K]
MILDRED, ABBESS Physician	(600s late) English	[K]
MILES, CATHARINE COX Psychologist	(1800s-1900s) American	[R1]
MILLARD, NAOMI ADELINE HELEN Zoologist	(1914-) South African	[W]
MILLER, AGNES E. Zoologist	(1900s) Scottish	[L3]
MILLER, BESSIE IRVING Mathematician	(1884-1931) American	[M8]
MILLER, CHRISTINA CRUICKSHANK Chemist	(1900s) Scottish	[L3]
MILLER, ELIZABETH CAVERT Biochemist/Oncologist	(1920-) American	[A,W] [NS]
MILLER, ELIZABETH KOCH Chemist/Home Economist	(1900s early) American	[B2]
MILLER, HARRIET MANN Ornithologist/Naturalist	(1831-1918) American	[N2,S1,Z,I5]
MILLER, HELEN AGNES Biologist	(1913-) American	[W]
MILLER, IRENE Physicist	(1933-) American	[O]
MILLER, JANICE MARGARET Veterinary Pathologist	(1938-) American	[A,O1]
MILLER, "OLIVE THORNE": *See* MILLER, HARRIET MANN		
MILNER, BRENDA Psychologist	(1900s) English/Canadian	[L3] [FR]
MINOKA-HILL, LILLIE R. Physician	(18??-19??) American	[D1] [MI]

MINOT, ANN STONE   (1894-)   [W]
  Chemist/Physiologist   American

MINTZ, BEATRICE   (1921-)   [A,O1]
  Biologist/Medical Geneticist   American   [NS]

MINUCIA   (1000s)   [K]
  Physician   Italian

MIRIAM SISTER OF MOSES: See MARIA THE JEWESS

MIRIAM THE JEWESS: See MARIA THE JEWESS

MITCHELL, EVELYN GROESBECK   (1800s-1900s)   [S1]
  Entomologist   American

MITCHELL, HELEN S.   (1895-)   [W]
  Nutritionist   American

MITCHELL, LUCY SPRAGUE: See SPRAGUE, LUCY

MITCHELL, MARIA   (1818-1889)   [C1,B1,W,H]
  Astronomer   American

MITCHELL, MILDRED   (1900s)   [G]
  Bionicist/Mathematician   American

MITTWOCH, URSULA   (1900s)   [W]
  Geneticist   German/English

MOELLER, HELENA SIBYLLA   (1600s)   [K]
  Naturalist   German

MOLLER, LILLIAN: See GILBRETH, LILLIAN EVELYN MOLLER

MOLZA, TARQUINIA   (1400s-1500s)   [Z,F2,R]
  Astronomer/Mathematician/Scholar   Italian

MONCRIEFF, SCOTT   (1900s early)   [D2]
  Biochemist/Geneticist   English

MONICA, SAINT   (332-386)   [K,R]
  Physician/Philosopher   North African

MONTAGU, MARY WORTLEY (PIERREPONT)   (1689-1762)   [Z,O1,I3,I4]
  Public Health Innovator   English

MONTANARO-GALLITELLI, EUGENIA   (1906-)   [C]
  Invertebrate Paleontologist   Italian

MONTESSORI, MARIA   (1870-1952)   [G4,D1,I3]
  Educator/Physician/Psychiatrist   Italian

MONTOYA, MATHILDE: See MONTOYA, MATILDE

MONTOYA, MATILDE   (18??-)   [D1,L6]
  Physician   Mexican

MOODY, AGNES CLAYPOLE   (1870-)   [Z,R1,R2,S2]
  Zoologist   American

MOODY, MARY BLAIR   (1837-)   [R1]
  Anatomist   American

MOOERS, EMMA WILSON DAVIDSON   (18??-1911)   [I3]
  Pathologist   American

MOOG, FLORENCE   (1916-)   [W]
  Biologist   American

MOORE, CHARLOTTE: *See* SITTERLY, CHARLOTTE E. MOORE

MOORE, EMMELINE   (1872-1963)   [R1]
  Aquatic Biologist/Conservationist   American

MOORE, LUCY BEATRICE   (1900s)   [L3]
  Scientist   New Zealander

MORABITO, LINDA   (1900s)   [P7]
  Astronomer   American

MORAN, JULIETTE M.   (1917-)   [W2,O1]
  Chemist   American

MORANDI-MANZOLINI, ANNA   (1716-1774)   [Z,B1,D1,U1]
  Anatomist   Italian

MORAWETZ, CATHLEEN SYNGE   (1923-)   [A,M]
  Applied Mathematician   Canadian/American

MOREAU, MIREILLE   (1925-)   [W]
  Plant Pathologist   French

MORELLO, JOSEPHINE A.   (1936-)   [A]
  Microbiologist   American

MORGAN, AGNES FAY   (1884-1967)   [W,O1,N3,R1]
  Chemist/Nutritionist   American

MORGAN, ANN HAVEN   (1882-1966)   [N3,R1,A1]
  Zoologist/Ecologist   American

MORGAN, ISABEL   (1900s early)   [R1]
  Virologist   American

MORGAN, JULIA   (1900s early)   [O1]
  Architectural Engineer   American

MORGAN, LILLIAN SAMPSON   (1800s)   [R1]
  Zoologist   American

MORISAWA, MARIE ETHEL   (1919-)   [A,M1]
  Geologist/Geomorphologist   American   [*MI*]

MORIZAKI, H.   (1800s early)   [D1]
  Physician/Obstetrician/Scholar   Japanese

MORLEY, MARGARET WARNER   (1800s-1900s)   [S1]
  Biologist   American

MORRILL, ANNIE SMITH: *See* SMITH, ANNIE MORRILL

MORRIS, ELIZABETH   (1800s)   [O]
  Botanist   American

MORRIS, JOANNE M.   (1958-   )   [O]
  Civil Engineer   American   *[MI]*

MORRIS, MARGARET   (1800s)   [V]
  Geneticist   American

MORRIS, MARGARETTA   (1800s)   [R1]
  Entomologist   American

MORRIS, ROSEMARY SHULL   (1929-   )   [W]
  Biochemist   American

MORSE, ELLEN HASTINGS   (1908-   )   [W]
  Nutritionist   American

MORSE, MARGARET: *See* NICE, MARGARET MORSE

MOSHER, CLELIA DUEL   (18??-19??)   [K3,R1,R2]
  Physician   American

MOSHER, ELIZA M.   (1846-1928)   [K3,R1,I5]
  Physician/Educator   American

MOUFANG, RUTH   (1905-   )   [C]
  Mathematician   German

MOY, MAMIE WONG   (1900s)   [M1]
  Chemist   American   *[MI]*

MUELLER, KATE HEUVNER   (1900s early)   [R1]
  Psychologist   American

MUIR, ISABELLA HELEN MARY   (1900s)   [L3]
  Rheumatologist/Medical Scientist   English   *[FR]*

MULLER, FRAU   (1500s?)   [Z]
  Astronomer   German

MULLER, GERTRUDE AGNES   (1887-1954)   [N3]
  Inventor/Engineer   American

MUNECCIME   (1200s?)   [U1]
  Astronomer   Persian/Iranian

MURAT, CAROLINE BONAPARTE, QUEEN   (1782-1839)   [Z,I5]
  Archaeologist   French/Italian

MURATA, KIKU   (1912-   )   [W]
  Food Chemist   Japanese

MURFELDT, MARY E.: *See* MURTFELDT, MARY ESTHER

MURPHY, LOIS BARCLAY Psychologist	(1902–) American	[W]
MURRAY, DIANE Mathematician/Computer Scientist	(1900s) American	[O] [*MI*]

MURRAY, MARGARET: *See* HUGGINS, MARGARET LINDSAY, LADY

MURRAY, MARGARET RANSONE Cell Biologist	(1901–) American	[W]
MURRAY, NOREEN ELIZABETH Molecular Biologist	(1900s) English	[L3] [*FR*]
MURRAY, ROSEMARY Chemist/Educator	(1900s) English	[O1]
MURTFELDT, MARY ESTHER Entomologist/Botanist	(1848–1913) American	[Z,R1,I3,I5] [*HA*]
MUSSER, EMMA Botanist	(1800s) American	[O]
MYERS, MABEL ADELAIDE Biologist	(1900–) American	[W]
MYERS, SARAH KERR Geographer/Sociologist	(1940–) American	[O1]
MYIA Natural Philosopher/Mathematician	(BC 500s) Greek/Italian	[L6,P5,F2,R]
MYRDAL, ALVA REINER Economist/Social Scientist	(1900s) Swedish	[O1]
MYRO Philosopher/Poet	(BC or early AD) Greek	[R,P5]

N

NAAZ, SUZANNE: *See* NECKER, SUZANNE NAAZ

NAGEL, SUZANNE Ceramic Engineer	(1945–) American	[O]
NAGY, ESTHER MARIA KOVACS Paleobotanist/Palynologist	(1914–) Hungarian	[W]
NAKA, T. Physician	(1800s early) Japanese	[D1]

NAKANISHI, O. Physician	(1800s early) Japanese	[D1]
NAPADENSKY, HYLA Combustion Engineer	(1900s) American	[O] [NE]
NAYAR, SUSHILA Physician	(1900s) Indian	[I9]
NEAL, JOSEPHINE BICKNELL Physician	(1880-1955) American	[W]
NECKER, ANNE GERMAINE Sociologist/Author	(1768-1817) French	[K]
NECKER, SUSANNE NAAZ Physician	(1740-1794) Swiss	[W,K,L6]
NECRASOV, C. OLGA Biologist/Anthropologist	(1910-) Rumanian	[C]
NEEDHAM, DOROTHY MARY MOYLE Biochemist	(1896-) British	[W,L3] [FR]
NELKIN, DOROTHY Sociologist/Science Policy Analyst	(1933-) American	[O]
NESIBE, GEVHER, PRINCESS Physician	(11??-12??) Persian/Iranian	[U1]
NESTHEADUSA Philosopher/Mathematician	(BC 400s) Greek/Italian	[P5]
NEUFELD, ELIZABETH FONDAL Biochemist/Human Geneticist	(1928-) American	[A,O1] [NS]
NEUMANN, BERTHA Mathematician	(18??-19??) German	[J2]
NEUMANN, HANNA VON CAEMMERER Mathematician	(1914-1971) German/Australian	[W,O1,M8,M9]

NEWCASTLE, DUCHESS OF: *See* CAVENDISH, MARGARET, DUCHESS

NEWSON, MARY WINSTON Mathematician	(1869-1959) American	[M7,M8,R]
NEWTON, MARGARET Plant Pathologist	(1900s early) Canadian	[R1]
NEWTON, NILES RUMELY Behavioral Scientist	(1923-) American	[W]
NICARETE OF MEGARA Philosopher/Mathematician/Scientist	(BC 300s) Greek	[Z,R,P5]
NICE, MARGARET MORSE Psychologist/Ornithologist	(1883-1974) American	[N3,R1]

NICERATA, SAINT Physician	(200s-300s) Turkish	[Z]
NICHOLLS, DORIS MARGARET MCEWEN Biochemist	(1927-) Canadian	[W]
NICHOLSON, MARJORIE HOPE Science Historian	(1900s) American	[O]
NICKERSON, MARGARET L. Zoologist	(1870-??) American	[R1,A1,S2]
NICULESCU, MEDEA P. Physician	(1900s) Rumanian	[D1]
NIELSEN, NIELSINE MATHILDE Physician	(1800s-1900s) Danish	[D1]
NIGHTINGALE, DOROTHY VIRGINIA Organic Chemist	(1902-) American	[A,O1,W6]
NIGHTINGALE, FLORENCE Nurse/Statistician	(1820-1910) English	[W,H,B1,O1]
NOBEL, ANN C. Chemist/Food Scientist	(1900s) American	[O1]
NOBLE, MARY JESSIE MCDONALD Biologist	(1900s) Scottish	[L3]
NOBLES, MILDRED K. Scientist	(1900s) Canadian	[L3]
NODDACK, IDA EVA TACKE Chemist	(1896-) German/French	[W,I5,B4,D4]
NOETHER, EMMY (AMALIE) Mathematician	(1882-1935) German/American	[N,M,W,B1,H]
NORSWORTHY, NAOMI Psychologist	(18??-19??) American	[R1]
NORTH, MARIANNE Geographer/Botanist	(1830-1890) American	[I3,R]
NORTON, DORITA A. Biophysicist	(1931-) American	[W]
NORWOOD, JANET Statistician	(1900s) American	[O]
NORWOOD, VIRGINIA Physicist/Electronics Engineer	(1900s) American	[G]
NOVOSELOVA, ALEKSANDRA VASIL'EVNA Chemist	(1900-) Russian	[S,T,W,C,L3] [*SS*]

NOYES, MARY C. Physicist	(1800s-1900s) American	[R1]
NUTTALL, ZELIA MARIA MAGDALENA Archaeologist/Anthropologist	(1857-1933) American	[N2,T2,R1,Z]
NUTTING, MARY ADELAIDE Nurse/Educator	(1858-1948) American	[R1,N1,N2,K]

O

OBENG, LETITIA Aquatic Biologist/Physician	(1900s) Ghanian	[B1]
O'BRIEN, RUTH Textile Physicist	(1900s early) American	[R1]
OCELLO OF LUCANIA Natural Philosopher/Mathematician	(BC 400s) Greek/Italian	[R,P5]
OCLO, MAMA Inventor	(1000 c.) Inca/Peruvian	[Z]
O'CONNELL, MARJORIE Paleontologist/Geologist	(18??-19??) American	[F1,R1]
OCTAVIA Physician/Pharmacist	(000s) Roman/Italian	[K]
ODILIA OF HOHENBURG Ophthalmologist	(600s-700s) German	[K]
O'FALLON, NANCY MCCUMBER Physicist	(1938-) American	[A]
OGILVIE, IDA HELEN Geologist	(1874-1963) American	[F1,R1]
OGILVIE-GORDON, MARIA M. Geologist	(1800s-1900s) American	[S1,R]
OGINO, G. Physician	(1800s) Japanese	[D1]
O'GRADY, MARCELLA: *See* BOVERI, MARCELLA O'GRADY		
OKAMI, KAI Physician	(18??-19??) Japanese	[K3]
OKAMI, KYOKO Physician	(18??-19??) Japanese	[D1]

OKEY, RUTH
Biochemist/Nutritionist
(1900s early)   [R1]
American

OLSON, EDITH
Inorganic Chemist
(1900s)   [G,H3]
American

OLSZEWSKA, MARIA JOANNA
Cytologist
(1929-   )   [W]
Polish

OLYMPIA OF ANTIOCH
Physician
(300s)   [K]
Turkish

OLYMPIAS OF THEBES
Physician
(000s)   [K,L6]
Greek

OM SETI: See EADY, DOROTHY

ONDRACKOVA, JANA
Phonetist
(1924-   )   [W]
Czechoslovakian

OPPENHEIMER, ELLA HUTZLER
Pathologist
(1900s early)   [R1]
American

OPPENHEIMER, JANE MARION
Developmental Biologist
(1911-   )   [W]
American

ORCUTT, RUBY RIVERS
Industrial Chemist
(1900s early)   [R1]
American

ORENT, ELSA
Nutritionist
(1900s early)   [R1]
American

ORIGENIA
Physician
(100s)   [K,Z,S1,L6]
Greek/Roman

ORIGENIE: See ORIGENIA

ORMEROD, ELEANOR ANNE
Economic Entomologist
(1828-1901)   [W,Z,S1,I3]
English

ORR, M.A.
Astronomer
(1800s-1900s)   [Z]
English

ORZALESI, NICOLA
Ophthalmologist
(1938-   )   [W]
Italian

OSBORN, MARY JANE
Microbiologist/Biochemist
(1927-   )   [A]
American   [NS,NB]

OSTERHOUT, MARIAN IRWIN
Medical Scientist
(1800s-1900s)   [R1]
American

OTTILA: See ODILIA

P

PACHAUDE, DAME LEONARD Surgeon	(1400s) French	[K]
PACHCIARZ, JUDITH ANN Immunologist/Microbiologist	(1941-) American	[A] [HA]
PADMAVATI, S. Biomedical Scientist/Physician	(1900s) Indian	[I9]
PAGELSON, HENRIETTE Dentist	(1800s late) German	[B1]
PAK, ESTHER KIM Physician	(1800s-1900s) Korean	[D1,K3]

PALATINE, PRINCESS: *See* ELIZABETH OF BOHEMIA, PRINCESS

PALMER, ALICE EUGENIA Dermatologist	(1910-) American	[W]
PALMER, ALICE W. Chemist	(1800s late) American	[R1]
PALMER, DOROTHY K. Micropaleontologist/Geologist	(1897-1947) American	[R1]
PALMER, KATHERINE E.H. VAN WINKLE Paleontologist	(1895-) American	[W]
PALMER, MARGARETTA Astronomer	(1862-1924) American	[Z,R]
PALSER, BARBARA FRANCES Botanist	(1916-) American	[W]
PAMPHYLA OF EPIDAURUS Philosopher/Scholar/Author	(000s) Greek/Egyptian	[R,P5]

PANAJIOTATOU, ANGELIKI: *See* PANAYOTATOU, ANGELIQUE

PANAYOTATOU, ANGELIQUE Physician	(1875-1954) Greek/Egyptian	[D1,K,D4]
PANGBORN, ROSE MARIE VALDES Food Technologist	(1932-) American	[W]
PANT, RADHA Biologist	(1900s) Indian	[O1]
PANTACLEA Philosopher	(BC 300s) Turkish/Egyptian	[P5]

PANTELEEVA, SERAFIMA   (1800s)   [O]
  Physiologist   Russian

PANTHIA   (100s)   [G2,G3]
  Physician   Roman/Turkish

PANYPERSEBASTA   (12??-13??)   [R,P5]
  Philosopher   Byzantine/Turkish

PAPER, ERNESTINE   (1800s-1900s)   [D1,L6]
  Physician   Italian

PAPHNOUTIA: *See* PAPHNUTIA THE VIRGIN

PAPHNUTIA THE VIRGIN   (100s)   [C5,C9,E3]
  Alchemist   Egyptian

PARDUE, MARY LOU   (1933-)   [A]
  Cell Biologist/Geneticist   American   [NS]

PARKE, MARY   (1900s)   [L3]
  Psychologist   English   [FR]

PARKE, MARY   (1900s)   [E]
  Marine Biologist   English   [FR]

PARLOA, MARIA   (1843-1909)   [I3]
  Nutritionist   American

PARSONS, ELOISE   (1900s early)   [B2]
  Physiological Chemist/Physician   American

PARSONS, ELSIE WORTHINGTON CLEWS   (1875-1941)   [W,N2,L2,R1]
  Anthropologist/Sociologist   American

PARSONS, HELEN TRACY   (1900s early)   [R1]
  Biochemist/Nutritionist   American

PARTHENAI, CATHERINE DE: *See* PARTHENAY, CATHERINE DE

PARTHENAY, CATHERINE DE   (1554-1631)   [Z,M5,F4,R]
  Mathematician/Scholar/Author   French

PARUNGO, FARN   (1900s)   [P2]
  Meteorologist   American

PASTEUR, MARIE LAURENT   (1800s)   [Z,B5,R]
  Bacteriologist   French

PASTORI, GIUSSEPINA   (1900s)   [O1,M9]
  Biologist   Italian

PASTORI, MARIA   (1895-)   [O1,M9]
  Mathematician   Italian

PATCH, EDITH M.   (18??-19??)   [Z,R1]
  Entomologist   American

PATRICK, JENNIE R.   (1949-)   [O]
  Chemical Engineer   American   [MI]

PATRICK, RUTH   (1907-)   [A,C1,O1]
  Limnologist/Botanist/Ecologist   American   [NS]

PATRICK-YEBOAH, JENNIE: See PATRICK, JENNIE R.

PATTERSON, FLORA WAMBAUGH   (1847-1928)   [R1,S1,Z]
  Plant Physiologist/Mycologist   American

PATTULLO, JUNE GRACE   (1921-)   [W]
  Oceanographer   American

PAULA   (347-404)   [D1,K]
  Physician   Roman

PAULZE, MARIE ANNE PIERRETTE: See LAVOISIER, MARIE ANNE PIERRETTE

PAVENSTEDT, ELEANOR   (1903-)   [W]
  Psychiatrist   American

PAVRI, K.M.   (1900s)   [I9]
  Biomedical Scientist   Indian

PAYNE, MARJATTA STRANDELL   (1900s)   [O1]
  Cost Engineer   Finnish/American

PAYNE-GAPOSCHKIN, CECILIA HELENA   (1900-1979)   [W,O1,R,K2]
  Astronomer/Astrophysicist   American

PAZ, ELVIRA L.   (1900s)   [M1]
  Biologist   American   [MI]

PEAK, HELEN   (1899-)   [R1]
  Psychologist   American

PEARCE, LOUISE   (1885-1959)   [W,N3,R1,D1]
  Pathologist/Research Physician   American

PEARL, MAUD DEWITT   (1900s early)   [R1]
  Biologist   American

PEARSE, DOROTHY NORMAN SPICER   (1908-)   [I5]
  Engineer/Aeronautical Pioneer   English

PECK, ANNIE S.   (1850-1935)   [G4]
  Archaeologist/Explorer   American

PECKHAM, ELIZABETH W.   (1800s-1900s)   [Z,R]
  Entomologist   American

PEDEN, IRENE CARSWELL   (1925-)   [A,O1]
  Electrical Engineer   American

PEEBLES, FLORENCE   (1874-)   [R1,A1,S2]
  Zoologist   American

PELL, ANNA JOHNSON: *See* WHEELER, ANNA JOHNSON PELL

PELL-WHEELER, ANNA JOHNSON: *See* WHEELER, ANNA JOHNSON PELL

PENA, DEAGELIA M. (1900s) [O]
  Statistician/Computer Scientist Philippine/American

PENDLETON, ELLEN FITZ (1800s) [R1]
  Mathematician American

PENNINGTON, MARY ENGLE (1872-1952) [X,Z,O1,N3]
  Chemist/Bacteriologist/Engineer American

PENROSE, EDITH TILTON (1914-) [W]
  Economist American/English

PERAZA, GILDA (1900s) [D1]
  Physician Cuban

PERCIVAL, ETHEL ELIZABETH (1900s) [L3]
  Chemist Scottish

PEREJASZLAVZENA, SOFJA: *See* PEREYASLAWZEWA, SOPHIA

PERETTE (1300s late) [K]
  Physician/Midwife French

PERETTI, ZAFFIRA (1700s) [K,L6,R]
  Anatomist/Educator/Physician Italian

PEREY, MARGUERITE (1909-1974) [B1,O1,D4]
  Nuclear Chemist/Physicist French

PEREYASLAWZEWA, SOPHIA (18??-1904) [Z,I3,R]
  Zoologist Russian

PEREZ, ERNESTINA (18??-) [D1]
  Physician Chilean

PERICTIONE (BC 400s) [Z,F2,L6,P5]
  Philosopher/Mathematician/Author Greek

PERICTYONE: *See* PERICTIONE

PERILLO, LANCELOTTI: *See* SPAGNUOLA, TERESA (Pseud.)

PERLMANN, GERTRUDE (19??-1974) [O1,R1,W6]
  Biochemist American

PERNA (1400s) [J1]
  Physician Italian

PERONELLE (1300s early) [K]
  Herbalist/Pharmacist French

PEROVSKAYA, SOFIA (1800s) [O]
  Physician Russian

PEROZO, EVANGELINE RODRIGUEZ Physician	(18??-) Dominican	[D1]
PERSON, LUCY WU Chemist/Computer Scientist	(1934-) American	[A,M1] *[MI]*
PERT, CANDACE Biologist/Pharmacologist	(1900s) American	[O]
PETER, ROZSA Mathematician/Logician	(18??-19??) Hungarian	[M8]
PETERMANN, MARY LOCKE Biochemist/Physiological Chemist	(1908-1976) American	[W,O1,W6]

PETRACCINI-TERRETTI, MARIA: *See* PETTRACINI, MARIA

PETROVA, MARIA KONSTANTINOVNA Physiologist	(1874-??) Russian	[W]
PETRUCCINI, MARIA Physician	(1300s) Italian	[K]
PETRY, LUCILE Nurse	(1903-) American	[N1]
PETTIT, HANNAH STEELE Astronomer	(1800s-1900s) American	[R1]
PETTRACINI, MARIA Anatomist/Educator/Physician	(1600s/1700s) Italian	[K,L6,R,Z]
PFAFFLIN, SHEILA Psychologist	(1900s) American	[O]
PFEIFFER, IDA MEYER Geographer/Naturalist	(1797-1858) Austrian	[Z,U1,S1,F3]
PHAENARETE Midwife/Obstetrician/Scholar	(BC 400s) Greek	[D1,L6]
PHANOSTRATE Physician/Midwife	(BC 300s) Greek	[G2]
PHELIPPE Physician	(12??-13??) French	[K,H2]
PHELPS, ALMIRA HART LINCOLN Botanist/Science Educator	(1793-1884) American	[F1,N2,R1,Z]
PHELPS, MARTHA AUSTIN Chemist	(18??-19??) American	[R1]

PHELPS, SUSANNA: *See* GAGE, SUSANNA S. PHELPS

PHENARETE: *See* PHAENARETE

PHILISTA   (BC 300 c.)   [K,L6]
  Obstetrician   Greek

PHILLIPS, CAROLYN F.   (1900s)   [O1]
  Mechanical Engineer   American

PHILLIPS, MELBA NEWELL   (1907-)   [A,R1]
  Physicist   American

PHILOMELA, SAINT   (200s-300s)   [K]
  Physician   Roman Empire

PHILTATIS   (BC 400s)   [R,P5]
  Natural Philosopher/Mathematician   Greek/Italian

PHINTIS: See PHINTYS

PHINTYS   (BC 400s)   [L6,R,P5]
  Philosopher/Author/Mathematician   Greek

PICCARD, SOPHIE   (1904-)   [W,C,M9]
  Mathematician   Russian/Swiss

PICK, RUTH HOLUB   (1913-)   [W]
  Physician   American

PICKETT, LUCY W.   (1900s)   [O1,W6]
  Chemist   American

PICKFORD, LILLIAN MARY   (1902-)   [E,L3]
  Physiologist/Endocrinologist   English/Scottish   [FR]

PICOTTE, SUSAN LAFLESCHE   (1865-1915)   [N2,D1,K3]
  Physician   American   [MI]

PIERCE, MADELENE EVANS   (1904-)   [W]
  Biologist   American

PIERRY, MME. DU: See DU PIERRY, MME.

PILSTEIN, SALOMEE ANNE: See RUSIECKA, SALOMEA

PINCKNEY, ELIZA LUCAS   (1723-1793)   [H,N2]
  Agronomist   American

PINERO, DOLORES M.   (1900s early)   [D1]
  Physician   American

PINTASSILGO, MARIA DE LOURDES   (1930-)   [O1]
  Chemical Engineer/Politician   Portuguese

PISAN, CHRISTINE DE   (1363-1431)   [Z,K,F2,D4]
  Scholar/Scientist/Poet/Author   Italian/French

PISCOPIA, ELENA CORNARO   (1600s-1700s)   [Z]
  Astronomer/Mathematician/Scholar   Italian

PITCHER, HARRIET BROOKS: *See* BROOKS, HARRIET

PITELKA, DOROTHY RIGGS Zoologist	(1920-) American	[W]
PITT-RIVERS, ROSALIND VENETIA Biochemist	(1900s) English	[L3] [*FR*]
PITTMAN, MARGARET Bacteriologist	(1901-) American	[W,R1]
PKIKHOT'KO, ANTONINA FYODOROVNA Solid State Physicist	(1900s) Russian	[O1]

PLATEARIUS, TROTULA: *See* TROTULA

PLATT, BERYL Aeronautical Engineer	(1900s) British	[O]
PLEIKE, ROSSING Physician	(18??-19??) Finnish	[L6]
PLESS, VERA STEPEN Mathematician	(1931-) American	[A]
PLUMMER, HELEN JEANNE Micropaleontologist/Geologist	(1891-1951) American	[R1]
POCKELS, AGNES Physicist/Physical Chemist	(18??-19??) German	[L1,H3,S3]
PODVYSOTSKAIA, OLGA NIKOLAEVNA Dermatologist	(1884-) Russian	[S]
POGSON, MISS Astronomer	(1800s-1900s) Indian/English	[Z,R]
POLYDAMNA Physician/Educator	(BC 1900s-1800s) Egyptian	[Z,K,W4,L6]
PONSE, KITTY Endocrinologist	(1897-) Swiss	[C]
POOL, JUDITH GRAHAM Physiologist	(1919-1975) American	[W,N3]
POPESCU, GEORGETA Virologist	(1925-) Rumanian	[W]
PORADA, EDITH Archaeologist	(1900s) Austrian/American	[O1]
PORCIA Philosopher	(BC 000s) Roman/Italian	[P5]
PORTER, HELEN KEMP Physiologist/Plant Physiologist	(1900s) English	[E,L3] [*FR*]

PORTER, MARY Crystallographer	(1800s-1900s) American	[F1]
POSSANNER-EHRENTHAL, GABRIELLE Physician	(1800s-1900s) Austrian	[D1]
POSTEL, SANDRA Botanist/Ecologist	(1900s) American	[O]
POTTER, BEATRIX Botanist/Author	(1866-1934) English	[H,R]
POTTER, EDITH LOUISE Fetal Pathologist	(1901-) American	[W,O1]
POTTS, MARY FLORENCE Inventor	(1800s) American	[O]
POUPARD, MARY E. Inventor	(1800s) English	[Z]
POUR-EL, MARIAN BOYKAN Mathematician/Logician	(1900s) American	[A,O1,K2]
PRATT, ANNE Botanist	(1806-1893) English	[S1]
PREDELLA, LIA Mathematician	(1800s-1900s) French/Italian	[M8,R]
PRESSEY, LUELLA COLE Psychologist	(1800s-1900s) American	[R1]
PRESSMAN, IDA I. Power Control System Engineer	(1900s) American	[O1]
PRESTON, ANN Physician	(1813-1872) American	[N2,L2,D1]
PRICE, DOROTHY Reproductive Endocrinologist	(1900s early) American	[B2]
PRICE, KATHERINE MILLS Medical Research Scientist	(1900s early) American	[R1]
PRICHARD, MARJORIE MABEL LUCY Physiologist	(1906-) English	[W]
PRIGOSEN, ROSA ELIZABETH Bacteriologist/Pediatrician	(1900s early) American	[I5]
PRIMILLA Physician	(000s-100s) Roman	[G2,G3]
PRIMILLA Physician	(400s-500s) Roman	[K]

PRINCE, HELEN DODSON Solar Astronomer	(1905-) American	[W,O1]
PRITA, MARIA Physician	(1800s-1900s) Yugoslavian	[D1]
PROCHAZKA, ANNE Orthopedic Nurse	(1897-) American	[N1]
PROCTER, MARY Astronomer	(1800s) American	[S1]
PROCTOR, MARY Astronomer	(1800s-1900s) English	[Z]
PROTHRO, JOHNNIE H. WATTS Nutritionist	(1922-) American	[B3] [MI]
PRZELECKA, ALEKSANDRA Cytologist	(1920-) Polish	[W]
PRZEWORSKA-ROLEWICZ, DANUTA Mathematician	(1931-) Polish	[W]
PTAH, MERIT Physician	(BC 2700 c.) Egyptian	[K,B1]
PTOLEMAIS THE CYRENEAN Philosopher/Musician/Mathematician	(100s-200s) Roman/Greek/Libyan	[R,P5]
PUCHTLER, HOLDE Physician	(1920-) American	[W]
PUFFER, ETHEL: See HOWES, ETHEL D. PUFFER		
PUGA, MARIA LUZ Botanist	(1900s) Mexican	[O]
PULCHERIA Natural Scientist/Physician	(399-453) Roman/Italian	[F2]
PULCHERIA Physician	(1400s) Italian	[K]
PULLMAN, A. Quantum Chemist	(1920-) French	[W]
PUTNAM, MARY CORINNA: See JACOBI, MARY CORINNA PUTNAM		
PUTNAM, MARY LOUISE DUNCAN Scientist	(1832-1903) American	[I3]
PYE, JULIA Physician	(000s-100s) Roman	[G2]
PYTHIAS OF ASSOS Biologist/Embryologist/Histologist	(BC 300s) Greek	[K,H5]

Q

QUEDLINBURG, ABBESS OF: *See* ANNA SOPHIA OF HESSE OR MATHILDA
  OF QUEDLINBURG, ABBESS

QUICK, HAZEL IRENE   (1900s early)   [I5]
  Engineer   American

QUIGGLE, DOROTHY   (1903-)   [I5]
  Chemical Engineer   American

QUIMBY, EDITH HINCKLEY   (1891-)   [W,Y,R1,C3]
  Biophysicist/Radiologist   American

QUINTIUS, JULIA   (400s)   [K]
  Physician   Spanish

QUIRK, AGNES   (1900s early)   [R1,R2]
  Botanist/Plant Pathologist   American

QUIROGA, MARGARITA DELGADO D.   (1900s)   [D1]
  Physiologist   Mexican

R

RAABE, MARIE   (1900s)   [L3]
  Scientist   German

RABINOVITCH-KEMPNER, LYDIA: *See* RABINOWITSCH-KEMPNER, LYDIA

RABINOWITSCH, LYDIA: *See* RABINOWITSCH-KEMPNER, LYDIA

RABINOWITSCH-KEMPNER, LYDIA   (1871-1935)   [W,I5,K3,J2]
  Bacteriologist   Lithuanian/German

RACE, RUTH ANN SANGER: *See* SANGER, RUTH ANN

RADEGONDE   (500s)   [K,F3]
  Physician   German/French

RADEGUNDE: *See* RADEGONDE

RADNITZ, GERTY: *See* CORI, GERTY THERESA RADNITZ

RAHAL, KHEIRA   (1900s)   [I8]
  Clinical Bacteriologist   Algerian

RAHMAN, YUEH ERH (JADY)   (1930-)   [A]
  Medical Scientist/Cell Biologist   American

RAMALEY, JUDITH AITKEN   (1941–)   [A]
Endocrinologist   American

RAMART-LUCAS, PAULINE   (1900s early)   [R1]
Chemist   French

RAMEY, ESTELLE ROSEMARY   (1917–)   [A,W,C3,Q1]
Endocrinologist/Biophysicist   American

RAMOS, SYLVIA M.   (1900s)   [M1]
Surgeon   American   [*MI*]

RAMSEY, ELIZABETH MAPELSDEN   (1906–)   [W]
Physician   American

RANADIVE, KAMAL JAYASING   (1917–)   [W]
Biologist   Indian

RAND, MARIE GERTRUDE   (1886–1970)   [N3,W,R1]
Psychologist/Engineer/Physicist   American

RANDOLPH, HARRIET   (18??–19??)   [Z,R]
Zoologist/Embryologist   American

RANNEY, HELEN M.   (1920–)   [A,O1]
Hematologist/Oncologist   American   [*NS*]

RAO, KAMALA S. JAYA   (1900s)   [I9]
Nutritionist   Indian

RASIOWA, HELENE ALINA   (1917–)   [C,E]
Mathematician/Mathematical Logician Polish

RASKOVA, HELENA   (1900s)   [L3]
Scientist   Czechoslovakian

RASMUSON, MARIANNE   (1900s)   [L3]
Zoologist   Swedish

RATHBUN, MARY JANE   (1860–1943)   [N2,S1,R1,Z]
Marine Zoologist   American

RATNER, SARAH   (1903–)   [A,W,O1,W6]
Biochemist   American   [*NS*]

RAUSCHER, ELIZABETH ANN   (1943–)   [A]
Physicist/Cosmologist   American

RAY, DIXY LEE   (1914–)   [A,L2,C3,O1]
Marine Biologist/Zoologist   American   [*AE*]

READ, LADY   (1700s)   [K]
Eye Surgeon   English

REAMES, ELEANOR   (1800s–1900s)   [R1]
Physicist   American

REBECCA VON SALERNO Physician/Educator/Author	(1200s) Italian	[J2]
REDDY, MUTHULAKSHMI Physician/Legislator	(1900s) Indian	[I9]
REED, EVA M. Botanist	(18??-1901) American	[I3]
REED, MARGARET: *See* LEWIS, MARGARET REED		
REES, FLORENCE GWENDOLINE Parisitologist/Zoologist	(1906-) English	[E,L3] [*FR*]
REES, MINA SPIEGEL Mathematician	(1902-) American	[A,O1,I5] [*NB*]
REICHARD, GLADYS AMANDA Anthropologist	(1893-1955) American	[N3,R1]
REIF, MILDRED: *See* DRESSELHAUS, MILDRED S. REIF		
REIMER, MARIE Chemist	(1900s early) American	[R1]
REINHARDT, ANNA BARBARA Mathematician	(1700s) Swiss	[Z,R]
RESNIK, JUDITH A. Electrical Engineer	(1950-) American	[O1] [*AS*]
REYNOLDS, DORIS LIVESEY Geologist	(1900s) Scottish	[L3]
RHINE, LOUISA ELLA Parapsychologist	(1891-) American	[W]
RHODOPE Natural Philosopher/Mathematician	(BC 400s) Greek	[R,P5]
RICE, KATHERINE Biochemist	(1900s) American	[L1]
RICE-WRAY, EDRIS Physician	(1904-) American/Mexican	[W]
RICHARDIS Medical Author	(11??-1168) German	[K]
RICHARDS, C. AUDREY Forestry Scientist/Pathologist	(1900s early) American	[R1]
RICHARDS, ELLEN HENRIETTA SWALLOW Chemist/Sanitary Engineer	(1842-1911) American	[Z,X,W,H,B1]
RICHARDS, ESTHER Psychiatrist	(1900s early) American	[R1]

RICHARDS, MILDRED HODGE   (1800s)   [V]
  Geneticist/Zoologist   American

RICHEUT   (12??-13??)   [K,H2]
  Physician   French

RICHMOND, COUNTESS OF: See BEAUFORT, MARGARET, COUNTESS

RICKETTS, LOUISE DAVIDSON   (1887-1940)   [I5]
  Mining Engineer   American

RIDDLE, ESTELLE MASSEY   (1903-)   [N1]
  Nurse   American

RIDE, SALLY K.   (1951-)   [O1]
  Physicist   American   [AS]

RIPAN, C. RALUCA   (1894-1978)   [C]
  Inorganic Chemist   Rumanian

RISING, MARY: See STIEGLITZ, MARY RISING

RITTLE, EDINA   (1000s-1100s)   [K,B1]
  Physician   English/Byzantine

ROBB, JANE SANDS   (1800s-1900s)   [R1]
  Medical Scientist   American

ROBBINS, MARY LOUISE   (1912-)   [W]
  Microbiologist   American

ROBERTS, CHARLOTTE FICH   (1859-1917)   [I3]
  Chemist   American

ROBERTS, DOROTHEA KLUMPKE: See KLUMPKE, DOROTHEA

ROBERTS, LYDIA JANE   (1879-1965)   [N3,R1]
  Nutritionist/Educator   American

ROBERTSON, ANNE STRACHAN   (1900s)   [L3]
  Archaeologist   Scottish

ROBERTSON, MURIEL   (1883-1973)   [B1]
  Medical Researcher   British

ROBESON, ESLANDA (CORDOZA) GOODE (1896-)   [I5]
  Anthropologist   American

ROBINSON, JULIA BOWMAN   (1919-)   [A,M,P7]
  Mathematician   American   [NS]

ROBINSON, MARGARET KING   (1906-)   [W]
  Oceanographer   American

ROBINSON, MARION FRANCES   (1900s)   [L3]
  Scientist   New Zealander

ROBSCHEIT-ROBBINS, FRIEDA Pathologist/Medical Researcher	(19??-1973) American	[R1]
ROCCATI, CRISTINA Physicist/Educator/Mathematician	(1600s-1700s) Italian	[Z]
ROCKWELL, MABEL MACFERRAN Electrical Engineer	(1902-) American	[I5]
RODRIGUEZ, MARIE LUISA SALDUNDE Pediatrician/Physician	(1900s early) Uruguayan	[D1]
RODRIGUEZ-DULANTO, LAURA ESTHER Physician	(1900s early) Peruvian	[D1]
ROE, ANN Psychologist	(1904-) American	[Q1,W]
ROEBLING, EMILY Civil Engineer	(1844-1902) American	[E1,V1,R]
ROEMER, ELIZABETH Astronomer	(1929-) American	[W,O1]
ROENNAU, LAUREL VAN DER WAL Bioastronauticist	(1900s) American	[G]
ROGERS, MARTHA ELIZABETH Nursing Educator	(1914-) American	[W]

ROHAN, PRINCESS DE: *See* PARTHENAY, CATHERINE DE

ROHAN-SOUBISE, PRINCESS OF: *See* PARTHENAY, CATHERINE DE

ROLAND, MANON JEANNE PHILIPON Pharmacologist/Psychologist	(1756-1793) French	[K,L6,R]
ROLF, IDA Biochemist/Applied Physiologist	(1900s early) American	[R1]
ROMAN, NANCY GRACE Astronomer	(1925-) American	[W,G,O1,I5]
ROMIEU, MARIE Physiologist	(1500s) French	[K]
RONCHETTI-ROSSI, CARLA Paleontologist	(1900s) Italian	[E]
RONCHI, VITTORIA NUTI Geneticist/Botanist	(1900s) Italian	[O1]
RONTO, GYORGYI Biophysicist	(1900s) Hungarian	[I8]
ROOKS, JUNE M. Physicist	(1900s) American	[D3] [HA,MI]

ROPER, MARGARET Physician/Scholar	(1505-1544) English	[K,D4]
ROSANOFF, LILLIAN Physicist	(1800s-1900s) American	[R1]
ROSCHER, NINA MATHENY Chemist	(1938-) American	[A,W6]
ROSE, FLORA Home Economist	(18??-19??) American	[R1,R2]
ROSE, GLENOLA BEHLING Chemist	(1900s early) American	[R1]
ROSE, HILARY Sociologist	(1900s) English	[O]
ROSE, MARY DAVIES SWARTZ Chemist/Nutritionist/Home Economist	(1874-1941) American	[N2,L2,R1,V]
ROSENBLATT, JOAN RAUP Statistician/Mathematician	(1926-) American	[F,A,O1]
ROSENTHAL, SINAIDA Scientist	(1900s) German	[L3]
ROSOFF, BETTY Physiologist	(1920-) American	[W]
ROSS, MARION AMELIA SPENCE Physicist	(1903-) Scottish	[W,L3]
ROSSI, ALICE Social Scientist	(1900s) American	[O]
ROSSITER, MARGARET Science Historian	(1900s) American	[O1]
ROTH, GRACE MARGUERITE Clinical Investigator	(1894-) American	[W]
ROTH, LAURA MAURER Solid State Physicist	(1930-) American	[A,O1]
ROTHSCHILD, MIRIAM LOUIS A. Zoologist/Parasitologist	(1908-) British	[O1,H3,D4]
ROTOMAGO, CLARISSE DE: *See* CLARISSE OF ROTOMAGO		
ROUDNEVA, MME. B.K. KACHEVAROVA Physician/Surgeon	(18??-19??) Russian	[L6]
ROUSSIETSKI, SALOMEE ANNE: *See* RUSIECKA, SALOMEA		
ROWLEY, JANET DAVIDSON Cytogeneticist/Physician	(1925-) American	[A] *[NS]*

ROYER, CLEMENCE AUGUSTINE   (1830-1902)   [Z,I3,I5,D4]
  Anthropologist/Physicist/Naturalist French

ROZOVA, EVDOKIA ALEKSANDROVNA   (1899-)   [S]
  Seismologist   Russian

RUBIN, VERA COOPER   (1928-)   [A,F,O1,P7]
  Astronomer   American   [NS]

RUBINSTEIN, SUSANNE   (18??-19??)   [J2]
  Psychologist/Author   Swiss

RUDNICK, DOROTHEA   (1907-)   [Y,I5]
  Embryologist   American

RUMKER, MADAME   (1800s)   [Z,R]
  Astronomer   German

RUSIECKA, SALOMEA   (1717-1786 c.)   [K,B1,L6]
  Oculist/Physician/Surgeon   Polish/Turkish

RUSIECKI, SALOMEE ANNE: See RUSIECKA, SALOMEA

RUSK, EVELYN TERESA CARROLL   (1900-1964)   [M8]
  Mathematician   American

RUSSELL, ELIZABETH SHULL   (1913-)   [A,Y,O1,C3]
  Geneticist/Zoologist   American   [NS]

RUSSELL, JANE ANNE   (1911-1967)   [N3]
  Biochemist/Endocrinologist   American

RUSSELL, OLIVE RUTH   (1900s)   [O1]
  Psychologist/Euthanasia Activist   Canadian/American

RUSSO, NANCY FELIPE   (1900s)   [O1]
  Psychologist   American

RUYS, A. CHARLOTTE   (1900s early)   [D1]
  Microbiologist/Physician/Educator   Dutch

RUYSCH, RACHEL   (1700 c.)   [K]
  Anatomist/Pathologist   Dutch

RYDSTROM, PAT   (1900s)   [G]
  Histopathologist   American

S

SAADAWI, NAWAL EL: See EL SAADAWI, NAWAL

SABIN, FLORENCE RENA   (1871-1953)   [B,D,X,Z,C1]
  Anatomist/Immunologist/Physician   American   [NS]

SABLIERE, MARGUERITE DE LA   (1636-1693)   [Z,I5,D4,R]
  Astronomer   French

SABUCO, OLIVIA: See BARRERA, OLIVA SABUCO

SAGALYN, RITA   (1924-)   [A,P4]
  Geophysicist/Space Physicist   American

SAGER, RUTH   (1918-)   [A,W,O1,L2]
  Geneticist/Biologist   American   [NS]

SAINT-GILLES, SARAH DE: See SARAH OF SAINT GILLES

SALERNO, REBECCA VON: See REBECCA VON SALERNO

SALOME   (1200s)   [K]
  Physician   Polish

SALPE   (BC 300s)   [K,L6]
  Physician/Ophthalmologist   Greek

SALUTER, ARLENE   (1900s)   [O]
  Statistician   American

SALUZZIO, MARGUERITE   (1400s)   [K,L6]
  Botanist/Pharmacologist/Physician Italian

SALUZZO, MARGUERITE: See SALUZZIO, MARGUERITE

SALVAGGIA, NICHOLA   (1600s)   [K]
  Physician   Italian

SALVINA   (300s)   [K]
  Physician   Roman

SAMISH, ZDENKA   (1900s)   [B1]
  Food Technologist   Israeli

SAMITHRA   (100s)   [K,L6]
  Physician   Roman

SAMMETT, JEAN E.   (1928-)   [A]
  Computer Scientist/Engineer   American   [NE]

SAMMURAMAT: See SEMIRAMIS, QUEEN

SAMPSON, LILLIAN: See MORGAN, LILLIAN SAMPSON

SANCTA CATHARINA OF ALEXANDRIA: See CATHERINE OF ALEXANDRIA,
  SAINT

SANDERSON, MILDRED LENORA   (1889-1914)   [M8]
  Mathematician   American

SANDI, ANA-MARIA   (1900s)   [I8]
  Mathematician/Systems Analyst   Rumanian

SANDLER, BERNICE   (1900s)   [O1]
  Psychologist/Educator   American

SANDS, JANE: *See* ROBB, JANE SANDS

SANFORD, KATHERINE KOONTZ Biologist	(1915-) American	[W]
SANFORD, VERA Mathematician/Science Historian	(1891-1914) American	[M8]
SANGER, MARGARET HIGGINS Nurse/Birth Control Reformer	(1883-1966) American	[H,B1,O1,L1]
SANGER, RUTH ANN Pathologist	(1900s) English	[E,L3] [*FR*]
SARA Natural Philosopher/Mathematician	(BC 500s) Greek/Italian	[R,P5]
SARA Physician	(13??-14??) German	[K,H2,J2]
SARACHIK, MYRIAM PAULA Solid State Physicist	(1933-) American	[A]

SARA DE ST. GILLES: *See* SARAH OF SAINT GILLES

SARAH: *See also* SARA

SARAH LA MIRGESSE Physician	(12??-13??) French	[J1]

SARAH OF SAINT GILES: *See* SARAH OF SAINT GILLES

SARAH OF SAINT GILLES Physician/Educator	(12??-13??) French	[W4,U1,K,H2]
SARAH OF WURZBURG Physician	(13??-14??) German	[J1]
SARGANT, ETHEL Botanist	(1864-1918) English	[I3,I7]
SARRE Physician	(12??-13??) French	[K,H2]
SARROCHI, MARGARETA Physician	(1600s) Italian	[K]
SARTRE, MARQUISE DE Mathematician/Naturalist/Physician	(1600s) French	[K]
SARUHASHI, KATSUKO Geochemist	(1900s) Japanese	[O1]
SATURNIA, JULIA Physician	(400s) Spanish	[K]
SAUER, MARIE ELIZABETH Physician/Midwife/Surgeon	(1700s) German	[K]

SAUNDERS, DOROTHY CHAPMAN Biologist	(1912–) American	[W]
SAUNDERS, E.R., MISS Botanist	(1900s early) English	[I7]
SAVITZ, MAXINE LAZARUS Chemist	(1937–) American	[A]
SAVOLAINEN, ANN W. Reactor Engineer	(1900s) American	[O1]
SAVULESCU, I. ALICE Mycologist/Plant Pathologist	(1905–) Rumanian	[C,W]
SAWYER, CONSTANCE BRAGDON Astronomer	(1926–) American	[W]

SAWYER, HELEN: See HOGG, HELEN BATTLES SAWYER

SAXE-GOTHA, LOUISE OF, DUCHESS Astronomer	(1700s) German	[Z]

SAXONY, PRINCESS OF: See ERDMUTHE, SOPHIE

SAY, LUCY WAY Entomologist/Natural Scientist	(1800s) American	[R1]
SCANLON, JANE CRONIN Mathematician	(1922–) American	[W]
SCARPELLINI, CATERINA Astronomer/Statistician/Geologist	(1808–) Italian	[Z,R]
SCHABANOFF, ANNA N. Physician	(1800s) Russian	[D1]

SCHARFF-GOLDHABER, GERTRUDE: See GOLDHABER, GERTRUDE SCHARFF

SCHARRER, BERTA VOGEL Anatomist/Neurobiologist	(1906–) American	[A,W,O1] [NS]
SCHELLHAMMER, MARIE SOPHIE CONRING Food Chemist	(1600s) German	[K]
SCHLIEMANN, SOPHIA ENGASTROMENOS Archaeologist	(1800s) Greek/German	[Z,D5]
SCHMIDT, INGEBORG Physician	(1899–) American	[W]
SCHMIDT, JOHANNA GERTRUD ALICE Topographer	(1909–) German	[W]
SCHMIDT, NATHALIE JOAN Microbiologist	(1928–) American	[W]

SCHMIDT-NIELSEN, BODIL MIMI (1918-)   [W,O1]
  Physiologist/Zoologist   Danish/American

SCHOBER, RITA   (1900s)   [L3]
  Scientist   German

SCHOENTAL, REGINA   (1906-)   [W]
  Cancer Research Worker   Polish/English

SCHOLASTICA, SAINT   (400s-500s)   [K,W4]
  Physician   Italian

SCHRADER, SALLY HUGHES: *See* HUGHES-SCHRADER, SALLY

SCHULZ, KAROLINE   (1800s late)   [J2]
  Physician   French

SCHUPAK, LENORE H.   (1955-)   [O1]
  Environmental Engineer   American

SCHURMAN, ANNA MARIA VAN: *See* VON SCHURMANN, ANNA MARIA

SCHURMANN, ANNA MARIA VON: *See* VON SCHURMANN, ANNA MARIA

SCHUTZMEISTER, LUISE: *See* MEYER-SCHUTZMEISTER, LUISE

SCHWAN, JUDITH   (1900s)   [O]
  Engineer   American   [*NE*]

SCHWARTZ, EDITH: *See* CLEMENTS, EDITH SCHWARTZ

SCHWARTZ, NEENA BETTY   (1926-)   [A]
  Neurobiologist/Physiologist American

SCHWARZER, THERESA FLYNN   (1940-)   [A,O1]
  Geologist/Geochemist   American

SCHWEBER, MIRIAM SCHURIN   (1900s)   [A,O1]
  Biochemist/Cell Biologist American

SCHWIDETZKY, ILSE   (1907-)   [C]
  Anthropologist/Human Biologist German

SCOTT, CHARLOTTE ANGAS   (1858-1931)   [N2,O1,M7,Z]
  Mathematician   English/American

SCOTT, FLORA MURRAY   (1891-)   [W,R1]
  Botanist   Scottish/American

SCOTT, FLORENCE MARIE, SISTER (1900s early)   [R1]
  Biologist   American

SCOTT, KATHERINE   (1900s early)   [R1]
  Biologist   American

SCOTT-MACINTYRE, SHEILA: *See* MACINTYRE, SHEILA SCOTT

SEDDON, MARGARET RHEA
Physician
(1900s)   [O1]
American   [AS]

SEEGAL, BEATRICE CARRIER
Immunologist
(1898-)   [W]
American

SEGA, MONA
Physician
(1300s)   [K]
Italian

SEIBERT, FLORENCE BARBARA
Biochemist/Microbiologist
(1897-)   [X,Z,O1,B2]
American   [HA]

SELEKEID
Physician
(13??-14??)   [J1]
German

SE-LING-SHE
Inventor
(BC 3000 c.)   [Z]
Chinese

SEMIRAMIS, QUEEN
Technologist/Engineer/Architect
(BC 800s)   [W5,E2,F4]
Assyrian/Iraqi

SEMPLE, ELLEN CHURCHILL
Anthropo-Geographer
(1863-1932)   [W,N2,L2,O1]
American

SEN, LOURMINIA CARINO
Biochemist
(1900s)   [M1,R1]
American   [MI]

SENGERS, JOHANNA M.H. LEVELT
Thermal Physicist
(1929-)   [A]
Dutch/American

SERINA, LAURA CERETA
Physician/Philosopher/Educator
(1300s)   [K,L6]
Italian

SERLIN: *See* ZERLIN

SERRANA, JOANNE
Obstetrician
(1300s)   [K]
Italian

SETH, NANDINI ANIL
Biomedical Scientist
(1900s)   [I9]
Indian

SFORZA, CATHERINE
Alchemist/Pharmacologist
(14??-15??)   [R3,F4,R]
Italian

SHABANOVA, ANNA
Physician/Pediatrician/Feminist
(1848-1932)   [D4]
Russian

SHAFER, HELEN
Mathematician
(1800s)   [R1]
American

SHAFTSBURY, ABBESS OF: *See* FERRAR, AGNES

SHAIBANY, HOMA
Surgeon
(1900s early)   [D1]
Persian/Iranian

SHAPIRO, FRANCES: *See* HERSKOVITS, FRANCES SHAPIRO

SHARP, JANE   (1600s)   [K]
Midwife/Obstetrician/Author   English

SHARPLESS, NANSIE SUE   (1932-)   [A,D3]
Biochemist/Neurochemist   American   [*HA*]

SHATTUCK, LYDIA WHITE   (1822-1889)   [N2,R1,I3,R]
Botanist/Chemist/Naturalist   American

SHAW, MARGERY WAYNE SCHLAMP   (1923-)   [W]
Geneticist   American

SHEININ, ROSE   (1930-)   [A,L3]
Biochemist/Virologist   Canadian

SHELDON, J.M. ARMS   (1800s-1900s)   [Z]
Entomologist   American

SHEONYNSTON, ALICE   (1300s)   [K]
Ophthalmologist   English

SHERMAN, ALTHEA ROSINA   (1853-1943)   [R1]
Ornithologist   American

SHERMAN, PATSY O'CONNELL   (1930-)   [A]
Polymer Chemist/Inventor   American

SHERRILL, MARY LURA   (19??-1968)   [O1,W6]
Chemist/Educator   American

SHIELDS, LORA MANEUM   (1912-)   [A,O1]
Biologist/Botanist   American   [*MI*]

SHIELDS, MARGARET   (1800s-1900s)   [R1]
Physicist   American

SHIH MAI-YU (DR. MARY STONE)   (1800s late)   [D1,O1,K3]
Physician   Chinese

SHINN, MILICENT WASHBURN   (1858-1940)   [N2]
Psychologist   American

SHOAF, MARY LA SALLE   (1932-)   [A]
Physicist   American

SHOHNO, NAOMI   (1925-)   [W]
Physicist   Japanese

SHORT, BARBARA   (1900s)   [G]
Aerospace Engineer   American

SHOTWELL, ODETTE LOUISE   (1922-)   [A,O1,D3]
Organic Chemist/Analytical Chemist   American   [*HA,MI*]

SHRAUNER, BARBARA ABRAHAM   (1934-)   [A]
Physicist/Biophysicist   American

SHREEVE, JEAN'NE MARIE Inorganic Chemist	(1933-) American	[A,O1,W6]
SHTERN, LINA SOLOMONOVNA Physiologist	(1878-) Russian	[S,T,W] [*SS*]

SHUBNIKOV, OLGA: *See* TRAPEZNIKOVA, OLGA

SICHELGAITA Toxicologist	(1000s-1100s) Italian	[K]
SIEBERT, KATHARINE BURR Physicist	(1897-) American	[I5]

SIEBOLD: *See* VON SIEBOLD, REGINA JOSEPH

SIEGEMUNDIN, JUSTINE DITTRICHIN Midwife/Obstetrician/Educator	(1650-1705) German	[K,W4,K3,L6]

SIEGMUND, JUSTINA DIETRICH: *See* SIEGEMUNDIN, JUSTINE DITTRICHIN

SIGEA, ALOYSIA Scholar/Physician/Linguist/Author	(1522-1560) Spanish/Portuguese	[K,R4,F4]

SIGEA, LUISA: *See* SIGEA, ALOYSIA

SILBERBERG, RUTH KATZENSTEIN Pathologist	(1906-) American	[W]
SILVERMAN, HILDA FREEMAN Biostatistician/Epidemiologist	(18??-1953) American	[R1]
SIMMONDS, SOFIA Biochemist	(1917-) American	[A,O1,W6]
SIMON, DOROTHY MARTIN Physical Chemist	(1919-) American	[A]
SIMONS, LAO GENEVRA Mathematician/Science Historian	(1870-1949) American	[M7,M8]
SIMPSON, JOANNE GEROULD Meteorologist	(1923-) American	[O1,K2,C3]
SINCLAIR, MARY EMILY Mathematician	(1878-1955) American	[M8]
SINGER, ELIZABETH Physician	(1700s) English	[K]
SINGER, MAXINE FRANK Biochemist	(1931-) American	[A,O1] [*NS*]
SINK, MARY Chemical Engineer	(1900s early) American	[R1]
SINKFORD, JEANNE C. Dentist/Educator	(1933-) American	[M1,B3] [*MI*]

SISON, HONORIE: *See* ACOSTA-SISON, HONORIA

SITTERLY, CHARLOTTE E. MOORE   (1898-)   [W,R1,P4,S2]
 Astrophysicist/Physicist/Astronomer American

SKALKOVA-PROCHAZKOVA, JARMILA   (1900s)   [L3]
 Scientist   Czechoslovakian

SKIRGIELLO, ALINA   (1911-)   [C]
 Botanist/Mycologist/Taxonomist   Polish

SKLODOWSKA, MANYA: *See* CURIE, MARIE SKLODOWSKA

SLATER, ROSE C.L. MOONEY   (1902-1983)   [A]
 Physicist   American

SLOSSON, ANNIE TRUMBULL   (1836-1926)   [Z,S1,R1,I5]
 Entomologist/Naturalist   American

SLYE, MAUD   (1879-1954)   [W,N3,C1,O1]
 Biologist/Geneticist/Pathologist American

SMIRNOVA-ZAMKOVA, ALEKSANDRA I.   (1880-)   [S]
 Pathological Anatomist   Russian

SMITH, ADELIA: *See* CALVERT, ADELIA SMITH

SMITH, ANNIE MORRILL   (1800s late)   [R1]
 Bryologist/Botanist   American

SMITH, CHARLOTTE R.   (1900s)   [O]
 Aerospace Physiologist   American   [HA]

SMITH, CHERYLE C.   (1900s)   [G]
 Operations Research Analyst   American

SMITH, CLARA ELIZA   (1865?-1943)   [M7,I5,M8]
 Mathematician   American

SMITH, DOROTHY GORDON   (1918-)   [W]
 Microbiologist   American

SMITH, EDITH LUCILE   (1913-)   [W]
 Biochemist   American

SMITH, ELIZABETH H.   (18??-1933)   [R1]
 Plant Pathologist   American

SMITH, ELSKE VAN PANHUYS   (1929-)   [A,O1]
 Astronomer/Solar Physicist   Monacoan/American

SMITH, EMILY A.   (1800s-1900s)   [Z]
 Entomologist   American

SMITH, ERMINNIE ADELLE PLATT   (1836-1886)   [W,N2,R1,S1]
 Anthropologist   American

SMITH, ISABEL (1800s-1900s) [F1]
Geologist American

SMITH, JANICE MINERVA (1906-) [W]
Nutritionist American

SMITH, JOANNA (1614-1687) [K]
Physician English/American

SMITH, KATHLEEN (1922-) [W]
Psychiatrist American

SMITH, MARIAN WESLEY (1907-1961) [R1]
Anthropologist American [HA]

SMITH, MRS. PLEASANCE (1773-1877) [I3]
Botanist English

SNETHLAGE, EMILIE (1868-1929) [W5]
Zoologist German/Brazilian

SNOW, JULIA W. (18??-19??) [Z,R1]
Botanist American

SOBEL, EDNA H. (1918-) [A]
Pediatrician/Endocrinologist American [HA]

SOEBANDRIO, HURUSTIATI: *See* SUBANDRIO, HURUSTIATI

SOLIS, MANUELA (1800s late) [D1]
Physician Spanish

SOMERVILLE, MARY FAIRFAX GREIG (1780-1872) [H,M,N,W,Z]
Mathematician/Physicist/Astronomer Scottish

SOONG MEI-LING: *See* CHIANG KAI-SHEK, MADAME

SOPHIA AUGUSTA FREDERICA: *See* CATHERINE THE SECOND, QUEEN

SOPHIA, ELECTRESS OF HANOVER: *See* SOPHIE, ELECTRESS OF HANOVER

SOPHIA ELIZABETH OF BRAUNSCHWEIG (1600s) [K]
Medical Practitioner/Scholar German

SOPHIA OF MECHLENBURG (1500s) [K]
Medical Reformer/Sanitary Pioneer German

SOPHIE, ELECTRESS OF HANOVER (1630-1714) [M5,T1,R]
Mathematician/Scientist/Scholar German

SOPHIE-CHARLOTTE OF PRUSSIA (1700s) [M5,R]
Mathematician/Scientist/Scholar German

SOPHISTRIA: *See* ASPASIA OF MILETUS

SORMOVA, ZORA (1900s) [L3]
Scientist Czechoslovakian

SOROR Physician	(8??-9??) Italian	[K]
SORU, D. EUGENIA Biochemist/Geneticist/Immunologist	(1901-) Rumanian	[C]
SOS, GYORGYI Construction Engineer	(1900s) Hungarian	[I8]
SOSIPATRA Philosopher/Scholar	(BC or early AD) Turkish/Syrian	[R,P5]
SOSIS, VENULEIA Physician	(000s-100s) Roman	[G2,G3]
SOTIRA Midwife/Obstetrician	(BC 300s?) Greek	[K,D1,L6]
SOUSLOVA, NADEJDA, MME. Physician	(18??-19??) Russian	[L6]
SOUTH, LILLIAN Bacteriologist	(1878-) American	[I5]

SOUTHWORTH, EFFIE: *See* SPALDING, EFFIE SOUTHWORTH

SPAGNUOLA, TERESA (pseud.) Medicinal Botanist	(1600s) Spanish	[K]
SPALDING, EFFIE SOUTHWORTH Plant Pathologist	(1800s-1900s) American	[R1]
SPANGBERG-HOLTH, MARIE Physician	(1800s-1900s) Norwegian	[D1]
SPARLING, REBECCA H. Metallurgical Engineer	(1900s) American	[O1]
SPENCER, MARY Plant Biochemist	(1923-) Canadian	[A,L3]
SPERRY, PAULINE Mathematician	(1885-1967) American	[M8]
SPETTOWA, STANISAWA MARIA J. Physician	(1902-) Polish	[W]
SPIEGEL-ADOLF, MONA Biochemist	(1893-) American	[W]
SPONER, HERTHA Physicist	(18??-19??) German/American	[R1]

SPONER-FRANCK, HERTHA: *See* SPONER, HERTHA

SPRAGUE, FRIEDA: *See* ROBSCHEIT-ROBBINS, FRIEDA

SPRAGUE, LUCY   (18??-19??)   [R2]
Child Psychologist   American

STADNICHENKO, MARIA   (18??-1958)   [F1,R1]
Geologist   American

STADNICHENKO, TAISIA: See STADNICHENKO, MARIA

STADTMAN, THRESSA CAMPBELL   (1920-)   [A]
Biochemist/Microbiologist   American   [NS]

STAEL-HOLSTEIN, BARONESS OF: See NECKER, ANNE GERMAINE

STAFFORD, HELEN ADELE   (1922-)   [W]
Biologist   American

STANLEY, LOUISE   (1883-1954)   [N3,R1,V]
Chemist/Home Economist   American

STEARNER, (SIGRID) PHYLLIS   (1919-)   [W,D3]
Radiobiologist   American   [HA]

STEARNS, GENEVIEVE   (1892-)   [W]
Chemist   American

STEARNS, MARY BETH GORMAN   (1925-)   [A,O1]
Physicist   American

STEELE, HANNAH: See PETTIT, HANNAH STEELE

STEELE, LOIS G. FISTER   (1900s)   [M1]
Physician   American   [MI]

STEEVENS, MADAME   (1700s)   [K]
Physician   Irish

STEITZ, JOAN ARGETSINGER   (1941-)   [A]
Molecular Biologist/Biochemist   American   [NS]

STENDLER, CELIA BURNS   (1911-)   [W]
Psychologist   American

STEPHENS, JEANNE   (1500-1600s)   [L6]
Physician   English

STEPHENS, MABEL C.   (1800s-1900s)   [Z]
Astronomer   American

STEPHENSON, MARJORY   (1900s early)   [I7]
Biologist   English   [FR]

STERLIN: See ZERLIN

STERN, CATHERINE BRIEGER   (1894-1973)   [N3]
Mathematician/Educator   Polish/American

STETSON, CHARLOTTE PERKINS: See GILMAN, CHARLOTTE PERKINS

STETTEN, MARJORIE ROLOFF   (1915–)   [W]
  Biochemist   American

STETTER, LETA: *See* HOLLINGWORTH, LETA ANNA STETTER

STEVENS, NETTIE MARIA   (1861–1912)   [N2,L2,D4,V]
  Cytologist/Geneticist/Zoologist   American

STEVENSON, MATILDA COXE EVANS   (1849–1915)   [W,N2,L2,R1]
  Anthropologist/Ethnologist   American

STEVENSON, SARAH HACKETT   (1841–1909)   [O1,K3]
  Physician   American

STEVENSON, SARAH YORK   (1847–1921)   [Z,S1,I5]
  Archaeologist   American

STEWARD, SUSAN SMITH MCKINNEY   (1847–1918)   [O1]
  Physician/Surgeon   American   [MI]

STEWART, GRACE ANN   (1893–1970)   [R1]
  Geologist   Canadian/American

STEWART, ISABEL M.   (1878–)   [N1]
  Nurse   American

STEWART, MAUDE   (1800s–1900s)   [R1]
  Physicist/Educator   American

STEWART, SARAH ELIZABETH   (1906–1976)   [W,O1,R1]
  Microbiologist/Viral Oncologist   American

STICKEL, LUCILLE FARRIER   (1915–)   [A,O1]
  Wildlife Research Zoologist   American

STIEBELING, HAZEL KATHERINE   (1896–)   [X,Z,I5]
  Physical Chemist/Food Chemist   American

STIEGLITZ, MARY RISING   (1800s–1900s)   [R1]
  Chemist   American

STIMSON, MIRIAM MICHAEL, SISTER   (1913–)   [W]
  Chemist   American

STINEWALT, MARGARET AMELIA   (1911–)   [W]
  Parisitologist   American

STINSON, MARGARET E.   (18??–1912)   [I3]
  Chemist   American

STIRLING, MARION   (1900s)   [O1]
  Archaeologist/Geographer   American

STOIBER, LENA ALLEN   (18??–19??)   [R1]
  Mining Engineer   American

STOICHITA, MICHAELA PAPILIAN   (1921–)   [W]
  Physician   Rumanian

STOKES, MARGARET Archaeologist	(18??-1900) Irish	[I3]
STOLL, ALICE MARY Biophysicist/Material Engineer	(1917-) American	[A,O1]
STOLZ, LOIS HAYDEN MEEK: *See* MEEK, LOIS HAYDEN		
STONE, CONSTANCE Physician	(1856-1902) Australian	[D1,B1,D4]
STONE, ISABELLE Physicist	(1800s-1900s) American	[R1,V]
STONE, MARY: *See* SHIH MAI-YU		
STOPES, MARIE CARMICHAEL Paleobotanist/Biologist	(1880-1958) English	[B1,O1,I5]
STOSE, ANNA JONAS: *See* JONAS, ANNA I.		
STOTT, ALICIA BOOLE Mathematician	(1860-1940) British	[M8]
STOVER, BETSY JONES Chemist	(1926-) American	[W]
STOWE, EMILY JENNINGS Physician	(1831-1903) Canadian	[W,D1,I5]
STOWE-GULLEN, AUGUSTA Physician	(1800s late) Canadian	[O1]
STOWELL, LOUISA REED Scientist	(1800s late) American	[R1]
STRACHEY, RAY Electrical Engineer/Author	(1887-1940) English	[I4]
STRATEN, FLORENCE: *See* VAN STRATEN, FLORENCE		
STRESHINSKY, NAOMI GOTTLIEB Sociologist	(1925-) American	[Q1]
STROBELL, ELLA C. Geneticist	(1800s) American	[V]
STRONG, DOROTHY HUSSEMANN Food Scientist	(1908-) American	[W]
STRONG, HELEN M. Geographer	(18??-19??) American	[R1]
STRONG, MIRIAM CARPENTER Botanist	(1800s-1900s) American	[R1]

STROUD-SCHMINK, F. AGNES NARANJO   (1922-)   [A,O1,M1]
  Radiation Biologist   American   [*MI*]

STROZZI, LORENZA   (1500s)   [Z]
  Scientist/Scholar   Italian

STUART, MIRANDA (aka JAMES BARRY)   (1795 c.-1865)   [B1,O1,G4]
  Physician/Surgeon   Scottish/English

SUBANDRIO, HURUSTIATI   (1900s)   [N5]
  Anthropologist/Physician   Indonesian

SUBBOTINA, MISS   (1800s)   [O]
  Physician   Russian

SULLIVAN, ELIZABETH (BETTY)   (1900s)   [O1,R1,W6]
  Cereal Chemist/Biochemist   American

SULLIVAN, KATHRYN D.   (1952-)   [O1]
  Geologist   American   [*AS*]

SUMMERSKILL, EDITH CLARA, BARONESS   (1901-)   [I5,Q1]
  Gynecologist/Physician   English

SUNDQUIST, ALMA   (18??-1940)   [D1,I5]
  Physician   Swedish

SUNDSTROM, ANNA C. PERSDOTTER   (1795-1871)   [C5,B4,W6]
  Chemist   Swedish

SURKO, PAMELA TONI   (1942-)   [A]
  Computer Scientist/Physicist   American

SUSLOVA, NADEZHDA   (1800s)   [B1,D1,Z]
  Physician   Russian

SUSLOWA, NADEJDA: *See* SUSLOVA, NADEZHDA

SUYIN, HAN   (1917-)   [Q1]
  Physician/Researcher   Chinese

SWAIN, CLARA A.   (1834-1910)   [N2,L2,D1]
  Physician   American

SWALLOW, ELLEN: *See* RICHARDS, ELLEN HENRIETTA SWALLOW

SWANSON, ANN BARRETT   (1948-)   [A,D3]
  Biochemist   American   [*HA*]

SWANSON, PEARL PAULINE   (1895-)   [W]
  Nutritionist   American

SWARTZ, MARY: *See* ROSE, MARY DAVIES SWARTZ

SWARUP, SUSHIELA SHYAM   (1925-)   [W]
  Hematologist   Indian

SWEENEY, BEATRICE MARY Botanist/Biologist	(1914–) American	[F,A]
SWIFT, MARY Naturalist/Science Educator	(1800s mid) American	[O]
SWINDLER, MARY Archaeologist	(1900s early) American	[R1]
SWOPE, GLADYS Chemist	(1900s) American	[O]
SYLVAIN, YVONNE Physician	(1900s) Haitian	[D1]
SZABOLCSI, GERTRUD Biological Scientist	(1900s) Hungarian	[L3]
SZEGO, CLARA MARIAN Zoologist	(1916–) American	[W]
SZENTGYORGYI, ZSUZSA Electrical Engineer	(1900s) Hungarian	[I8]
SZMIELEW, WANDA Mathematician	(1918–) Polish	[C]

T

TAEUBER, IRENE BARNES Demographer/Sociologist	(1906–1974) American	[W,N3,M8]
TAIT, SYLVIA AGNES SOPHIA Biochemist/Endocrinologist	(1900s) English	[E,L3] [FR]
TALBOT, MARION Home Economist/Science Educator	(18??–19??) American	[B2,R1,R2]
TALBOT, MARY Zoologist	(1903–) American	[W]
TALBOT, MIGNON Geologist	(1869–1950) American	[F1,I5]
TALIAFERRO, LUCY GRAVES Microbiologist/Immunologist	(1895–) American	[W,B5]
TALLIEN, MADAME Medico-Social Worker/Educator	(1700s late) French	[K,L6]
TAPP, JUNE L. Psychologist	(1930–) American	[Q1]

TAPPUTI-BELATEKALLIM (BC 1200s) [C5,C9]
Chemist Mesopotamian/Iraqi

TARZI, PAKIZE IZZET (1900s) [N5]
Physician/Gynecologist/Surgeon Turkish

TAUSSIG, HELEN BROOKE (1898-) [A,W,C1,L2]
Endocrinologist/Cardiologist American [NS]

TAUSSKY, OLGA (1906-) [W,A]
Mathematician German/American

TAYLOR, JANET (1800s early) [Z,R]
Nautical Astronomer/Author English

TAYLOR, LUCY BEAMAN HOBBS (1833-1910) [N2,L2,H]
Dentist/Physician American

TAYLOR, MONICA (1877-) [W]
Protozoologist English/Scottish

TAYLOR, ROSE H. (18??-1918) [I3]
Botanist American

TELKES, MARIA DE (1900-) [W,O1,R1,I5]
Physical Chemist/Engineer Hungarian/American

TERENTIA (400s) [K]
Physician Italian

TERENTIA PRIMA (000s-100s) [G2,G3]
Physician Roman

TERESA DE JESUS, SANTA (1515-1582 c.) [K,R]
Physician/Psychologist Spanish

TERRAS, AUDREY ANNE (1942-) [A]
Mathematician American

TERTRE, MARGUERITE DU: *See* DE LA MARCHE, MARGUERITE DU TERTRE

TESORO, GIULIANA (1921-) [A,O1]
Organic Polymer Chemist American

TESSA, MONA (1200s) [K]
Physician Italian

TETKA OF BOHEMIA (700s) [K]
Physician Czechoslovakian

THARP, MARIE (1900s) [P7]
Geologist American

THATCHER, MARGARET HILDA RICHARDS (1925-) [E2]
Chemist/Politican English

THEANO (BC 500s) [N,Z,F2,D4]
Mathematician/Physicist/Philosopher Egyptian/Greek

THEIN, MYA MYA Botanist	(1900s) Burmese	[I8]
THELANDER, HULDA EVELIN Pediatrician	(1896-) American	[W]
THELKA, SAINT Physician/Natural Philosopher	(200s-300s) Roman/Greek/Syrian	[K,R]

THEMISTA: *See* THEMISTO

THEMISTE OF LAMPSACUM: *See* THEMISTO

THEMISTO Philosopher/Natural Philosopher	(BC 300 c.) Greek	[R,P5,Z]
THEMISTOCLEA Natural Philosopher/Mathematician	(BC 500s) Greek/Italian	[R,P5]

THEOCLEA: *See* THEMISTOCLEA

THEODOLNDE Physician	(500s) French	[K]
THEODORA Philosopher/Mathematician/Poet	(500-548) Byzantine/Turkish	[R,P5,E2]
THEODOSIA, SAINT Physician/Surgeon	(200s-300s) Roman	[K,Z]
THEOGNIDA Philosopher	(BC 300s) Turkish/Egyptian	[P5]
THEOPHILA Philosopher/Scholar	(BC 000s) Greek/Roman	[R,P5]
THEOSEBEIA Alchemist/Author	(200s late) Egyptian	[C5,C9,E3]

THEOSEBIA THE HERMETIC: *See* THEOSEBEIA

THILLAYAMPALAM, EVANGELINE Zoologist/Educator	(1900s) Indian	[N5]
THOMANN, KAREN Computer Scientist	(1900s) American	[F]
THOMAS, CAROLINE BEDELL Physician	(1904-) American	[W]
THOMAS, DOROTHY SWAINE Sociologist/Demographer	(1899-) American	[W]
THOMAS, EVA MARIA B. Physicist	(1923-) American	[W]

THOMAS, MARTHA Chemical Engineer	(1900s) American	[O]
THOMAS, MARY FRAME MYERS Physician	(1816-1888) American	[K2,K3,I5]
THOMAS, MARY P. Botanist	(1800s) American	[O]
THOME, FRANCES Astronomer	(18??-1916) American	[I3]

THOMPSON, HELEN: *See* GAIGE, HELEN THOMPSON or WOOLLEY, HELEN
   BRADFORD THOMPSON

THOMPSON, LAURA Anthropologist	(1905-) American	[W]
THOMPSON, MARY HARRIS Physician/Surgeon	(1829-1895) American	[W,N2,O1,I5]
THOMS, ADAH BELLE Nurse	(1900s early) American	[O1] [*MI*]
THORSELL, WALBORG SUSANNA Chemist	(1919-) Swedish	[W]
THURMAN, ERNESTINE HOGAN Entomologist	(1920-) American	[W]
TIBURTIUS, FRANZISKA Research Physician	(18??-19??) Swiss/German	[K3]
TILDEN, EVELYN BUTLER Microbiologist	(1891-) American	[W]
TIMOTHY, ADRIENNE F. Solar Astronomer	(1900s) English/American	[O1]
TISHEM, CATHERINE Scholar/Physician/Linguist	(1500s) English/Dutch	[K,L6,F4]

TISSHEIM, CATHERINE: *See* TISHEM, CATHERINE

TODD, MABEL LOOMIS Astronomer	(1800s) American	[S1]

TODD, OLGA TAUSSKY: *See* TAUSSKY, OLGA

TOLLET, ELIZABETH Mathematician/Philosopher/Linguist	(1694-1754) English	[F4]
TOMASZEWICZOWNA, ANNA Physician	(1800s) Polish	[B1,L6]

TOMASZEWIEZ, ANNE: *See* TOMASZEWICZOWNA, ANNA

TONNELAT, MARIE ANTOINETTE BAUDOT   (1912–)   [C,W]
  Physicist   French

TORREY, MARIAN M.   (1900s early)   [R1]
  Mathematician   American

TOU, JENNIE   (1900s)   [F]
  Virologist   American

TOWNSEND, MARJORIE RHODES   (1930–)   [A,G,O1]
  Electronics Engineer   American

TRACY, MARTHA   (1876–1942)   [W,N2,K3,I5]
  Physician   American

TRAPEZNIKOVA, OLGA   (1900s)   [O]
  Low Temperature Physicist   Russian

TRAVIS, DOROTHY FRANCES   (1920–)   [W]
  Biologist   American

TREAT, MARY   (1800s)   [Z,R1,R]
  Botanist/Entomologist   American

TREDWAY, HELEN: *See* GRAHAM, HELEN TREDWAY

TRENTACAPILLI, LUISE   (1400s early)   [H2]
  Physician   Italian

TREVINO, BERTHA   (1900s)   [M1]
  Mathematician   American   *[MI]*

TREVINO, ELVA   (1900s)   [O]
  Mathematician/Computer Scientist   American   *[MI]*

TRIMBLE, VIRGINIA LOUISE   (1943–)   [A]
  Astronomer/Astrophysicist   American

TROTT, DAME: *See* TROTULA

TROTTER, MILDRED   (1899–)   [W]
  Anatomist   American

TROTULA   (1000 c.)   [K,H,M2,B1]
  Physician/Gynecologist/Obstetrician Italian

TROTULA OF SALERNO: *See* TROTULA

TRUEBLOOD, EMILY WALCOTT EMMART   (1898–)   [W]
  Cytologist   American

TSAI, TSU–TZU   (1900s)   [G]
  Chemist   American

TUBMAN, HARRIET ROSS   (1820?–1913)   [O1,G4]
  Medical Practitioner/Abolitionist   American   *[MI]*

TURBEVILLE, SARAH Oculist	(1700 c.) English	[K]
TURI, ZSUZSA F. Physicist	(1900s) Hungarian	[I8]
TURNER, ABBEY H. Zoologist	(1900s early) American	[R1]
TURNER, BIRD MARGARET Mathematician	(1896-1962) American	[M8]
TURNER, HENRIE M. Developmental Biologist	(1900s) American	[O] [*MI*]
TUTIN, WINIFRED ANNE Botanist	(1900s) English	[L3] [*FR*]
TWINING, LOUISE Archaeologist	(1820-1912) English	[I5]
TWISS, EDITH MINOT Botanist	(18??-19??) American	[R1]
TWITTY, GERALDINE WILLIAMS Zoologist	(1900s) American	[M1] [*MI*]

TYE, MRS. H.H.: *See* SOUTH, LILLIAN H.

TYMICHA THE LACEDAEMONIAN Natural Philosopher/Mathematician	(BC 400 c.) Greek	[R,P5]
TYRSENE OF SYBARIS Philosopher/Mathematician	(BC 400s) Greek/Italian	[P5]
TYURINA, GALINA NIKOLAEVNA Mathematician	(1800s-1900s) Russian	[M8]

U

UGON, MARIA ARMAND Physician	(1900s) Uruguayan	[D1]
UHLENBECK, KAREN K. Mathematician/Physicist	(1942-) American	[A,M]
ULRICH, MABEL Physician	(1882?-) American	[Q1]
UNDERHILL, ANNE BARBARA Astrophysicist	(1920-) Canadian/Dutch	[W]

UNDERHILL, RUTH MURRAY Anthropologist	(1884–) American	[R1,I5]
UNDSET, SIGRID Archaeologist	(1900s early) Scandinavian	[K]
UNZER, JOHANNA CHARLOTTE Science Historian	(1724–1782) German	[K]
URRACA Physician	(1200s) Portuguese	[K]
USHAKOVA, ELIZAVEVA IVANOVNA Agronomer	(1895–) Russian	[S]

V

VALIAE Physician	(200s–300s) Roman/Italian	[Z]
VAN BURKALOW, ANASTASIA Geologist	(1911–) American	[W]
VANDEN DRIESSCHE, THERESE Biologist	(1900s) Belgian	[O1]
VAN HOOSEN, BERTHA Physician/Educator	(1900s early) American	[K3]
VAN RENSSELAER, MARTHA Home Economist	(18??–19??) American	[R1,R2]
VAN SCHURMAN, ANNA MARIA: *See* VON SCHURMANN, ANNA MARIA		
VAN STRATEN, FLORENCE Meteorologist	(1913–) American	[Y]
VAN TUSSENBROEK, CATHARINE Physician	(1800s–1900s) Dutch	[D1]
VAN WAGENEN, GERTRUDE Endocrinologist/Medical Educator	(1900s early) American	[R1]
VARGA, EDIT Chemical Engineer	(1900s) Hungarian	[I8]
VARGA, MAGDOLNA Plant Physiologist	(1922–) Hungarian	[W]
VARSANOFIEVA, VERA ALEKSANDROVNA Geologist	(1889–) Russian	[S,W]

VAUGHAN, JANET MARIA, DAME Biologist	(1900s) English	[L3] [*FR*]
VAUGHAN, MARTHA Biochemist/Medical Scientist	(1926-) American	[A] [*NS*]
VEIJJABU, PIERRA HOON Physician	(1900s early) Thai	[D1,O1,H3]
VEJJABUL, PIERRA HOON: *See* VEIJJABU, PIERRA HOON		
VEIL, CATHERINE Physiologist	(1900s) French	[C]
VENKOVA, TOTA Physician	(1856-1921) Bulgarian	[F3]
VENNESLAND, BIRGIT Biochemist	(1913-) American	[W,O1,W6]
VENNING, ELEANOR HILL Biochemist	(1900-) Canadian	[W,L3]
VERDER, A. ELIZABETH Bacteriologist	(1900s early) American	[R1]
VERDER, ADA Pathologist	(1900s early) American	[B2]
VERMES, ERZSEBET Chemical Engineer	(1900s) Hungarian	[I8]
VERRETT, JOYCE M. Biologist	(1900s) American	[M1] [*MI*]
VICTORIA Physician	(300s) Roman/Italian	[Z,K,L6]
VICTORIA THE GYNECIA Physician	(BC 300s) Greek	[K]
VILLA, AMELIA CHOPITEA Physician	(18??-1942) Bolivian	[D1,I5]
VILLA-KOMAROFF, LYDIA Cell Biologist/Molecular Biologist	(1947-) American	[A,M1] [*MI*]
VILLARCEAU, YVON Astronomer/Mathematician	(1700s) French	[M5,R]
VIRDIMURA Physician	(1300s) Italian	[J1]
VISSCHER, ANNA ROEMERS Glass Engraving Innovator/Poet	(1584-1651) Dutch	[T3]
VIVAUT, SARRE Physician	(12??-13??) French	[L6]

VIVIAN, ROXANA HAYWARD   (1871-)   [I3]
Mathematician   American

VLADZIMIRSKAYA, ELENA VASIL   (1929-)   [W]
Chemist   Ukrainian/Russian

VOGT, MARTHE LOUISE   (1903-)   [W,L3]
Physiologist/Pharmacologist   English/Hungarian   [FR]

VOGT, MME.   (1900s early)   [K3]
Research Physician   German

VOLD, MARJORIE JEAN YOUNG   (1913-)   [W,O1,W6]
Chemist   American

VOLKOVA, ANNA ALEKSANDROVNA   (1902-)   [S]
Microbiologist   Russian

VON BORSTELL, FRAU GENERALIN   (1700s)   [K]
Botanist   German

VON CAEMMERER-NEUMANN, HANNA: See NEUMANN, HANNA VON CAEMMERER

VON CALISCH, BARONESS   (1700s)   [K]
Surgeon/Obstetrician/Physician   Hungarian

VON HILDEN, MARIE COLINET   (1600s)   [K,L6]
Physician/Surgeon/Obstetrician   Swiss/German

VON HORENBURG, ANNA ELIZABETH   (1500s-1600s)   [K]
Midwife/Obstetrician/Author   German

VON LOSER, MARGARET SIBYLLA   (1600s)   [K,R]
Physician/Scholar/Chemist   German

VON MISES, HILDA GEIRINGER: See GEIRINGER, HILDA

VON RODDE, DOROTHEA   (1770-1824)   [K,B1]
Scientist/Physician   German

VON SANDRART, ESTHER BARBARA   (1651-1729)   [K]
Naturalist   German

VON SCHURMANN, ANNA MARIA   (1607-1678)   [Z,K,D4,F3]
Scientist/Physician/Scholar   Dutch/German

VON SIEBOLD, CARLOTTA: See VON SIEBOLD, CHARLOTTE

VON SIEBOLD, CHARLOTTE   (1761-1859)   [K,Z,W4,D1]
Obstetrician/Physician   German

VON SIEBOLD, REGINA JOSEPH   (17??-18??)   [K,Z,W4,K3]
Obstetrician/Physician   German

VON ZAY, MARIA VON CALISCH   (1779-??)   [K]
Obstetrician/Surgeon/Physician   Hungarian

W

WAELSCH, SALOME GLUECKSOHN	(1907-)	[A,W]
Geneticist/Developmental Biologist	American	[NS]
WAGNER-FISCHER, ANNE-MARIE	(1918-)	[W]
Physician	German	
WAKEFIELD, PRISCILLA BELL	(1700s-1800s)	[R1]
Botanist	English	
WALCOTT, HELENE B.	(18??-1911)	[I3]
Geologist	American	
WALCOTT, MARY MORRIS VAUX	(1860-1940)	[N2,L2,R1]
Naturalist	American	
WALD, LILLIAN D.	(1867-1940)	[N2,N1,O1]
Public Health Nurse/Reformer	American	
WALKER, ELIZABETH	(1600s late)	[K]
Pharmacist	English	
WALKER, MARY EDWARDS	(1832-1919)	[L2,O1,H3]
Physician	American	
WALKER, MARY RICHARDSON	(1800s)	[W5]
Naturalist/Taxidermist/Pioneer	American	
WALKER, NORMA FORD	(1893-)	[W,I5]
Biologist	Canadian	
WALL, FLORENCE E.	(1900s early)	[R1]
Cosmetic Chemist	American	
WALLACE, EDITH	(1900s early)	[R1]
Geneticist	American	
WALPURGA, SAINT	(754-778)	[K,W4]
Physician/Educator	English/German	
WALTHAM, MARGARET	(1500s-1600s)	[K]
Physician	English	
WALWORTH, ELLEN HARDIN	(1800s late)	[R1]
Geologist	American	
WANG, CHI CHE	(1894-)	[W]
Biochemist	American	
WANG ZHENYI	(1768-1797)	[O]
Mathematician/Meteorologist	Chinese	
WARGA, MARY ELIZABETH	(1904-)	[W]
Physicist	American	

WARNER, ESTELLA FORD Physician/Public Health Specialist	(1900s early) American	[R1]
WARWICK, LADY Physician	(1600s) English	[K]
WASHBURN, MARGARET FLOY Psychologist	(1871-1939) American	[B,R,O1,N2] [NS]
WASSELL, HELEN Chemist	(1900s early) American	[R1]
WATKINS, DELLA Plant Pathologist	(19??-1977) American	[R1,R2]
WATKINS, WINIFRED MAY Biochemist/Immunologist	(1924-) English	[E,L3] [FR]
WATSON, ELLEN Mathematician	(1860?-1884?) English	[I3]
WATSON, JANET VIDA Geologist	(1923-) English	[E,L3] [FR]
WATSON, VERA Computer Scientist	(1900s) American	[O]
WATTS, BETTY MONAGHAN Chemist	(1907-) American	[W]
WAUNEKA, ANNIE DODGE Medical Innovator	(1900s early) American	[H3] [MI]
WAY, KATHARINE Physicist	(1903-) American	[A,O1,P4]
WAYMOUTH, CHARITY Cell Biologist	(1915-) American	[W]
WEAVER, MARY OLLIDEN Chemist/Inventor	(1900s) American	[O]
WEBB, MARTHA BEATRICE POTTER Sociologist	(1858-1943) English	[W,Q1]
WECKERIN, ANNA Pharmacist/Nutritionist	(15??-16??) German	[K]
WEEKS, DOROTHY Scientist	(1800s) American	[M1] [MI]
WEINER, RUTH Photochemist/Ecologist	(1900s) American	[O1,K2]

WEINTRAUB, BARBARA: See WEINTRAUBIN, BARBARA

WEINTRAUBIN, BARBARA Physician/Midwife/Author	(15??-16??) German	[K,R]

WEINZEIRL, LAURA LANE Paleontologist	(18??-1928) American	[R1]
WEISS, MARIE JOHANNA Mathematician	(1903-1952) American	[M8]
WEISS, MARY CATHERINE Mathematician	(1930-1966) American	[M8]
WEISSTEIN, NAOMI Psychologist	(1900s) American	[O1]
WELCH, WINONA HAZEL Botanist	(1896-) American	[W]
WELD, JULIA TIFFANY Bacteriologist/Medical Scientist	(19??-1973) American	[R1]
WELKIE, CAROL Geophysicist	(1900s) American	[O]
WELLS, AGNES ERMINA Mathematician/Astronomer	(1876-1959) American	[R1,I5]
WELLS, LOUISA D. Astronomer	(18??-19??) American	[Z,R]
WELLS, MARY EVELYN Mathematician	(1881-1965) American	[M8]
WELSH, JANE KILLY Geologist	(1800s early) American	[O]
WELSH, LILLIAN Physiologist/Zoologist/Physician	(18??-19??) American	[R1,K3,R2]
WEMBRIDGE, ELEANOR ROWLAND Psychologist/Physical Therapist	(1900s early) American	[R1]
WESTCOTT, CYNTHIA Botanist/Plant Pathologist	(1900s early) American	[R1]
WESTON, ELIZABETH Naturalist/Medical Scientist	(1600s) English/Czech	[K]
WHEELER, ANNA JOHNSON PELL Mathematician	(1883-1966) American	[N3,M7,M8,V]
WHEELER, B.E. Archaeologist	(1800s-1900s) American	[Z]
WHEELER, MARY FANETT Mathematician	(1938-) American	[A,M]
WHEELER, RUTH Chemist/Nutritionist	(1877-1948) American	[N2,R1,V]

WHITE, EDITH GRACE Ichthyologist	(1890-) American	[W]
WHITE, FLORENCE ROY Chemist	(1909-) American	[W]
WHITE, FRANCES EMILY Physiologist	(18??-19??) American	[K,R1]
WHITE, LAURA BRADSTREET Chemist	(18??-1919) American	[I3]
WHITING, SARAH FRANCES Physicist/Astronomer/Educator	(1847-1927) American	[J,O1,N2,D4]
WHITMORE, JOAN Hydrologist	(1900s) South African	[B1]
WHITNEY, JESSAMINE Statistician	(1900s early) American	[R1]
WHITNEY, MARY WATSON Astronomer	(1847-1921) American	[B1,N2,L2,Z]
WICK, FRANCES GERTRUDE Physicist	(1875-1941) American	[R1,I5]
WICKENS, ARYNESS JOY Statistician	(1900s early) American	[R1]
WIDDOWSON, ELSIE MAY Nutritionist/Medical Scientist	(1900s) English	[E,L3] [FR]
WIDERSTROM, KAROLINA Physician	(1800s-1900s) Swedish	[D1,L6]
WIDGOFF, MILDRED Elementary Particle Physicist	(1924-) American	[A,W]
WIDNALL, SHEILA EVANS Aeronautical Engineer	(1938-) American	[A,O1] [NE]
WIEBUSCH, AGNES TOWNSEND Physicist	(1900s early) American	[R1]
WIJTHOFF, A. GERTRUIDA Mathematician	(1859-) Dutch	[M8,R]
WILDER, INEZ WHIPPLE Zoologist	(1800s-1900s) American	[S1,R1]
WILDESEN, LESLIE Archaeologist/Anthropologist	(1900s) American	[O1]
WILLARD, MARY LOUISA Chemist	(1898-) American	[W]

WILLCOX, MARY   (18??-19??)   [R1]
  Zoologist/Biologist   American

WILLIAMS, ANNA C.   (18??-19??)   [D1]
  Bacteriologist   American

WILLIAMS, ANNA WESSELS   (1863-1954)   [N3,R1,K3]
  Bacteriologist/Physician   American

WILLIAMS, BLANCHE E.   (1800s-1900s)   [Z]
  Archaeologist   American

WILLIAMS, CICELY   (1893-)   [O1]
  Physician   English/American

WILLIAMS, VIRGINIA RICE   (1919-)   [W]
  Biochemist   American

WILLOCK-BRYANT, SOPHIE: *See* BRYANT, SOPHIE WILLOCK

WILLOUGHBY, LADY   (1600s)   [K]
  Medicinal Botanist/Physician   English

WILSDORF, DORIS KUHLMAN   (1922-)   [W]
  Physicist   American

WILSON, ALICE E.   (1881-1964)   [O1,R1]
  Geologist   Canadian

WILSON, IRENE MOSSOM   (1904-)   [W]
  Botanist   English

WILSON, KATHERINE WOODS   (1923-)   [W]
  Chemist   American

WILSON, LOIS   (1900s)   [O]
  Physician   American

WILSON, LUCY   (1800s-1900s)   [R1]
  Physicist   American

WINCKELMANN, MARGARETE: *See* KIRCH, MARIA MARGARITE WINCKELMANN

WINLOCK, ANNA   (1857-1904)   [Z,I3,N4]
  Astronomer   American

WINOGRADZKI, JUDITH   (1916-)   [W]
  Theoretical Physicist   French

WINSTON-NEWSON, MARY: *See* NEWSON, MARY WINSTON

WINTHROP, HANNAH   (1700s)   [F1]
  Astronomer   American

WITKIN, EVELYN MAISEL   (1921-)   [A]
  Microbial Geneticist/Geneticist   American   [*NS*]

WOKER, GERTRUDE JAN Biochemist	(1878-) Swiss	[W]
WOLF, KATHERINE Research Psychologist	(1900s early) American	[R1]
WOLLSTEIN, MARTHA Pathologist	(18??-19??) American	[S1,K3]
WOOD, ELIZABETH ARMSTRONG Crystallographer	(1912-) American	[W]
WOODHOUSE, ELEANOR Surgeon	(1600s late) English	[K]
WOOLEY, ANN Physician/Pharmacist/Nutritionist	(1623-) English	[K,V2]
WOOLEY, HANNAH: See WOOLEY, ANN		
WOOLLEY, HANNAH: See WOOLEY, ANN		
WOOLLEY, HELEN BRADFORD THOMPSON Research Psychologist	(1874-1947) American	[N2,R1,V,A1]
WORNER, RUBY K. Chemist	(1900s early) American	[R1]
WORTHINGTON, EUPHEMIA Mathematician	(1900s early) American	[R1]
WORTLEY-MONTAGU, LADY: See MONTAGU, MARY WORTLEY (PIERREPONT)		
WOZNICKA, URSZULA Nuclear Physicist	(1900s) Polish	[O]
WRIGHT, BARBARA EVELYN Biochemist	(1926-) American	[W]
WRIGHT, FRANCES WOODWORTH Astronomer	(1897-) American	[W]
WRIGHT, HELEN Astronomer	(1914-) American	[W,I5]
WRIGHT, JANE C. Physician/Cancer Researcher	(1919-) American	[O1] [MI]
WRIGHT, MABEL OSGOOD Naturalist	(1859-1934) American	[N2]
WRIGLEY, GLADYS MARY Geographer	(1885-1975) American	[R1]
WRINCH, DOROTHY M. Biochemist/Mathematician/Physicist	(1894-1976) Argentinian/American	[W,P1,R1,I5]

WU, CHIEN SHIUNG   (1912-)   [A,W,Y,H,C1]
  Nuclear Physicist   American   [*NS*]

WYCKOFF, DELAPHINE GRACE ROSA   (1906-)   [W]
  Microbiologist   American

WYCKOFF, DOROTHY   (1800s-1900s)   [F1]
  Geologist   American

WYMAN, IRMA   (1900s)   [O]
  Engineer   American

WYTTENBACH, JEANNE   (17??-1830)   [K]
  Physician/Medical Historian   German

X

XANITA   (100s)   [K,L6]
  Physician   Greek/Roman

XIE XI-DE   (1900s)   [O]
  Physicist   Chinese

Y

YA MEI KIN   (18??-19??)   [D1]
  Physician/Microscopist   American/Chinese

YALOW, ROSALYN SUSSMAN   (1921-)   [A,L,W1,O1]
  Medical Physicist/Endocrinologist   American   [*NL,NS*]

YAMAMOTO, MATSUYO   (1900s)   [O1]
  Home Economist   Japanese

YANG, MARION   (1900s early)   [D1]
  Public Health Physician   Chinese

YANOVSKAYA, SOFIYA ALEKSANDROVNA: *See* JANOVSKAJA, SOF'JA
  ALEKSANDROVNA

YARROS, RACHEL   (18??-19??)   [K3]
  Obstetrician/Educator   American

YASUI, KONO   (1900s early)   [O1]
  Botanist   Japanese

YOSHIOKA, YA YOI   (1872-)   [D1,O1]
  Physician/Medical Educator   Japanese

YOUNG, ANNIE S.   (1800s-1900s)   [R1,Z]
  Astronomer   American

YOUNG, CHARLOTTE MARIE   (1910-)   [W]
  Nutritionist   American

YOUNG, GRACE CHISHOLM   (1868-1944)   [M,M7,M8,R1]
  Mathematician   English/American

YOUNG, HOYLANDE D.: *See* FAILEY, HOYLANDE D. YOUNG

YOUNG, MABEL MINERVA   (1872-1963)   [M8]
  Mathematician   American

YOUNG, MARY SOPHIE   (18??-1919)   [I3]
  Botanist   American

YOUNG, LEONA ESTHER   (1893-)   [W]
  Chemist   American

YSABEL   (12??-13??)   [K,H2]
  Physician   French

YSABIAU   (12??-13??)   [H2]
  Physician   French

YUASA, TOSHIKO   (1900s)   [O1]
  Nuclear Physicist   Japanese/French

Z

ZACHRY, CAROLINE BEAUMONT   (1894-1945)   [N2]
  Educational Psychologist   American

ZAIMIS, ELEANOR CRISTIDES   (1915-)   [W,L3]
  Pharmacologist   Greek/English

ZAKRZEWSKA, MARIE ELIZABETH   (1829-1902)   [W,N2,B1,L2]
  Physician   German/American

ZALESKA, KATHERINA   (1900s)   [B1]
  Physician/Nurse   Polish/Nigerian

ZAMES, FRIEDA   (1900s)   [O]
  Mathematician   American   [*HA*]

ZAMIR, AVA   (1900s)   [O]
  Scientist   Israeli

ZAND, NATHALIE   (1800s-1900s)   [D1]
  Pathologist   Polish

ZECKWER, ISOLDE THERESE Pathologist	(1892-) American	[W]
ZENIAS, SAINT Physician	(200s-300s) Roman Empire	[K]
ZENOBIA, QUEEN Scholar	(240-300) Syrian/Roman	[F2,F3,E2]
ZERLIN Physician/Oculist/Ophthalmologist	(1400s early) German	[K,W4,H2,J1]
ZERLINE: *See* ZERLIN		
ZIEMIECKA, JADWIGA Microbiologist	(1891-) Polish	[C]
ZIMMERMAN, CAROL Geophysicist	(1900s) American	[O]
ZIPPORAH Physician	(BC 1200 c.) Egyptian/Judean	[K,W4]
ZOK KYONS CHANG Physician	(1900s early) Chinese	[D1]
ZORUBIN, R., MISS Physicist	(1800s) English	[I7]
ZUCKER, MARJORIE BASS Physiologist	(1919-) American	[W]
ZUCKERMAN, HARRIET Sociologist	(1900s) American	[O]

WOMEN SCIENTISTS
LISTED BY FIELD

AERONAUTICAL ENGINEERS

FLUGGE-LOTZ, IRMGARD
MACGILL, ELSIE GREGORY
PEARSE, DOROTHY NORMAN SPICER
PLATT, BERYL
WIDNALL, SHEILA EVANS

AGRICULTURAL SCIENTISTS

ANNO, KIMIKO
BAI, A.R. KASTURI
BAILEY, CATHERINE HAYES
BAILEY, LIBERTY HYDE
BARDINA, SOFIA
CHILTON, MARY DELL MATCHETT
CLARKE, ELIZABETH L.
LAUCHIS, BETTIE E.
LEKCZYNSKA, JADWIGA
PINCKNEY, ELIZA LUCAS
USHAKOVA, ELIZAVEVA IVANOVNA

ANATOMISTS

BASSI, LAURE MARIA CATARINA
BIHERON, MLLE.
BISHOP, KATHARINE SCOTT
BURY, ELIZABETH
CROSBY, ELIZABETH CAROLINE
D'ARCONVILLE, GENEVIEVE
    CHARLOTTE
DEANE, HELEN WENDLER
DELAUNEY, MARGUERITE DE STAEL

DE WITT, LYDIA MARIA ADAMS
FIFKOVLA, EVA
GAGE, SUSANNA S. PHELPS
GILIANI, ALESSANDRA
HAY, ELIZABETH DEXTER
HINES, MARION
JACOBS, PATRICIA ANN
LEWIS, MARGARET REED
LEWIS, MRS. WARREN H.
LOGAN, MYRA ADELE
LONGSHORE, HANNAH E. MYERS
LUSE, SARAH AMANDA
MOODY, MARY BLAIR
MORANDI-MANZOLINI, ANNA
PERETTI, ZAFFIRA
PETTRACINI, MARIA
PYTHIAS OF ASSOS
RUYSCH, RACHEL
SABIN, FLORENCE RENA
SCHARRER, BERTA VOGEL
SMIRNOVA-ZAMKOVA,
    ALEXSANDRA I.
TROTTER, MILDRED

ANTHROPOLOGISTS

ABERLE, SOPHIE BLEDSOE
BARRERA, ANA M. GALVEZ
BECKWITH, MARTHA
BENEDICT, RUTH FULTON
BRUES, ALICE MOSSIE
BUNZEL, RUTH L.
BURLIN, NATALIE CURTIS
CODERE, HELEN FRANCES

ANTHROPOLOGISTS (cont'd)

COLSON, ELIZABETH FLORENCE
DE LAGUNA, FREDERICA ANNIS
DENSMORE, FRANCES THERESA
DU BOIS, CORA
DUNHAM, KATHERINE
ELLIS, FLORENCE HAWLEY
EMERSON, ELLEN RUSSELL
FLETCHER, ALICE CUNNINGHAM
FRIEDL, ERNESTINE
GEERTZ, HILDRED
GOLDFRANK, ESTHER S.
GONZALEZ, NANCIE LOUDON
GOODMAN, MARY ELLEN HOHEISEL
GUNTER, ERNA
HAAS, MARY ROSAMOND
HAMMOND, DOROTHY BRAMSON
HEARST, PHOEBE APPERSON
HERSKOVITS, FRANCES SHAPIRO
HURSTON, ZORA NEALE
KATAKURA, MOTOKO
KINGSLEY, MARY HENRIETTA
LEACOCK, ELEANOR BURKE
LEAKEY, MARY
LEGEY, LA DOCTORESSE
LUOMALA, KATHARINE
MARRIOTT, ALICE LEE
MEAD, MARGARET
NECRASOV, C. OLGA
NUTTALL, ZELIA MARIA MAGDALENA
PARSONS, ELSIE WORTHINGTON
  CLEWS
REICHARD, GLADYS AMANDA
ROBESON, ESLANDA (CORDOZA)
  GOODE
ROYER, CLEMENCE AUGUSTINE
SCHWIDETZKY, ILSE
SEMPLE, ELLEN CHURCHILL
SMITH, ERMINNIE ADELLE PLATT
SMITH, MARIAN WESLEY
STEVENSON, MATILDA COXE EVANS
SUBANDRIO, HURUSTIATI
THOMPSON, LAURA
UNDERHILL, RUTH MURRAY
WILDESEN, LESLIE

ARCHAEOLOGISTS

ARDITI, MICHELE
CAETANI-BOVATELLI, DONNA
  ERSILIA
DIEULAFOY, JEANNE PAULE MAGRE
EADY, DOROTHY
EDWARDS, AMELIA ANN BLANFORD
EL SADEEK, WAFAA
ESTE, ISABELLA D'
GIBSON, MARGARET DUNLOP
GOLDMAN, HETTY
HALL, EDITH H.
HANSEN, HAZEL D.
HARRISON, JANE ELLEN
HAWES, HARRIET A. BOYD
HAWKES, JACQUETTA HOPKINS
HELENA, EMPRESS
HORSFORD, CORNELIA
JAMESON, ANNA BROWNELL MURPHY
KENYON, KATHLEEN
LEAKEY, MARY
LEWIS, AGNES SMITH
MERITT, LUCY TAXIS SHOE
MESTORF, JOHANNA
MURAT, CAROLINE BONAPARTE,
  QUEEN
NUTTALL, ZELIA MARIA MAGDALENA
PECK, ANNIE S.
PORADA, EDITH
ROBERTSON, ANNE STRACHAN
SCHLIEMANN, SOPHIA ENGASTROMENOS
STEVENSON, SARAH YORK
STIRLING, MARION
STOKES, MARGARET
SWINDLER, MARY
TWINING, LOUISE
UNDSET, SIGRID
WHEELER, B.E.
WILDESEN, LESLIE
WILLIAMS, BLANCHE E.

ASTRONOMERS
  See also ASTROPHYSICISTS

AGANICE
AGLAONICE
ANTHUSA
ASHLEY, MARY
BARDWELL, ELIZABETH M.
BAUTZ, LAURA PAT
BAYNARD, ANNE
BELL, BARBARA
BIGELOW, HARRIET
BOBINSKI, COUNTESS
BOYD, MARY E.
BRAHE, SOPHIA
BRIERE, NICOLE-REINE ETABLE
  DE LA
BROWN, ALICE
BROWN, ELIZABETH
BRUCE, CATHERINE WOLFE
BRYAN, MARGARET
BURBIDGE, (ELEANOR) MARGARET
  PEACHEY
BURNELL, JOCELYN BELL
BYRD, EMMA
CANNON, ANNIE JUMP
CARTER, ELIZABETH
CLERKE, AGNES MARY
CLERKE, ELLEN M.
COWLEY, ANNE PYNE
CUNITZ, MARIA
CUNNINGHAM, SUSAN
CUSHMAN, FLORENCE
DUMEE, JEANNE
DU PIERRY, MME.
EIMMART, MARIE CLAIRE
ELVIUS, AINA
EUDOCIA (ATHENAIS)
EVERETT, ALICE
FABER, SANDRA MOORE
FARNSWORTH, ALICE
FAYE, MME.
FLAMMARION, CAMILLE
FLEMING, WILLIAMINA PATON
  STEVENS
FURNESS, CAROLINE ELLEN
GILL, JOCELYN RUTH

GOKDOGEN, NUZHET
HARWOOD, MARGARET
HAYES, ELLEN AMANDA
HERSCHEL, CAROLINE LUCRETIA
HEVELIUS, ELIZABETH KOOPMAN
HOFFLEIT, ELLEN DORRUT
HOGG, HELEN BATTLES SAWYER
HUGGINS, MARGARET LINDSAY, LADY
IWANOWSKA, WILHELMINA
JANSEN, MME.
JONES-FORMAN, CHRISTINE
KIRCH, MARIA MARGERITE
  WINCKELMANN
KLUMPKE, DOROTHEA
LALANDE, MARIE LEFRANCAIS DE
LEAVITT, HENRIETTA SWAN
LELAND, EVA F.
LEPAUTE, HORTENSE
LEWIS, FLORENCE PARTHENIA
LICHTENSTEIN, PEARL RUBENSTEIN
LYNDS, BEVERLY TURNER
MACE, HANNA
MAKEMSON, MAUD WORCESTER
MAUNDER, ANNIE SCOTT DILL
  RUSSELL
MAURY, ANTONIA CAETANA
MEDICI, CATHERINE DE
MEINEL, MARJORIE PETTIT
MIDDLEHURST, BARBARA MARY
MITCHELL, MARIA
MOLZA, TARQUINIA
MORABITO, LINDA
MULLER, FRAU
MUNECCIME
ORR, M.A.
PALMER, MARGARETTA
PAYNE-GAPOSCHKIN, CECILIA
  HELENA
PETTIT, HANNAH STEELE
PISCOPIA, ELENA CORNARO
POGSON, MISS
PRINCE, HELEN DODSON
PROCTER, MARY
PROCTOR, MARY
RAUSCHER, ELIZABETH ANN
ROEMER, ELIZABETH
ROENNAU, LAUREL VAN DER WAL

ASTRONOMERS (cont'd)

ROMAN, NANCY GRACE
RUBIN, VERA COOPER
RUMKER, MADAME
SABLIERE, MARGUERITE DE LA
SAWYER, CONSTANCE BRAGDON
SAXE-GOTHA, LOUISE OF, DUCHESS
SCARPELLINI, CATERINA
SITTERLY, CHARLOTTE E. MOORE
SMITH, ELSKE VAN PANHUYS
SOMERVILLE, MARY FAIRFAX GREIG
STEPHENS, MABEL C.
TAYLOR, JANET
THOME, FRANCES
TIMOTHY, ADRIENNE F.
TODD, MABEL LOOMIS
TRIMBLE, VIRGINIA LOUISE
VILLARCEAU, YVON
WELLS, AGNES ERMINA
WELLS, LOUISA D.
WHITING, SARAH FRANCES
WHITNEY, MARY WATSON
WINLOCK, ANNA
WINTHROP, HANNAH
WRIGHT, FRANCES WOODWORTH
WRIGHT, HELEN
YOUNG, ANNIE S.

ASTROPHYSICISTS

BURNELL, JOCELYN BELL
CRANNELL, CAROL JO ARGUS
DRAPER, MARY ANNA PALMER
IWANOWSKA, WILHELMINA
JONES-FORMAN, CHRISTINE
MASSEVITCH, ALLA GENRIKHOVNA
PAYNE-GAPOSCHKIN, CECILIA
  HELENA
SITTERLY, CHARLOTTE E. MOORE
TRIMBLE, VIRGINIA LOUISE
UNDERHILL, ANNE BARBARA

BACTERIOLOGISTS
  See also MICROBIOLOGISTS

ALEXANDER, HATTIE ELIZABETH
ANTHONY, BERTHA VAN HOUTEN
BENGTSON, IDA
BLISS, ELEANOR ALBERT
BRANHAM, SARA
BRUCE, MARY, LADY
CALDWELL, MARY E.
CAUSEY, CALISTA ELIOT
DOWNS, CORA
ENGELBRECHT, MILDRED AMANDA
EVANS, ALICE CATHERINE
FLEMING, AMALIA C., LADY
GENUNG, ELIZABETH F.
GILBERT, RUTH
HILL, JUSTINE HAMILTON
JEZKOVA, ZDENKA
KIRKBRIDE, MARY
LANCEFIELD, REBECCA CRAIGHILL
LANGE, LINDA B.
MACNAMARA, JEAN
MENDOZA-GUAZON, MARIA PAZ
PASTEUR, MARIE LAURENT
PENNINGTON, MARY ENGLE
PITTMAN, MARGARET
PRIGOSEN, ROSA ELIZABETH
RABINOWITSCH-KEMPNER, LYDIA
RAHAL, KHEIRA
SOUTH, LILLIAN
VERDER, A. ELIZABETH
WELD, JULIA TIFFANY
WILLIAMS, ANNA C.
WILLIAMS, ANNA WESSELS

BIOCHEMISTS

APGAR, B. JEAN
ASKONAS, BRIGITTE ALICE
BANGA, ILONA
BAZIN, SUZANNE
BLOMBAEK, M. WETTER
BLUM, ARLENE
BREYER, MARIA GERDINA BRANDWIJK
BRISCOE, ANNE M.

BROWN, RACHEL FULLER
BUELL, MARY VAN RENSSELAER
CALDWELL, MARY L.
CARSTEN, MARY E.
CHAIX, PAULETTE AUDEMARD
CHILTON, MARY DELL MATCHETT
CHMIELEWSKA, IRENA
CLARKE, PATRICIA HANNAH
CLEMENT, JACQUELINE
COHN, MILDRED
CORI, GERTY THERESA RADNITZ
DANIEL, LOUISE JANE
DAVIDSON, BETTY
DE MEURON-LANDOLT, MONIQUE
DYER, HELEN M.
EICHELBERGER, LILLIAN
ELION, GERTRUDE BELLE
EMERSON, GLADYS ANDERSON
FARR, WANDA KIRKBRIDE
FINK, KAY FERGUSON
FLOCK, EUNICE VERNA
FORREST, IRENE STEPHANIE
  NEUBERG
FOX, MATTIE RAE SPIVEY
GOLDSCHMIDT, LEONTINE
GRAHAM, HELEN TREDWAY
GREEN, ARDA A.
HAYES, DORA KRUSE
HEILBRONN-WIKSTROM, EDITH
HIMMS-HAGEN, JEAN
HOLLANDER, NINA
HORNING, MARJORIE G.
HUBBARD, RUTH
JONES, MARY ELLEN
KAUFMAN, JOYCE J.
KENNEDY, CORNELIA
KRASNOW, FRANCES
LOW, BARBARA WHARTON
LUCID, SHANNON W.
MACY-HOOBLER, ICIE GERTRUDE
MAN, EVELYN BROWER
MANDL, INES
MARTIN, ARLENE PATRICIA
MATHEWS, JESSICA TUCHMAN
MCDONALD, MARGARET RITCHIE
MELCHIOR, JACKLYN BUTLER
MENTON, MAUD

MILLER, ELIZABETH CAVERT
MONCRIEFF, SCOTT
MORRIS, ROSEMARY SHULL
NEEDHAM, DOROTHY MARY MOYLE
NEUFELD, ELIZABETH FONDAL
NICHOLLS, DORIS MARGARET MCEWEN
OKEY, RUTH
OSBORN, MARY JANE
PARSONS, HELEN TRACY
PERLMANN, GERTRUDE
PETERMANN, MARY LOCKE
PITT-RIVERS, ROSALIND VENETIA
RATNER, SARAH
RICE, KATHERINE
ROLF, IDA
RUSSELL, JANE ANNE
SCHWEBER, MIRIAM SCHURIN
SEIBERT, FLORENCE BARBARA
SEN, LOURMINIA CARINO
SHARPLESS, NANSIE SUE
SHEININ, ROSE
SIMMONDS, SOFIA
SINGER, MAXINE FRANK
SMITH, EDITH LUCILE
SORU, D. EUGENIA
SPENCER, MARY
SPIEGEL-ADOLF, MONA
STADTMAN, THRESSA CAMPBELL
STEITZ, JOAN ARGETSINGER
STETTEN, MARJORIE ROLOFF
SULLIVAN, ELIZABETH (BETTY)
SWANSON, ANN BARRETT
TAIT, SYLVIA AGNES SOPHIA
VAUGHAN, MARTHA
VENNESLAND, BIRGIT
VENNING, ELEANOR HILL
WANG, CHI CHE
WATKINS, WINIFRED MAY
WILLIAMS, VIRGINIA RICE
WOKER, GERTRUDE JAN
WRIGHT, BARBARA EVELYN
WRINCH, DOROTHY M.

BIOLOGISTS
  See also CELL BIOLOGISTS,
  MICROBIOLOGISTS, BOTANISTS,
  ZOOLOGISTS

ACCAME-MURATORI, ROSANNA
AGASSIZ, ELIZABETH CABOT CARY
ALPER, TIKVAH
ALVARINO DE LEIRA, ANGELES
ARBER, AGNES
ASHBY, WINIFRED MAYER
ASKONAS, BRIGITTE ALICE
AUERBACH, CHARLOTTE
BARNES, MARGARET
BEHRE, ELLINOR H.
BRIGHTWEN, MRS. ELIZA ELDER
BROADHURST, JEAN
BROOKS, MATILDA MOLDENHAUER
CAHOON, MARY ODILE, SISTER
CARSON, RACHEL LOUISE
CHMIELEWSKA, IRENA
CLAPP, CORNELIA MARIA
CLAYPOLE, EDITH JANE
CORREL, HELEN B.
COUSIN, GERMAINE
DUNNING, WILHELMINA FRANCES
EARLE, SYLVIA
ESTON, VERONICA RAPP
EVANS, VIRGINIA JOHN
FIELDE, ADELE MARION
FINKEL, MIRIAM POSNER
GANTT, ELISABETH
GAY, HELEN
GREGORY, EMILY RAY
GRIFFITHS, MRS.
GRUNBERG-MANAGO, MARIANNE
HALBERG, JULIA
HALLIDAY, NELLIE
HARDESTY, MARY
HEWITT, DOROTHY
HILDEGARD OF BINGEN, SAINT
HINCKLEY, MARY H.
HOWARD, ALMA
HUBBARD, RUTH
HUMMEL, KATHARINE PATTEE
JACARUSO, KAREN M.
JACOBS, PATRICIA ANN
JAHN, ELSE

JAKOWSKA, SOPHIE
KELLER, EVELYN FOX
KERLING, LOUISE
KIELAN-JAWOROWSKA, ZOFIA
KING, GLADYS FLORENCE SMITH
KOPEC, MARIA
KUJALOVA, VERA
LAIRD, ANNA KANE
LATHROP, KATHERINE AUSTIN
LEPESHINSKAIA, OLGA BORISOVNA
LEVI-MONTALCINI, RITA
LINDSAY, MISS B.
LOSTROH, ARDIS JUNE
LYON, MARY FRANCES
MAATHAI, WANGARI
MACLEOD, ANNA MACGILLIVRAY
MARSHALL, SHEINA MACALISTER
MATEYKO, GLADYS MARY
MCDOWELL, MARGARET ANN,
  SISTER
MCLAREN, ANNE LAURA
MCVEIGH, IDA
MCWHINNIE, MARY ALICE
MICHELET, MME. JULES
MILLER, HELEN AGNES
MINTZ, BEATRICE
MOOG, FLORENCE
MOORE, EMMELINE
MORLEY, MARGARET WARNER
MURRAY, NOREEN ELIZABETH
MYERS, MABEL ADELAIDE
NECRASOV, C. OLGA
NOBLE, MARY JESSIE MCDONALD
OBENG, LETITIA
OPPENHEIMER, JANE MARION
PANT, RADHA
PARKE, MARY
PASTORI, GIUSEPPINA
PAZ, ELVIRA L.
PEARL, MAUD DEWITT
PERT, CANDACE
PIERCE, MADELENE EVANS
PYTHIAS OF ASSOS
RANADIVE, KAMAL JAYASING
RAY, DIXY LEE
ROENNAU, LAUREL VAN
  DER WAL
SAGER, RUTH

SANFORD, KATHERINE KOONTZ
SAUNDERS, DOROTHY CHAPMAN
SCHARRER, BERTA VOGEL
SCHWARTZ, NEENA BETTY
SCHWIDETZKY, ILSE
SCOTT, FLORENCE MARIE, SISTER
SCOTT, KATHERINE
SHIELDS, LORA MANEUM
SKIRGIELLO, ALINA
SLYE, MAUD
STAFFORD, HELEN ADELE
STEARNER, (SIGRID) PHYLLIS
STEITZ, JOAN ARGETSINGER
STEPHENSON, MARJORY
STOPES, MARIE CARMICHAEL
STROUD-SCHMINK, F. AGNES
   NARANJO
SWEENEY, BEATRICE MARY
SZABOLCSI, GERTRUD
TRAVIS, DOROTHY FRANCES
TURNER, HENRIE M.
VANDEN DRIESSCHE, THERESE
VAUGHAN, JANET MARIA, DAME
VERRETT, JOYCE M.
VILLA-KOMAROFF, LYDIA
WAELSCH, SALOME GLUECKSOHN
WALKER, NORMA FORD
WILLCOX, MARY

BIOMEDICAL SCIENTISTS
See also PHYSICIANS

BAKER, SARA JOSEPHINE
DASTIDAR, SUJATA D.
EDDY, BERNICE ELAINE
FRIEND, CHARLOTTE
GEY, MARGARET
GHAFARUNISSA, DR.
GUILD, ELIZABETH (BETSY)
HOLLINSHEAD, ARIEL CAHILL
JAMESON, DOROTHEA
JOHNSON, VIRGINIA ESHELMAN
MILLER, ELIZABETH CAVERT
PADMATAVI, S.
PAVRI, K.M.
RANNEY, HELEN M.
ROTH, GRACE MARGUERITE

SCHOENTAL, REGINA
SETH, NANDINI ANIL
STEWART, SARAH ELIZABETH
WARNER, ESTELLA FORD
WRIGHT, JANE C.

BIOPHYSICISTS

COHN, MILDRED
FRANKLIN, ROSALIND (ELSIE)
GRIFFITHS, MARY
GUTTMAN, RITA
HAYES, DORA KRUSE
MCSHERRY, DIANA HARTRIDGE
NORTON, DORITA A.
QUIMBY, EDITH HINCKLEY
RAMEY, ESTELLE ROSEMARY
RONTO, GYORGYI
SHRAUNER, BARBARA ABRAHAM
STOLL, ALICE MARY

BOTANISTS

AGAMEDE
ALBERTSON, MARY A.
AMES, MARY L. PULSIFER
ANNA SOPHIA OF DENMARK,
   PRINCESS
ANNA SOPHIA OF HESSE
ANTONIA, DUCHESS OF WURTEMBERG
ARTEMESIA OF CARIA
BAILEY, ETHEL
BEACH, MARTHA
BECKER, LYDIA
BENCE, THALIA
BENHAM, RHODA
BENNETT, ERNA
BENSON, MARGARET J.
BITTING, KATHERINE E. GOLDEN
BLACKWELL, ELIZABETH
BLUKET, NINA ALEKSANDROVNA
BODLEY, RACHEL LITTLER
BORISOVA, ANTONIA
   GEORGIEVNA
BRANDEGEE, MARY
BRAUN, EMMA LUCY

BOTANISTS (cont'd)

BRENCHLEY, WINIFRED ELSIE
BRITTON, ELIZABETH GERTRUDE
  KNIGHT
CAULLEY, MARY M.
CHASE, MARY AGNES MEARA
CHUTE, HETTIE MORSE
CLARK, ARABELLA
CLARKE, CORA HUIDEKOPER
CLEAVE, MARY
CLEMENTS, EDITH SCHWARTZ
COLDEN, JANE
COMSTOCK, ANNA BOTSFORD
CONWAY, ELSIE
COOK, ALICE CARTER
COOKSIN, ISABEL CLINTON
CREIGHTON, HARRIET
CUMMINGS, CLARA EATON
CURRAN, MARY
CUTTER, ELIZABETH GRAHAM
DAY, MARY
DECANDOLLE, ANNE CASIMIR
DE FERRE, YVETTE
DETMERS, FREDA
DIETRICH, (KONKORDIE) AMALIE
  NELLE
DOKHMAN, GENRIETTA ISAAKOVNA
DORETY, ANGELA, SISTER
DU BONNAY, MARCHIONESS
DUNN, LOUISE BRISBIN
EASTMAN, ALICE
EASTWOOD, ALICE
ECKERSON, SOPHIA H.
ELLIS, ARVILLA J.
ESAU, KATHERINE
FELL, ELIZA
FELL, SARAH ANN
FERGUSON, MARGARET CLAY
FERNANDES, ROSETTE MERCEDES B.
FOSDICK, NELLIE
FRANCINI, ELEANORA
FULFORD, MARGARET HANNAH
FURBISH, KATE
GERRY, ELOISE
GILCHRIST, MAUDE
GOLDRING, WINIFRED

GRAY, MARIA EMMA
GREGORY, EMILY L.
GRIFFITHS, MRS.
HALLOWELL, SUSAN MARIA
HASKINS, ALICE
HASLE, GRETHE R.
HAZEN, ELIZABETH LEE
HEDGES, FLORENCE
HIRSCHBOECK, KATHERINE
HOLDEN, RUTH
HOLLEY, MARY A.
HOLTON, NINA
HOOKER, HENRIETTA
HOOKER, MRS. HENSLOW
HOOPER, LUCY
HUTTON, MRS.
JOBE, MARY L.
JOHNSON, LAURA
JOHNSON, LOUISA
JONES, MARGARET
KABLICK, JOSEPHINE
KAEISER, MARGARET
KARPOWICZ, LUDMILA
KIMBER, ABAGAIL
KINGSLEY, MARY HENRIETTA
LANGDON, LADEMA M.
LANKESTER, MRS.
LARSON, GERALDINE
LAUCHIS, BETTIE E.
LECLERCQ, SUZANNE CELINE
LEMMON, SARAH A. PLUMMER
LEOPOLD, ESTELLA BERGERE
LOUDON, JANE
MANTON, IRENE
MARCELLO-MOCENIGO, LOREDANA
MARCET, JANE HALDIMAN
MATHIAS, MILDRED ESTHER
MCCLINTOCK, BARBARA
MERIAN, MARIA SIBYLLA
MORRIS, ELIZABETH
MURTFELDT, MARY ESTHER
MUSSER, EMMA
NAGY, ESTHER MARIA
  KOVACS
NORTH, MARIANNE
PALSER, BARBARA FRANCES
PATRICK, RUTH

PATTERSON, FLORA WAMBAUGH
PHELPS, ALMIRA HART LINCOLN
PORTER, HELEN KEMP
POSTEL, SANDRA
POTTER, BEATRIX
PRATT, ANNE
PUGA, MARIA LUZ
QUIRK, AGNES
REED, EVA M.
RONCHI, VITTORIA NUTI
SALUZZIO, MARGUERITE
SARGANT, ETHEL
SAUNDERS, E.R., MISS
SAVULESCU, I. ALICE
SCOTT, FLORA MURRAY
SHATTUCK, LYDIA WHITE
SHIELDS, LORA MANEUM
SKIRGIELLO, ALINA
SMITH, ANNIE MORRILL
SMITH, MRS. PLEASANCE
SNOW, JULIA W.
SPAGNUOLA, TERESA (pseud.)
STOPES, MARIE CARMICHAEL
STRONG, MIRIAM CARPENTER
SWEENEY, BEATRICE MARY
TAYLOR, ROSE M.
THEIN, MYA MYA
THOMAS, MARY P.
TREAT, MARY
TUTIN, WINIFRED ANNE
TWISS, EDITH MINOT
VON BORSTELL, FRAU GENERALIN
WAKEFIELD, PRISCILLA BELL
WELCH, WINONA HAZEL
WESTCOTT, CYNTHIA
WILLOUGHBY, LADY
WILSON, IRENE MOSSOM
YASUI, KONO
YOUNG, MARY SOPHIE

CARTOGRAPHERS

COUDREAU, OCTAVIE, MADAME
FISCHER, IRENE KAMINKA
SCHMIDT, JOHANNA GERTRUD
  ALICE

CELL BIOLOGISTS
  See also CYTOLOGISTS

FARQUHAR, MARILYN GIST
FOOT, KATHERINE
GONZALEZ, ELMA
GRUNBERG-MANAGO, MARIANNE
HARVEY, ETHEL BROWNE
LE BRETON, ELAINE
MARGULIS, LYNN
MURRAY, MARGARET RANSONE
PARDUE, MARY LOU
RAHMAN, YUEH ERH (JADY)
SCHWEBER, MIRIAM SCHURIN
VILLA-KOMAROFF, LYDIA
WAYMOUTH, CHARITY

CHEMICAL ENGINEERS

DAI, MINH THI
GARCIA, ELIZABETH
HUTCHINSON, MARGARET H.
JUILLARD, JACQUELINE
PATRICK, JENNIE R.
PINTASSILGO, MARIA DE LOURDES
QUIGGLE, DOROTHY
SINK, MARY
THOMAS, MARTHA
VARGA, EDIT
VERMES, ERZSEBET

CHEMISTS
  See also BIOCHEMISTS, GEO-
  CHEMISTS, PHYSICAL CHEMISTS

ADAMS, MILDRED
ALLEN, MALWINA (INKA) GERSON
ALMASI, LUCRETIA ROTSCHILD
ANCHEL, MARJORIE WOLFF
ANGEL, ANDREA
ANNE OF DENMARK
ANNO, KIMIKO
APSLEY, LUCY, LADY
ARMBRUSTER, MARION
BAI, BIJUR TARA
BARNARD, EDITH ETHEL

CHEMISTS (cont'd)

BECKE-GOEHRING, MARGOT LINE
   KLARA
BELETSKAYA, I.P.
BEVIER, ISABEL
BILGER, LEONORA NEUFFER
BISHOP, ANN
BISHOP, HAZEL GLADYS
BLUNT, KATHARINE
BODLEY, RACHEL LITTLER
BOGDANOFSKY, VERA EVSTAFJEVNA
BOJANOVIC, JELENA
BREED, MARY BIDWELL
BROCK, SYLVIA
BROWN, JEANETTE E.
BURTON, BEVERLY S.
CAPEN, BESSIE
CARR, EMMA PERRY
CARTER, MARY EDDIE
CASEIRO, MARJORIE C.
CAUCHOIS, YVETTE
CAUQUIL, GERMAINE ANNE
CHAKRAVARTI, DEBI MUKERJI
CHANG, MARGUERITE SHUE-WEN
CHATTERJEE, ASHIMA MUKHERJEE
CHILTON, MARY DELL MATCHETT
CIORANESCU-NENITZESCU,
   ECATERINA
CLAYTON, BARBARA
CLEOPATRA
CLEOPATRA THE ALCHEMIST
CLIFFORD, ANN, LADY
COBB, ROSALIE M. KARAPETOFF
CORTESE, ISABELLA
CRAWFORD, JEAN VEGHTE
CURIE, MARIE SKLODOWSKA
DANIELS, AMY
D'ARCONVILLE, GENEVIEVE
   CHARLOTTE
DAWSON, MERNA
DORABIALSKA, ALICE DOMENICA
DUNBAR, ALICE DAVIS
EVANS, MARJORIE WOODARD
EVERARD, MS.
FAILEY, HOYLANDE D. YOUNG
FENSELAU, CATHERINE

FENWICK, FLORENCE
FERRY, EDNA LOUISE
FIESER, MARY
FISCHER-HJALMARS, INGA MARGRETE
FLAMEL, PERRENELLE
FOSSLER, MARY
FOSTER, MARGARET D.
FOSTER, MARY LOUISE
FREIDLINA, RAKHIL' KHATSKELEVNA
FREUND, IDA
FULHAME, ELIZABETH
GADEGBEKU, TONI
GIBLIN, LOUISE
GILMAN, ELIZABETH
GOLDTHWAITE, NELLIE
GOOD, MARY LOWE
HAHN, DOROTHY ANNA
HALL, DOROTHY
HALL, JULIA BRAINERD
HATHAWAY, MILLICENT LOUISE
HODGKIN, DOROTHY MARY CROWFOOT
HOKE, CALM MORRISON
IONESCU-SOLOMON, IRINA
ISIS
JEANES, ALLENE ROSALIND
JERNOW, JANE
JEZOWSKA-TRZEBIATOWSKA,
   BOGUSLAWA
JOLIOT-CURIE, IRENE
KAILA, ARMI KAARINA
KELLEY, LOUISE
KELLY, LENA
KIELY, HELEN U.
KNOCK, FRANCES ENGELMANN
KRAUS, IDA RAGINA
LAVOISIER, MARIE ANNE PIERRETTE
LEE, LUCY
LEFEBRE, MME.
LEMARCHAND-BERAUD, THERESE
   MARIE
LERMONTOVA, JULIA
LEWES, VIVIAN BYNAM
LINDNER, KATALIA SZOTYORI
LLOYD, RACHEL
LOCHMANN, CHRISTINA
LOEWE, LOTTE LUISE FRIEDERICKE
LYON, MARY

MACGILLAVRY, CAROLINA
  HENRIETTE
MACK, PAULINE BEERY
MACY-HOOBLER, ICIE GERTRUDE
MARCET, JANE HALDIMAN
MARIA KOPT
MARIA THE JEWESS
MCGEER, EDITH GRAEF
MCGRATH, LOUISE
MCKINLEY, SUZANNE
MCNEAL, CATHERINE J.
MEDES, GRACE
MEDICIS, MARIE DE
MESHKE, EDNA DOROTHY
METZGER, HELENE
MEURDRAC, MARIA
MILDMAY, GRACE SHERRINGTON
MILLER, CHRISTINA CRUICKSHANK
MILLER, ELIZABETH KOCH
MINOT, ANN STONE
MORAN, JULIETTE M.
MORGAN, AGNES FAY
MOY, MAMIE WONG
MURATA, KIKU
MURRAY, ROSEMARY
NIGHTINGALE, DOROTHY VIRGINIA
NOBEL, ANN C.
NODDACK, IDA EVA TACKE
NOVOSELOVA, ALEKSANDRA
  VASIL'EVNA
OLSON, EDITH
ORCUTT, RUBY RIVERS
PALMER, ALICE W.
PAPHNUTIA THE VIRGIN
PARSONS, ELOISE
PENNINGTON, MARY ENGLE
PERCIVAL, ETHEL ELIZABETH
PEREY, MARGUERITE
PERSON, LUCY WU
PETERMANN, MARY LOCKE
PHELPS, MARTHA AUSTIN
PICKETT, LUCY W.
PULLMAN, A.
RAMART-LUCAS, PAULINE
REIMER, MARIE
RICHARDS, ELLEN HENRIETTA
  SWALLOW

RIPAN, C. RALUCA
ROBERTS, CHARLOTTE FICH
ROSCHER, NINA MATHENY
ROSE, GLENOLA BEHLING
ROSE, MARY DAVIES SWARTZ
SAVITZ, MAXINE LAZARUS
SCHELLHAMMER, MARIE SOPHIE
  CONRING
SFORZA, CATHERINE
SHARPLESS, NANSIE SUE
SHATTUCK, LYDIA WHITE
SHERMAN, PATSY O'CONNELL
SHERRILL, MARY LURA
SHOTWELL, ODETTE LOUISE
SHREEVE, JEAN'NE MARIE
STANLEY, LOUISE
STEARNS, GENEVIEVE
STIEGLITZ, MARY RISING
STIMSON, MIRIAM MICHAEL,
  SISTER
STINSON, MARGARET E.
STOVER, BETSY JONES
SULLIVAN, ELIZABETH (BETTY)
SUNDSTROM, ANNA C. PERSDOTTER
SWOPE, GLADYS
TAPPUTI-BELATEKALLIM
TESORO, GIULIANA
THATCHER, MARGARET HILDA
  RICHARDS
THEOSEBEIA
THORSELL, WALBORG SUSANNA
TSAI, TSU-TZU
VLADZIMIRSKAYA, ELENA VASIL
VOLD, MARJORIE JEAN YOUNG
VON LOSER, MARGARET SIBYLLA
WALL, FLORENCE E.
WASSELL, HELEN
WATTS, BETTY MONAGHAN
WEAVER, MARY OLLIDEN
WEINER, RUTH
WHEELER, RUTH
WHITE, FLORENCE ROY
WHITE, LAURA BRADSTREET
WILLARD, MARY LOUISA
WILSON, KATHERINE WOODS
WORNER, RUBY K.
YOUNG, LEONA ESTHER

CIVIL ENGINEERS

BARNEY, NORA STANTON
    BLATCH
EAVES, ELSIE
JONES, VELDA CYNTHIS
MORRIS, JOANNE M.
ROEBLING, EMILY

COMPUTER SCIENTISTS

AVRAM, HENRIETTE
BURKS, MARTHA A.
BUTLER, MARGARET K.
CADE, RUTH ANN
CHARTZ, MARCELLINE
DAVIS, RUTH MARGARET
EASLEY, ANNIE
EBERLEIN, PATRICIA JAMES
EVENS, MARTHA WALTON
FISCHER, CHARLOTTE FROESE
FOX, PHYLLIS
FRIEDMAN, JOYCE BARBARA
HEDGPETH, MARY
HOPPER, GRACE MURRAY
LEWIS, ISABEL MARTIN
LOVELACE, ADA AUGUSTA BYRON,
    LADY
MANN, HELEN
MASKEWITZ, BETTY F.
MCSHERRY, DIANA HARTRIDGE
MURRAY, DIANE
PENA, DEAGELIA M.
PERSON, LUCY WU
SAMMETT, JEAN E.
SURKO, PAMELA TONI
THOMANN, KAREN
TREVINO, ELVA
WATSON, VERA

CRYSTALLOGRAPHERS

FRANKLIN, ROSALIND (ELSIE)
HODGKIN, DOROTHY MARY CROWFOOT
KARLE, ISABELLA LUGOSKI

LONSDALE, KATHLEEN YARDLEY
MACGILLAVRY, CAROLINA HENRIETTE
PORTER, MARY
WOOD, ELIZABETH ARMSTRONG

CYTOLOGISTS
    See also CELL BIOLOGISTS

ALLEN, RUTH FLORENCE
BOCHANTSEVA, ZINAIDA PETROVNA
GRAHAM, RUTH MOORE
GUTHRIE, MARY JANE
OLSZEWSKA, MARIA JOANNA
PRZELECKA, ALEKSANDRA
STEVENS, NETTIE MARIA
TRUEBLOOD, EMILY WALCOTT EMMART

ECOLOGISTS

ANDERSON, CAROL A.
BALFOUR, ELIZABETH JEAN
BRAUN, EMMA LUCY
CARSON, RACHEL LOUISE
CLEMENTS, EDITH SCHWARTZ
DAVIS, MARGARET BRYAN
EARLE, SYLVIA
KARPOWICZ, LUDMILA
MCCAMMON, HELEN
MOORE, EMMELINE
MORGAN, ANN HAVEN
PATRICK, RUTH
POSTEL, SANDRA
WEINER, RUTH

ELECTRICAL ENGINEERS

CLARKE, EDITH
DRESSELHAUS, MILDRED S. REIF
ESTRIN, THELMA A.
HAAS, VIOLET BUSHWICK
HARMON, ELISE F.
HASLETT, CAROLINE, DAME
HICKS, BEATRICE ALICE
LAMME, BERTHA

MAGANA, MARIA
PEDEN, IRENE CARSWELL
RESNIK, JUDITH A.
ROCKWELL, MABEL MACFERRAN
STRACHEY, RAY
SZENTGYORGI, ZSUZSA

ELECTRONICS ENGINEERS

NORWOOD, VIRGINIA
TOWNSEND, MARJORIE RHODES

EMBRYOLOGISTS

GAGE, SUSANNA S. PHELPS
HARVEY, ETHEL BROWNE
KING, HELEN DEAN
LEWIS, MARGARET REED
PYTHIAS OF ASSOS
RANDOLPH, HARRIET
RUDNICK, DOROTHEA

ENDOCRINOLOGISTS

ANDERSON, EVELYN
JUHN, MARY
LEACH, CAROLYN
PICKFORD, LILLIAN MARY
PONSE, KITTY
PRICE, DOROTHY
RAMALEY, JUDITH AITKEN
RAMEY, ESTELLE ROSEMARY
RUSSELL, JANE ANNE
SOBEL, EDNA H.
TAIT, SYLVIA AGNES SOPHIA
TAUSSIG, HELEN BROOKE
VAN WAGENEN, GERTRUDE
YALOW, ROSALYN SUSSMAN

ENGINEERS

See also AERONAUTICAL
ENGINEERS, CHEMICAL EN-
GINEERS, CIVIL ENGINEERS,
ELECTRICAL ENGINEERS,
ELECTRONICS ENGINEERS,
INDUSTRIAL ENGINEERS,
MECHANICAL ENGINEERS,
MINING ENGINEERS, SYSTEMS
ENGINEERS

ANCKER-JOHNSON, BETSY
ASBOTH, JUDIT TORMA
BALLOWE, KANCHANA
CAPO, MARY ANN
CEAUSESCU, ELENA
CHAMBERS, ANNETTE
CHATHAM, ALICE
CHEN, OLIVIA L.
CONWELL, ESTHER MARLEY
CURBY, NORMA
DENNIS, OLIVE WETZEL
DUIGNAN-WOODS, EILEEN
EDGEWORTH, MARIA
ESTRIN, THELMA A.
FISCHER, IRENE KAMINKA
FLETCHER, ANN
FLETCHER, SHIRLEY
FORBES-RESHA, JUDITH
FROST, ROSA F.
GILBRETH, LILLIAN EVELYN
    MOLLER
GOLD, LORNE W.
GORDON, RUTH VIDA
HALL, JULIA BRAINERD
HEISING-GOODMAN, CAROLINE
HOWARD-LOCK, HELEN ELAINE
JOHNSON, BARBARA CRAWFORD
JONES, VELDA CYNTHIS
KANKUS, ROBERTA A.
KELLEMS, VIVIEN
KOCHANOVSKA, ADELA
LATTIRI, ZUBEIDA
LECKBAND, SUSANNE M.
MATTHEWS, ALVA T.
MCAFEE, NAOMI J.
MCNALLY, MARGARET

ENGINEERS (cont'd)

MEYER, EDITHNA PAULA CHART-
  KOFF
MORGAN, JULIA
MULLER, GERTRUDE AGNES
NAGEL, SUZANNE
NAPADENSKY, HYLA
PAYNE, MARJATTA STRANDELL
PEARSE, DOROTHY NORMAN
  SPICER
PENNINGTON, MARY ENGLE
PRESSMAN, IDA I.
QUICK, HAZEL IRENE
RAND, MARIE GERTRUDE
RICHARDS, ELLEN HENRIETTA
  SWALLOW
SAMMETT, JEAN E.
SAVOLAINEN, ANN W.
SCHUPAK, LENORE H.
SCHWAN, JUDITH
SEMIRAMIS, QUEEN
SHORT, BARBARA
SOS, GYORGYI
SPARLING, REBECCA H.
STOLL, ALICE MARY
TELKES, MARIE DE
WYMAN, IRMA

ENTOMOLOGISTS

AGENJO, CECILIA RAMON
CLARKE, CORA HUIDEKOPER
COMSTOCK, ANNA BOTSFORD
DREBENEVA-UKHOVA, VARVARA
  PAVLOVNA
FIELDE, ADELE MARION
HERRICK, SOPHIE
MERIAN, MARIA SIBYLLA
MITCHELL, EVELYN GROESBECK
MORRIS, MARGARETTA
MURTFELDT, MARY ESTHER
ORMEROD, ELEANOR ANNE
PATCH, EDITH M.
PECKHAM, ELIZABETH W.
SAY, LUCY WAY

SHELDON, J.M. ARMS
SLOSSON, ANNIE TRUMBULL
SMITH, EMILY A.
THURMAN, ERNESTINE HOGAN
TREAT, MARY

EPIDEMIOLOGISTS

HORSTMANN, DOROTHY MILLICENT
MACDONALD, ELEANOR J.
SILVERMAN, HILDA FREEMAN

ETHOLOGISTS

FOSSEY, DIAN
GOODALL, JANE
KLEIMAN, DEVRA
KOHTS, MME.

FOOD SCIENTISTS
  See also HOME ECONOMISTS,
  NUTRITIONISTS

BASSE, MARIE-THERESE
BEAN, MAURA
NOBEL, ANN C.
PANGBORN, ROSE MARIE VALDES
SAMISH, ZDENKA
SCHELLHAMMER, MARIE SOPHIE
  CONRING
STIEBLING, HAZEL KATHERINE
STRONG, DOROTHY HUSSEMANN

FORESTRY SCIENTISTS

GERRY, ELOISE
LARSON, GERALDINE
LEKCZYNSKA, JADWIGA
MAATHAI, WANGARI
RICHARDS, C. AUDREY

GENETICISTS

ALEXANDER, MARY LOUISE
ALLEN, SALLY LYMAN
ANDERSON, CAROL A.
AUERBACH, CHARLOTTE
BAILEY, CATHERINE HAYES
BAKHTADZE, KSENIA ERMOLAEVNA
BEGAK, MARIA LUIZA
BENNETT, DOROTHEA
BENNETT, ERNA
BORING, ALICE M.
CAROTHERS, E. ELEANOR
CHANG, ANNIE C.Y.
CLAYTON, FRANCES ELIZABETH
ERDMANN, RHODA
FOOT, KATHERINE
GABE, DINA RUFINOVNA
KING, HELEN DEAN
LYON, MARY FRANCES
MACKLIN, MADGE THURLOW
MCCLINTOCK, BARBARA
MCLAREN, ANNE LAURA
MINTZ, BEATRICE
MITTWOCH, URSULA
MONCRIEFF, SCOTT
MORRIS, MARGARET
NEUFELD, ELIZABETH FONDAL
PARDUE, MARY LOU
RICHARDS, MILDRED HODGE
RONCHI, VITTORIA NUTI
ROWLEY, JANET DAVIDSON
RUSSELL, ELIZABETH SHULL
SAGER, RUTH
SHAW, MARGERY WAYNE SCHLAMP
SLYE, MAUD
SORU, D. EUGENIA
STEVENS, NETTIE MARIA
STROBELL, ELLA C.
WAELSCH, SALOME GLUECKSOHN
WALLACE, EDITH
WITKIN, EVELYN MAISEL

GEOCHEMISTS

IUSOPOVA, SARADZHAN
  MIKHAILOVNA

SARUHASHI, KATSUKO
SCHWARZER, THERESA FLYNN

GEOGRAPHERS

AMARAL, MARIA LUISA GARCIA
BEAUJEU, JACQUELINE MARTHE G.
BINGHAM, MILLICENT
BISHOP, ISABELLA BIRD
BOYD, LOUISE ARNER
CARLSON, LUCILE
CHALUBINSKA, AMIELA
DENNING, DELIA
ECKERT, MARION
GENTHE, MARTHA KRUG
HOL, JACOBA BRIGITTA LOUISA
JOBE, MARY L.
JOHNSON, HILDEGARD BINDE
KACZOROWSKA, ZOFIA
MARTIN, VIVIAN S.
MYERS, SARAH KERR
NORTH, MARIANNE
PFEIFFER, IDA MEYER
SEMPLE, ELLEN CHURCHILL
STIRLING, MARION
STRONG, HELEN M.
WRIGLEY, GLADYS MARY

GEOLOGISTS

ALDRICH, MICHELE L.
ALLARDYCE, CONSTANCE
APPLIN, ESTHER RICHARDS
ATWATER, TANYA
BALK, CHRISTINA LOCHMAN
BASCOM, FLORENCE
BELYEA, HELEN R.
BORG, IRIS Y.
BOYD, ELLA F.
BUCKLAND, MRS. WILLIAM
CASE, ERMINE COWLES
DAVIDSON, ADA D.
DONALD, MARY JANE
DUSEL-BACON, CYNTHIA
EBERS, EDITH HEIRICH

GEOLOGISTS (cont'd)

EDSON, FANNY CARTER
ELLISOR, ALVA CHRISTINE
FISHER, ELIZABETH F.
FOSTER, MARGARET D.
FOWLER-BILLINGS, KATHARINE
GLASS, JEWELL JEANNETTE
GOLD, LORNE W.
HALL, DOLLIE RADLER
HARRIS, ANITA
HILL, DOROTHY
HIRSCHBOECK, KATHERINE
HOLMES, MARY E.
HOMMAIRE DE HELL, MME.
JONAS, ANNA I.
JORDAN, LOUISE
KINGSLEY, LOUISE
KLADVIKO, EILEEN
KLIBURSKY, MARIA VOGL
KLINE, VIRGINIA HARRIET
KNOPF, ELEANORA FRANCES
  BLISS
LEHMANN, INGE
LEOPOLD, ESTELLA BERGERE
LESLEY, SUSAN INCHES
LONGSTAFF, MRS. GEORGE
  BLUNDELL
LUNN, KATHERINE FOWLER
LYELL, MRS.
MARVIN, URSULA BAILEY
MAURY, CARLOTTA JOAQUINA
MORISAWA, MARIE ETHEL
NAGY, ESTHER MARIA KOVACS
O'CONNELL, MARJORIE
OGILVIE, IDA HELEN
OGILVIE-GORDON, MARIA M.
PALMER, DOROTHY K.
PLUMMER, HELEN JEANNE
REYNOLDS, DORIS LIVESEY
SCARPELLINI, CATERINA
SCHWARZER, THERESA FLYNN
SMITH, ISABEL
STADNICHENKO, MARIA
STEWART, GRACE ANN
SULLIVAN, KATHRYN D.
TALBOT, MIGNON

THARP, MARIE
VAN BURKALOW, ANASTASIA
VARSANOFIEVA, VERA
  ALEKSANDROVNA
WALCOTT, HELENE B.
WALWORTH, ELLEN HARDIN
WATSON, JANET VIDA
WELSH, JANE KILLY
WILSON, ALICE E.
WYCKOFF, DOROTHY

GEOPHYSICISTS

ATWATER, TANYA
BLINOVA, EKATERINA NIKITICHNA
BUNCE, ELIZABETH THOMPSON
FISCHER, IRENE KAMINKA
FREDGA, KERSTIN
KEEN, CHARLOTTE ELIZABETH
SAGALYN, RITA
WELKIE, CAROL
ZIMMERMAN, CAROL

GYNECOLOGISTS

AL-MALLAH, SAMIRA
AZARMIE, SOGHRA
BALFOUR, MARGARET IDA
BARNARDINO, CONSUELO
BARRINGER, EMILY DUNNING
CHINNATAMBY, SIVA
CLEOPATRA
DICKENS, HELEN OCTAVIA
FARRAR, LILLIAN K.P.
FRANCOISE
LEOPARDA
MEARS, ELEANOR COWIE LOUDON
MEARS, MARTHA
METRODORA
SUMMERSKILL, EDITH CLARA,
  BARONESS
TARZI, PAKIZE IZZET
TROTULA

HOME ECONOMISTS
See also FOOD SCIENTISTS, NUTRITIONISTS

BAI, BIJUR TARA
BATCHELDER, ESTHER L.
BEVIER, ISABEL
DANIELS, AMY
GREGORY, LOUISA CATHERINE ALLEN
JUSTIN, MARGARET
MARLATT, ABBY LILLIAN
MILLER, ELIZABETH KOCH
ROSE, FLORA
ROSE, MARY DAVIES SWARTZ
STANLEY, LOUISE
TALBOT, MARION
VAN RENSSELAER, MARTHA
YAMAMOTO, MATSUYO

HYDROLOGISTS

WHITMORE, JOAN

ICHTHYOLOGISTS

ACCAME-MURATORI, ROSANNA
CLARK, EUGENIE
EIGENMANN, ROSA SMITH
FISH, MARIE POLAND
LAMONTE, FRANCESCA RAYMOND
MELLEN, IDA
WHITE, EDITH GRACE

IMMUNOLOGISTS

ASKONAS, BRIGITTE ALICE
FLUME, JIMMIE
HERZENBERG, LEONORE
JEZKOVA, ZDENKA
KOSHLAND, MARIAN ELLIOTT
PACHCIARZ, JUDITH ANN
SABIN, FLORENCE RENA
SEEGAL, BEATRICE CARRIER

SORU, D. EUGENIA
TALIAFERRO, LUCY GRAVES
WATKINS, WINIFRED MAY

INDUSTRIAL ENGINEERS

FOLLETT, MARY PARKER
SMITH, CHERYLE C.

INVENTORS

ALDEN, CYNTHIA WESTOVER
ALLISON, EMMA
ASKINS, BARBARA S.
BASSANI, SIGNORA
CHANG, MARGUERITE SHUE-WEN
CLEOPATRA THE ALCHEMIST
COSTON, MARTHA J.
EGLUI, ELLEN
GLEASON, KATE
GREENE, CATHERINE LITTLEFIELD
HARMON, ELISE F.
HOWE, MRS.
HYPATIA
JACQUARD, MADAME
JONES, AMANDA THEODOSIA
KIES, MARY
KNIGHT, MARGARET E.
LAZARENKO, NATALIA IOASAFOVNA
LEFEBRE, MME.
MANNING, MRS. A.H.
MARIA THE JEWESS
MASTERS, SYBILLA
MATHER, SARAH
METCALF, BETSEY
MULLER, GERTRUDE AGNES
OCLO, MAMA
POTTS, MARY FLORENCE
POUPARD, MARY E.
SE-LING-SHE
SHERMAN, PATSY O'CONNELL
WEAVER, MARY OLLIDEN

LIMNOLOGISTS

PATRICK, RUTH

MATHEMATICIANS

ABETE-SCARAFIOTTI, ANNA ROSA
ABROTELIA
AESARA OF LUCANIA
AGANICE
AGNESI, MARIA GAETANA
ALTERMAN, ZIPORA STEPHANIA
ANDERSON, JANET
ANDREIAN, CABIRIA
ANHALT-DESSAU, PRINCESS
ARDINGHELLI, MARIA ANGELA
ARIGNOTE OF SAMOS
ARMFELDT, NATALIA
BACON, CLARA LATIMER
BAILAR, BARBARA ANN
BAILIE, ANN ECKELS
BALCELLS, MARIAM
BALELYMA
BARI, NINA KARLOVNA
BARNUM, CHARLOTTE CYNTHIA
BATES, GRACE ELIZABETH
BAYNARD, ANNE
BENSCHOTEN, ANNA LAVINIA VAN
BLANCHE, MARIE DE COSTE
BORROMEO, CLELIA GRILLO
BREDIHANA, EVGENIJA
  ALEKSANDROVNA
BRYANT, SOPHIE WILLOCK
BUDENBACH, MARY H.
BURGESS, MARY AYRES
BURY, ELIZABETH
BUTLER, MARGARET K.
BYO
CARLSON, ELIZABETH
CAROLINE OF BRANDENBURG
  ANSPACH
CARTWRIGHT, MARY LUCY, DAME
CARUS, MARY HEGELER
CASTELLANI, MARIA
CATHERINE OF ALEXANDRIA,
  SAINT

CHATELET, GABRIELLE-EMILIE DU
CHILONIS
CHRISTINA, QUEEN OF SWEDEN
CHRISTINA OF HESSE
CINQUINI, MARIA DEI CONTI
  CIBRARIO
CLEAECHMA
COBBE, ANNE PHILIPPA
COLE, ISABELLA J.
COMNENA, ANNA
COOK, MARGUERITE
COOPER, ELIZABETH MORGAN
COPELAND, LENNIE PHOEBE
CORNERO, ELLENA LUCRETIA
CULLUM, JANE KEHOE
CUMMINGS, LOUISE DUFFIELD
CUNNINGHAM, SUSAN
DAMO
DANTE, THEODORA
DAVIS, RUTH MARGARET
DI NOVELLA, MARIA
DONAJ, CECILIA KRIEGER
DUBREIL-JACOTIN, MARIE-LOUISE
DU PIERRY, MME.
ECCELLO OF LUCANIA
ECHECRATIA THE PHILIASIAN
EDDY, IMOGEN W.
ELDERTON, ETHEL MARY
ELIZABETH OF BOHEMIA,
  PRINCESS
ELY, ACHSAH M.
EUDOCIA (ATHENAIS)
FABRI, CORNELIA
FIELDS, EWAUGH FINNEY
FISCHER, CHARLOTTE FROESE
FITCH, ANNE LOUISE MACKINNON
FLUGGE-LOTZ, IRMGARD
GEIRINGER, HILDA
GENTRY, RUTH
GERMAIN, SOPHIE
GRIERSON, CONSTANTIA
GRIFFIN, HARRIET MADELINE
GRUBB, GERD
HAMILL, FRANCES
HARDCASTLE, FRANCES
HAYES, ELLEN AMANDA
HAZLETT, OLIVE C.

HELOISE
HENNEL, CORA BARBARA
HESTIAEA
HIGHTOWER, RUBY USHER
HOPPER, GRACE MURRAY
HROSVITHA OF GANDERSHEIM
HUDSON, HILDA PHOEBE
HYPATIA
JANOVSKAJA, SOF'JA
  ALEKSANDROVNA
JOHANSSON, INGEBRIGT
JOHN, DOROTHY B.
KARP, CAROL RUTH
KATSURADA, YOSHI
KELDYSH, LUDMILLA
  VSEROLODOVNA
KENDALL, CLARIBEL
KHUSU, AMILIYA PAVLOVNA
KLUMPKE, DOROTHEA
KOVALEVSKY, SOFIA VASILIYEVNA
KRUPSKAYA, NADEZHDA
LADD-FRANKLIN, CHRISTINE
LALANDE, MARIE LEFRANCAIS DE
LASTHENIA OF ARCADIA
LATYSHEVA, KLAVDIYA
  YAKOLEVNA
LEHR, MARGUERITE
LELONG, JACQUELINE FERRAND
LEPAUTE, HORTENSE
LERNER, EMMA
LEWIS, FLORENCE PARTHENIA
LIBERMANN, PAULETTE
LITVINOVA, ELIZAVETA
  FEDOREVNA
LITZINGER, MARIE
LOGSDON, MAYME IRWIN
LOVELACE, ADA AUGUSTA BYRON,
  LADY
LUCHINS, EDITH HIRSCH
LUTZ, ELIZABETH
MACINTYRE, SHEILA SCOTT
MADDISON, ISABEL
MARCHIONNA-TIBILETTI,
  CESARINA
MARQUET, SIMONE
MARTIN, EMILIE NORTON
MASKEWITZ, BETTY F.

MATTHEWS, ALVA T.
MCDONALD, JANET
MEDAGLIA, DIAMANTE
MELISSA
MERRILL, HELEN ABBOT
MILLER, BESSIE IRVING
MITCHELL, MILDRED
MOLZA, TARQUINIA
MORAWETZ, CATHLEEN SYNGE
MOUFANG, RUTH
MURRAY, DIANE
MYIA
NESTHEADUSA
NEUMANN, BERTHA
NEUMANN, HANNA VON CAEMMERER
NEWSON, MARY WINSTON
NICARETE OF MEGARA
NOETHER, EMMY (AMALIE)
OCELLO OF LUCANIA
PARTHENAY, CATHERINE DE
PASTORI, MARIA
PENDLETON, ELLEN FITZ
PERICTIONE
PETER, ROZSA
PHILTATIS
PHINTYS
PICCARD, SOPHIE
PISCOPIA, ELENA CORNARO
PLESS, VERA STEPEN
POUR-EL, MARIAN BOYKAN
PREDELLA, LIA
PRZEWORSKA-ROLEWICZ, DANUTA
PTOLEMAIS THE CYRENEAN
RASIOWA, HELENE ALINA
REES, MINA SPIEGEL
REINHARDT, ANNA BARBARA
RHODOPE
ROBINSON, JULIA BOWMAN
ROCCATI, CRISTINA
ROSENBLATT, JOAN RAUP
RUSK, EVELYN TERESA CARROLL
SANDERSON, MILDRED LENORA
SANDI, ANA-MARIA
SANFORD, VERA
SARA
SARTRE, MARQUISE DE
SCANLON, JANE CRONIN

MATHEMATICIANS (cont'd)

SCOTT, CHARLOTTE ANGAS
SHAFER, HELEN
SIMONS, LAO GENEVRA
SINCLAIR, MARY EMILY
SMITH, CLARA ELIZA
SOMERVILLE, MARY FAIRFAX
  GREIG
SOPHIE, ELECTRESS OF HANOVER
SOPHIE-CHARLOTTE OF PRUSSIA
SPERRY, PAULINE
STERN, CATHERINE BRIEGER
STOTT, ALICIA BOOLE
SZMIELEW, WANDA
TAUSSKY, OLGA
TERRAS, AUDREY ANNE
THEANO
THEMISTOCLEA
THEODORA
TOLLET, ELIZABETH
TORREY, MARIAN M.
TREVINO, BERTHA
TREVINO, ELVA
TURNER, BIRD MARGARET
TYMICHA THE LACEDAEMONIAN
TYRSENE OF SYBARIS
TYURINA, GALINA NIKOLAEVNA
UHLENBECK, KAREN K.
VILLARCEAU, YVON
VIVIAN, ROXANA HAYWARD
WANG ZHENYI
WATSON, ELLEN
WEISS, MARIE JOHANNA
WEISS, MARY CATHERINE
WELLS, AGNES ERMINA
WELLS, MARY EVELYN
WHEELER, ANNA JOHNSON PELL
WHEELER, MARY FANETT
WIJTHOFF, A. GERTRUIDA
WORTHINGTON, EUPHEMIA
WRINCH, DOROTHY M.
YOUNG, GRACE CHISHOLM
YOUNG, MABEL MINERVA
ZAMES, FRIEDA

MECHANICAL ENGINEERS

CLARK, YVONNE
FITZROY, NANCY DELOYE
GLEASON, KATE
GLENNON, NAN
HOLMES, VERENA
INGELS, MARGARET
PHILLIPS, CAROLYN F.

MEDICAL SCIENTISTS--DENTAL

CHANIN, MARGARET
HOBBS, LUCY B.
PAGELSON, HENRIETTE
SINKFORD, JEANNE C.
TAYLOR, LUCY BEAMAN HOBBS

MEDICAL SCIENTISTS--
  VETERINARY

CRUZ, ZENAIDA G.
CUST, AILEEN
HINSON, LOIS E.
KENNEDY, SUZANNE
MATIKASHVILI, NINA
MELLEN, IDA
MILLER, JANICE MARGARET

MEDICAL WOMEN
  See also *PHYSICIANS, NURSES*

ADELBERGER OF LOMBARDY
ARETHUSA
ASHBY, WINIFRED MAYER
BARROWS, ISABEL C.
BAUCYN, JULIANA
BEAUFORT, MARGARET, COUNTESS
BENHAM, RHODA
BERTHILDIS OF CHELLES, ABBESS
CATHERINE THE SECOND, QUEEN
CATHERINE URSULA OF BADEN
CELLIER, ELIZABETH
CHINCHON, COUNTESS OF

COMBES, FRANCES
CONNOR, JEAN
DASTIDAR, SUJATA D.
DERSCHEID-DELCOURT, MARIE
ELIOT, MARTHA M.
ERDMUTHE, SOPHIE
ESTRIN, THELMA A.
FAUSTINA
FERRAR, AGNES
FLOREY, MARY ETHEL
FOQUET, MARIE, VICOMTESSE
  DE VAUX
FOUQUET, MARIE, VICOMTESSE
FRIEND, CHARLOTTE
FULTON, MARY
GHAFARUNISSA, DR.
GIBBS, ERMA LEONHARDT
GUION, CONNIE
HEDWIG, WILHELMINA, PRINCESS
HUTCHINSON, ANNE
ISABEL
JACKSON, JACQUELYNE JOHNSON
JOAN
JOHNSON, KRISTEN
KAPLAN, JOAN C.
KENDRICK, PEARL
KOCH, MARIE LOUISE
LACEY, ELLA PHILLIPS
LEPINSKY, MELANIE
LINCOLN, EDITH MAAS
MAYOR, HEATHER DONALD
MINTZ, BEATRICE
MUIR, ISABELLA HELEN MARY
OSTERHOUT, MARIAN IRWIN
PADMAVATI, S.
PAVRI, K.M.
PRICE, KATHERINE MILLS
RAHMAN, YUEH ERH (JADY)
RICHARDIS
ROBB, JANE SANDS
ROBERTSON, MURIEL
ROBSCHEIT-ROBBINS, FRIEDA
SETH, NANDINI ANIL
SOPHIA ELIZABETH OF
  BRAUNSCHWEIG
SOPHIA OF MECHLENBURG
TUBMAN, HARRIET ROSS

VAN WAGENEN, GERTRUDE
VAUGHAN, MARTHA
WAUNEKA, ANNIE DODGE
WELD, JULIA TIFFANY
WESTON, ELIZABETH
WIDDOWSON, ELSIE MAY
WYTTENBACH, JEANNE
YALOW, ROSALYN SUSSMAN
YOSHIOKA, YA YOI

METALLURGISTS

HOKE, CALM MORRISON

METEOROLOGISTS

ACKERMAN, BERNICE
ANTHUSA
AUSTIN, PAULINE MORROW
BACON-BERCEY, JUNE
BLINOVA, EKATERINA NIKITICHNA
KACZOROWSKA, ZOFIA
LEMONE, MARGARET ANNE
PARUNGO, FARN
SIMPSON, JOANNE GEROULD
VAN STRATEN, FLORENCE
WANG ZHENYI

MICROBIOLOGISTS
  See also BACTERIOLOGISTS

ALLEN, DORIS TWITCHELL
ALLEN, MARY BELLE
BENHAM, RHODA
BERGQUIST, LOIS MARIE
BITTING, KATHERINE E. GOLDEN
BUNTING, MARY INGRAHAM
COLWELL, RITA R.
DICK, GLADYS ROWENA HENRY
DOWNS, CORNELIA MITCHELL
EDDY, BERNICE ELAINE
ERMOLIEVA, ZINAIDA
  VISSARIONOVNA
EVANS, ALICE CATHERINE

MICROBIOLOGISTS (cont'd)

FENNEL, DOROTHY I.
FRIEND, CHARLOTTE
GABE, DINA RUFINOVNA
GEORG, LUCILLE KATHARINE
GOLINEVICH, ELENA MIKHAILOVNA
GUTTMAN, HELENE AUGUSTA
  NATHAN
HAZEN, ELIZABETH LEE
HESSE, FRAU
HUTCHISON, DORRIS JEANNETTE
JOLY, SEBASTIANA
JONES, RENA TALLEY
KOCH, MARIE LOUISE
KORSHUNOVA, OLGA STEPANOVNA
LAMBIN, SUZANNE
LANCEFIELD, REBECCA CRAIGHILL
MATIKASHVILI, NINA
MCCOY, ELIZABETH
MORELLO, JOSEPHINE A.
OSBORN, MARY JANE
PACHCIARZ, JUDITH ANN
ROBBINS, MARY LOUISE
RUYS, A. CHARLOTTE
SAVULESCU, I. ALICE
SCHMIDT, NATHALIE JOAN
SEIBERT, FLORENCE BARBARA
SMITH, DOROTHY GORDON
STADTMAN, THRESSA CAMPBELL
STEWART, SARAH ELIZABETH
TALIAFERRO, LUCY GRAVES
TAYLOR, MONICA
TILDEN, EVELYN BUTLER
VOLKOVA, ANNA ALEKSANDROVNA
WYCKOFF, DELAPHINE GRACE
  ROSA
ZIEMIECKA, JADWIGA

MICROSCOPISTS

BOOTH, MARY ANN ALLARD
BRUCE, MARY, LADY
YA MEI KIN

MIDWIVES
  See also OBSTETRICIANS

BOURSIER, MADAME
CELLIER, ELIZABETH
COBBE, MARGARET
CRAMER, CATHERINE GERTRUDE
DE CHANTAL, MME.
DE LA MOTTE, MADAME
DUGES, MARIE-JONET
FUSS, MARGARITA
IBERIN, VERONICA
JONES, MARGARET
KALTENBEINER, VICTORINE
KEIL, ELIZABETH MARGARETA
LAVINDER, MARY
MAMMANA, CONSTANTIA
MEURODACIA
PERETTE
PHAENARETE
PHANOSTRATE
SAUER, MARIE ELIZABETH
SHARP, JANE
SIEGEMUNDIN, JUSTINE
  DITTRICHIN
SOTIRA
VON HORENBURG, ANNA
  ELIZABETH
WEINTRAUBIN, BARBARA

MINERALOGISTS

BARLETT, HELEN BLAIR
BORG, IRIS Y.
DU CHATELET, MARTINE DE
  BIRTEREAU
FOSTER, MARGARET D.
KORN, DORIS ELFRIEDE
MACKOWSKY, MARIE THERESE
MARVIN, URSULA BAILEY

MINING ENGINEERS

DU CHATELET, MARTINE DE
  BIRTEREAU

GREENE, EVA HIRDLER
RICKETTS, LOUISE DAVIDSON
STOIBER, LENA ALLEN

NATURAL PHILOSOPHERS

ABROTELIA
ARIGNOTE OF SAMOS
BEHN, APHRA
CAVENDISH, MARGARET, DUCHESS
CHILONIS
DAMO
ECCELLO OF LUCANIA
HIPPO
LEONTIUM
MELISSA
MYIA
OCELLO OF LUCANIA
PHILTATIS
RHODOPE
SARA
THELKA, SAINT
THEMISTO
THEMISTOCLEA
TYMICHA THE LACEDAEMONIAN

NATURAL SCIENTISTS

ANNA SOPHIA OF HESSE
CARPEGNA, COUNTESS, OF ROME
D'ARCONVILLE, GENEVIEVE
    CHARLOTTE
DIANA OF POITIERS
DIOTIMA
PULCHERIA
SAY, LUCY WAY

NATURALISTS

AGASSIZ, ELIZABETH CABOT CARY
ALBIN, MISS
ANTONIA, DUCHESS OF
    WURTEMBURG
COUDREAU, OCTAVIE, MADAME

DIETRICH, (KONKORDIE) AMALIE
    NELLE
DOUBLEDAY, NELTJE B. DE GRAFF
ECKSTORM, FANNIE PEARSON
    HARDY
GRINNELL, ELIZABETH
HAMMER, MARIE SIGNE
HEDWIG, WILHELMINA, PRINCESS
HOLLEY, MARY A.
HUBER, AIMEE
MARTIN, MARIA
MERIAN, DOROTHEA
MERIAN, HELENA
MICHELET, MME. JULES
MILLER, HARRIET MANN
MOELLER, HELENA SIBYLLA
PFEIFFER, IDA MEYER
ROYER, CLEMENCE AUGUSTINE
SARTRE, MARQUISE DE
SHATTUCK, LYDIA WHITE
SLOSSON, ANNIE TRUMBULL
SWIFT, MARY
VON SANDRART, ESTHER BARBARA
WALCOTT, MARY MORRIS VAUX
WALKER, MARY RICHARDSON
WESTON, ELIZABETH
WRIGHT, MABEL OSGOOD

NURSES

AGNES OF JERUSALEM
BAUCYN, JULIANA
BINGHAM, MILLICENT
BLAKE, FLORENCE G.
DELANO, JANE ARMINDA
DE MELUN, MLLE.
DIX, DOROTHEA LYNDE
FABIOLA
FERRAR, AGNES
FLOYD, THEODORA A.
FREEMAN, RUTH BENSEN
FULLER, MARGARET
GOODRICH, ANNIE WARBURTON
GOWAN, SISTER M. OLIVIA
KENNY, ELIZABETH (SISTER
    KENNY)

SHARP, JANE
SIEGEMUNDIN, JUSTINE
  DITTRICHIN
SOTIRA
TROTULA
VON CALISCH, BARONESS
VON HILDEN, MARIE COLINET
VON HORENBURG, ANNA ELIZABETH
VON SIEBOLD, CHARLOTTE
VON SIEBOLD, REGINA JOSEPH
VON ZAY, MARIA VON CALISCH
YARROS, RACHEL

OCEANOGRAPHERS

ALVARINO DE LEIRA, ANGELES
BRADFORD, JANET MARY
BRONGERSMA, MARGARETHA
  SANDERS
BUNCE, ELIZABETH THOMPSON
PATTULLO, JUNE GRACE
ROBINSON, MARGARET KING

OPHTHALMOLOGISTS

BOKOVA-SECHENOVA, MARIA
CARVILL, MAUD
DE FOSCHUA, ULRICHA
LITRICIN, OLGA
LUCIA, SAINT
MARGUERITE OF NAPLES
ODILIA OF HOHENBURG
ORZALESI, NICOLA
RUSIECKA, SALOMEA
SALPE
SHEONYNSTON, ALICE
TURBEVILLE, SARAH
ZERLIN

ORNITHOLOGISTS

BAILEY, FLORENCE AUGUSTA
  MERRIAM
BLACK, HORTENSIA

COMYNS-LEWER, ETHEL
ECKSTORM, FANNIE PEARSON
  HARDY
LEWIS, GRACEANNA
MILLER, HARRIET MANN
NICE, MARGARET MORSE
SHERMAN, ALTHEA ROSINA

PALEONTOLOGISTS

APPLIN, ESTHER RICHARDS
CASE, ERMINE COWLES
EDINGER, TILLY
EDSON, FANNY CARTER
ELLISOR, ALVA CHRISTINE
FRITZ, MADELEINE ALBERTA
GARDNER, JULIA ANNA
GOLDRING, WINIFRED
HALL, DOLLIE RADLER
JORDAN, LOUISE
KABLICK, JOSEPHINE
KEEN, ANGELINA MYRA
KIELAN-JAWOROWSKA, ZOFIA
KLINE, VIRGINIA HARRIET
LAMBORN, HELEN MORNINGSTAR
LEOPOLD, ESTELLA BERGERE
LOEBLICH, HELEN NINA TAPPAN
MAURY, CARLOTTA JOAQUINA
MONTANARO-GALLITELLI,
  EUGENIA
O'CONNELL, MARJORIE
PALMER, DOROTHY K.
PALMER, KATHERINE E.H. VAN
  WINKLE
PLUMMER, HELEN JEANNE
RONCHETTI-ROSSI, CARLA
WEINZEIRL, LAURA LANE

PARISITOLOGISTS

CRAM, ELOISE BLAINE
REES, FLORENCE GWENDOLINE
ROTHSCHILD, MIRIAM LOUIS A.
STINEWALT, MARGARET AMELIA

PATHOLOGISTS
See also *PLANT PATHOLOGISTS*

ANDERSEN, DOROTHY HANSINE
BASS, ELIZABETH
CATANI, GIUSEPPINA
CLAYPOLE, EDITH JANE
CLAYTON, BARBARA
CONE, CLARIBEL
DACK, GAIL
DE WITT, LYDIA MARIA ADAMS
FARQUHAR, MARILYN GIST
FRANTZ, VIRGINIA KNEELAND
GARDNER, HILDA FLOREY
GETZOWA, SOPHIE
HURDON, ELIZABETH
JONES, EVA ELIZABETH
L'ESPERANCE, ELISE DEPEW
    STRANG
LOCATELLI, PIERA
MENDOZA-GUAZON, MARIA PAZ
MILLER, JANICE MARGARET
MOOERS, EMMA WILSON
    DAVIDSON
OPPENHEIMER, ELLA HUTZLER
PEARCE, LOUISE
POTTER, EDITH LOUISE
ROBSCHEIT-ROBBINS, FRIEDA
RUYSCH, RACHEL
RYDSTROM, PAT
SANGER, RUTH ANN
SILBERBERG, RUTH KATZENSTEIN
SLYE, MAUD
VERDER, ADA
WOLLSTEIN, MARTHA
ZAND, NATHALIE
ZECKWER, ISOLDE THERESE

PEDIATRICIANS

ALEXANDER, HATTIE ELIZABETH
ANDERSEN, DOROTHY HANSINE
CALDICOTT, HELEN
DE LANGE, CORNELIA CATHARINA
DOMBROVSKAYA, YULIYA
    FOMINICHNA

GIANNINI, MARGARET JOAN
HARRISON-ROSS, PHYLLIS ANN
HORSTMANN, DOROTHY MILLICENT
HUNTER, GERTRUDE T.
JACOBI, MARY CORINNA PUTNAM
LAVINDER, MARY
LINCOLN, EDITH MAAS
PRIGOSEN, ROSA ELIZABETH
RODRIGUEZ, MARIE LUISA
    SALDUNDE
SHABANOVA, ANNA
SOBEL, EDNA H.
THELANDER, HULDA EVELIN

PETROLOGISTS

BORG, IRIS Y.
DUSEL-BACON, CYNTHIA
JONAS, ANNA I.
KNOPF, ELEANORA FRANCES BLISS

PHARMACISTS
    See also *PHARMACOLOGISTS*

ANNA SOPHIA OF DENMARK,
    PRINCESS
APSLEY, LUCY, LADY
ELEONORA, DUCHESS OF TROPPAU
ELIZABETH, COUNTESS OF KENT
EVERARD, MS.
HEBDEN, KATHERINE
HELLWIG, CHRISTINA REGINA
HUTTON, MRS.
JONES, MARGARET
KENWIX, MARGARET
MARILLAC, LOUISE
    OCTAVIA
PERONELLE
WALKER, ELIZABETH
WECKERIN, ANNA
WOOLEY, ANN

PHARMACOLOGISTS
See also PHARMACISTS

AGAMEDE
AHTEE, LIISA MARJATTA
BLISS, ELEANOR ALBERT
BULBRING, EDITH
ELION, GERTRUDE BELLE
FENSELAU, CATHERINE
GRAHAM, HELEN TREDWAY
GREIG, MARGARET ELIZABETH
HORNING, MARJORIE G.
KAUFMAN, JOYCE J.
KELSEY, FRANCES OLDHAM
LOCKETT, MARY FAURIEL
MALING, HARRIET FLORENCE
  MYLANDER
MARCELLO-MOCENIGO, LOREDANA
PERT, CANDACE
ROLAND, MANON JEANNE PHILIPON
SALUZZIO, MARGUERITE
SFORZA, CATHERINE
VOGT, MARTHE LOUISE
ZAIMIS, ELEANOR CRISTIDES

PHYSICAL CHEMISTS

BENERITO, RUTH ROGAN
BENSTON, MARGARET LOWE
BERKOWITZ, JOAN B.
BLODGETT, KATHARINE BURR
CREMER, ERIKA
DE BROUCKERE, LUCIA
GREER, SANDRA CHARLENE
HARRISON, ANNA JANE
JACOX, MARILYN ESTHER
JOLIOT-CURIE, IRENE
KARLE, ISABELLA LUGOSKI
LEPIN, LYDIA KARLOVNA
POCKELS, AGNES
SIMON, DOROTHY MARTIN
STIEBELING, HAZEL KATHERINE
TELKES, MARIA DE

PHYSICIANS

ABBOTT, MAUDE E.
ABELLA
ABIDH, STELLA
ABOUCHDID, EDNA
ACOSTA-SISON, HONORIA
ADAMS, SARAH E.
ADELLE OF THE SARACENS
ADELMOTA OF CARRARA,
  PRINCESS
ADINE
AELFLEDA, ABBESS
AEMILIA
AGAMEDE
AGNES, COUNTESS OF AIX
AGNES OF BOHEMIA
AGNES OF JERUSALEM
AGNES OF SILESIA
AGNES OF STRASBOURG
AGNODICE
AH MAE WONG
ALBRECHT, ROSEMARIE
ALBRINK, MARGARET JORALEMON
ALCOCK, SARAH
ALI, SAFIEH
AMALOSUNTA
AMBRUS, CLARA MARIA BAYER
AMELINE
AMLA, INDIRA
AMMUNDSEN, ESTHER
ANDERSON, CAROLINE VIRGINIA
ANDERSON, ELIZABETH GARRETT
ANDERSON, EVELYN
ANDRE, VALERIE EDMEE
ANDROMACHE
ANICIA
ANICIA, JULIA
ANN MEDICA OF YORK
ANNA OF BOHEMIA
ANTHONY, BERTHA VAN HOUTEN
ANTIOCHIS OF TARENTUM
ANTIOCHIS OF TLOS
ANTIOCHUS
ANTONIA, MAESTRA
APGAR, VIRGINIA
APSLEY, LUCY, LADY

PHYSICIANS (cont'd)

ARTEMESIA OF CARIA
ASPASIA
ASSTE, MINUCIA
ASYLLIA
AYRTON, MATILDA CHAPLIN
AZARMIE, SOGHRA
BAKER, SARA JOSEPHINE
BAKWIN, RUTH MORRIS
BALFOUR, MARGARET IDA
BARBARA
BARLOW, ANNE LOUISE
BARNARD, MARY
BARNARDINO, CONSUELO
BARRERA, OLIVA SABUCO
BARRINGER, EMILY DUNNING
BAUMGARTNER, LEONA
BEATRICE MEDICA OF CANDIA
BEATRICE OF SAVOY
BEDELL, ELIZABETH
BELOTA
BENDER, LAURETTA
BENNETT, ALICE
BERECUNDA, VALERIA
BERENGARIA OF CASTILE, QUEEN
BERTHAGYTA, ABBESS
BERTILE OF CHELLES
BERTRANDE
BIATRIS
BIRCH, CARROLL LAFLEUR
BISCOT, JEANNE
BLACKWELL, ELIZABETH
BLACKWELL, EMILY
BLAKE, MARY SAFFORD
BLANCHE, MARIE DE COSTE
BLANCHE OF CASTILE, QUEEN
BLOMBAEK, M. WETTER
BOAK, RUTH A.
BODLEY, RACHEL LITTLER
BOIVIN, MARIE ANNE VICTOIRE
BONONI, ESTHER
BOURGEOISE, LOUYSE
BRATKOWSKA-SENIOW, BARBARA
BRELA OF BOHEMIA (700s)
BRELA OF BOHEMIA (1400s)
BRES, MADELEINE

BRIDGET, SAINT, OF SCANDINAVIA
BRIDGET, SAINT, OF IRELAND
BROOMALL, ANNA E.
BROWN, CHARLOTTE
BROWN, ELLEN
BRUCKNER, FRAU DR.
BRUNETTA
BRUNFELS, FRAU
BRYANT, LOUISE STEVENS
BUCCA, DOROTEA
BUONSIGNORE, MADALENA
BURNS, LOUISA
BURY, ELIZABETH
BUTTELINI, MARCHESA
CALDERONE, MARY S.
CALDERONE, NOVELLA
CALDICOTT, HELEN
CALENDA, COSTANZA
CALENDA, LAURA
CALENDA, LAUREA CONSTANTIA
CALL, EMMA L.
CAMBRIERE, CLARICE
CARPEGNA, COUNTESS, OF ROME
CARVAJALES Y CAMINO, LAURA
    M. DE
CARVALHO, DOMITILA DE
CASSANDRA FIDELIS
CATHERINA
CATHERINE MEDICA OF CRACOW
CATHERINE OF BOLOGNA, SAINT
CATHERINE OF GENOA, SAINT
CATHERINE OF SIENA, SAINT
CECELIA OF OXFORD
CESNIECE-FREUDENFELDE, ZELMA
CHAUCER, MRS., DUCHESS OF
    SUFFOLK
CHAWLA, S.
CHELLIER-FUMAT, DOROTHEE
CHILIA, ELVIRA REY
CHINN, MAY E.
CHINNAPPA, LUCIA NARAMANIC V.
CLARA OF ASSISI, SAINT
CLARISSE OF ROTOMAGO
CLARKE, NANCY TALBOT
CLEOBULINA
CLEOPATRA
CLOTHILDE OF BURGANDY

COLE, REBECCA
COMNENA, ANNA
COMNENA, BERTHA
CONVERSE, JEANNE
CORNERO, ELLENA LUCRETIA
CORREIA, ELISA
CORTESE, ISABELLA
CRUTCHFIELD, MITSCH
CUNEGUNDE (Polish)
CUNEGUNDE (German)
DANIEL, ANNIE
DANIELLO, ANTONIA
DE ALMANIA, JACQUELINE FELICIE
DEBORAH OF JUDEA
DE BREAUTE, ELEONORE-NEIL-
  SUZANNE
DE CHAILLY, JEANNE
DE GORZANO, LEONETTA
DE GY, MARIE
DEJERINE-KLUMPKE, AUGUSTA
DE LANGE, CORNELIA
  CATHARINA
DE LEBRIX, FRANCOISE
DEL MUNDO, FE
DE MELUN, MLLE.
DE MONTANEIS, STEPHANIE
DEMUD
DE NOCHERA, MARIA TERESA MORA
DE NOLDE, HELENE ALDEGONDE
DERSCHEID-DELCOURT, MARIE
DE SALINS, GUIGNONNE
DE SEVIGNE, MADAME
DES WOLFFES, FRAULEIN
DE VALOIS, MADAME
DE WITT, LYDIA MARIA ADAMS
DIANA OF POITIERS
DIAZ, ELOIZA
DIBLAN, MAKBULE
DI CANDIA, BEATRICE
DICK, GLADYS ROWENA HENRY
DIMOCK, SUSAN
DOBREANU-ENESCU, VIORICA
DOLLEY, SARAH R. ADAMSON
DOMNINA
DONNE, MARIA DALLE
DRANT, PATRICIA HART
DUROCHER, MARIE JOSEFINA
  MATILDE

EDDY, MARY PIERSON
ELEANOR OF AQUITAINE, QUEEN
ELEANORA, DUCHESS OF MANTUA
ELEONORA, DUCHESS OF TROPPAU
ELIOT, MARTHA M.
ELIZABETH (Czechoslovakian)
ELIZABETH (Polish/Hungarian)
ELIZABETH, COUNTESS OF KENT
ELIZABETH OF ARAGON
ELIZABETH OF BOHEMIA,
  PRINCESS
ELIZABETH OF BRANDENBURG,
  PRINCESS
ELIZABETH OF HUNGARY, SAINT
ELIZABETH OF PORTUGAL, QUEEN
ELIZABETH OF SCHONAU
ELLIS, CONSTANCE
EL SAADAWI, NAWAL
ENG, HU KING
ENGERASIE
ERXLEBEN, DOROTHEA CHRISTIANE
ETHELDRIDA, QUEEN
EUGERASIA
EUPHEMIA OF WHERWELL, ABBESS
ESTRELA, MARIE AUGUSTA
  GENEROSO
FABIOLA
FABRI, CORNELIA
FARRAR, LILLIAN K.P.
FAVILLA
FEARN, ANNE WALTER
FEGAN, CLAUDIA DAVIS
FELICIE, JACOBA
FELICITAS, CLAUDIA
FEODOROWNA, MARIA
FERRERO, GINE LOMBROSO
FERRETTI, ZAFFIRA
FIGNER, VERA
FISHER, ANNE L.
FLORIAN
FOWLER, LYDIA FOLGER
FRANCES OF BRITTANY
FRANCESCA
FRANCOISE
FREI, TERESA
FULTON, MARY
GALINDO, BEATRIX
GHILIETTA

PHYSICIANS (cont'd)

GIANNINI, MARGARET JOAN
GIBLETT, ELOISE ROSALIE
GISELLE
GLASGOW, MAUDE
GLOUCESTER, DUCHESS OF
GOLDSMITH, GRACE ARABELL
GOLOVINA, ANASTASIA
GOULDING, ANNA
GRIERSON, CECILIA
GUARNA, REBECCA DE
GUARNA, SENTIA
GUION, CONNIE
GULLETT, LUCY E.
HAINAULT, COUNTESS OF
HALKETT, ANNE, LADY
HAMILTON, ALICE
HAOYS OF PARIS
HARPER, MARILYN HILL
HARWOOD, FANNY
HASTINGS, ALICIA E.
HATSHEPSUT, QUEEN
HEBDEN, KATHERINE
HEBEL, MEDICIENNE
HEDWIG, QUEEN OF SILESIA
HEIKEL, ROSINA
HEIM-VOGTLIN, MARIE
HELLWIG, CHRISTINA REGINA
HELOISE
HELOYS, DAME, OF PARIS
HENTSCHEL-GUERNTH, DOROTHEA
HEREFORD, COUNTESS
HERSENDE, ABBESS OF
  FONTEVRAULT
HERSENDE OF CHAMPAGNE
HEUREAUX, MERCEDES A.
HILDA OF WHITBY, ABBESS
HILDEGARD OF BINGEN, SAINT
HOBY, LADY
HOLLINSHEAD, ARIEL CAHILL
HROSVITHA OF GANDERSHEIM
HUETER, MME.
HUGONAY, VILMA
HUNT, HARRIOT K.
HURD-MEAD, KATE CAMPBELL
HURDON, ELIZABETH

HUTTON, MRS.
INGLIS, ELSIE
IRENE, QUEEN
ISABEL
ISABELLE
ISABIAU OF PARIS
ISIS
ISLAMBOOLI, MISS
JACKSON, MERCY BISBEE
JACOBI, MARY CORINNA PUTNAM
JACOBINA MEDICA OF BOLOGNA
JACOBINA OF FLORENCE
JACOBS, ALETTA HENRIETTE
JACOBSEN, CLARA
JACOPA
JACOPA OF PASSAU
JEFFERSON, MILDRED FAY
JEHANETTE
JEHANNETTE OF PARIS
JEX-BLAKE, SOPHIA
JOANNA
JOHANNA MEDICA
JOSHEE, ANANDIBAI YUMNA
JOTEYKO, JOSEPHINE
JUS, KAROLINA FRYST
KAHN, IDA
KALAPOTHAKIS, MINNIE
KALTENBEINER, VICTORINE
KASHEVAROVA-RUDNEVA, VARVARA
KELLER, FLORENCE
KELSEY, FRANCES OLDHAM
KIN-YIEN HSU
KLAPPER, MARGARET STRANGE
KLEIMAN, ANNA
KLUMPKE, AUGUSTA
KLUMPKE, DERJINE
KOPROWSKA, IRENE GRASBERG
KORSINI, NATALIA
KOVRIGINA, MARIA DMITRIEVNA
KULEY, MUFIDE
LA CHAPELLE, MARIE LOUISE
  DUGES
LAIS
LARRIEU, MARIE JOSETTE BOUBEE
LAS HUELGAS, ABBESS OF
LEE, REBECCA
LEGEY, LA DOCTORESSE

LEONETTA MEDICA OF TURIN
LEOPARDA
LEPINSKY, MELANIE
L'ESPERANCE, ELISE DEPEW
  STRANG
LEVI-MONTALCINI, RITA
LEWIS, JESSICA HELEN
LIBUSSA OF BOHEMIA
LIUBATOVICH, OLGA
LJOTCHITCH-MILOCHEVITCH,
  DRAGA
LOCUSTA
LOGAN, MYRA ADELE
LOLLINI, CLELIA
LONGSHORE, HANNAH E. MYERS
LOPEZ, RITA LOBATO VELHO
LOSA, ISABELLA
LOUGHLIN, WINIFRED CATHERINE
LOZIER, CLEMENCE SOPHIA
  HARNED
LUCY, ALICE, LADY
LUISI, PAULINA
LULBURENEN, MADAME
LUXOSE, MARY POONEN
MACHA, QUEEN
MACKLIN, MADGE THURLOW
MACMURCHY, HELEN
MACNAMARA, JEAN
MACRINA
MADONNA CATERINA, MEDICA
MAHOUT, COUNTESS OF ARTOIS
MAIA
MALAHLELE, MARY SUSAN
MALTRANERSA, ADELMOTA
MANCE, JEAN
MANCINI, ANNE MARIA
MANICATILDE, ELENA
MARCELLA
MARCET, JANE HALDIMAN
MARGARET OF GERMANY
MARGARET OF THE NETHERLANDS
MARGARET OF YPRES
MARGARET, QUEEN
MARGARET, QUEEN OF SCOTLAND
MARGARETA
MARGARITA
MARGUERITE OF BOURGOGNE,
  QUEEN

MARGUERITE OF NAPLES
MARIA FEODOROWNA, QUEEN
MARIE, DAME, OF PARIS
MASTELLARI, MARIE
MATHILDA OF QUEDLINBURG,
  ABBESS
MATILDA, QUEEN
MATTEO, THOMASIA DE
MAUD, QUEEN
MCGEE, ANITA NEWCOMB
MCKINNON, EMILY H.S.
MECHTHILD OF HACKECDORN
MEDICI, CATHERINE DE
MELITINE
MENDENHALL, DOROTHY REED
MENTUHETEP, QUEEN
METCHNIKOFF, MME.
METRODORA
MEURODACIA
MIGDALSKA, BARBARA CHOJNACKA
MILDMAY, GRACE SHERRINGTON
MILDRED, ABBESS
MINOKA-HILL, LILLIE R.
MINUCIA
MONICA, SAINT
MONTESSORI, MARIA
MONTOYA, MATILDE
MORIZAKI, H.
MOSHER, CLELIA DUEL
MOSHER, ELIZA M.
MUIR, ISABELLA HELEN MARY
NAKA, T.
NAKANISHI, O.
NAYAR, SUSHILA
NEAL, JOSEPHINE BICKNELL
NECKER, SUSANNE NAAZ
NESIBE, GEVHER, PRINCESS
NICERATA, SAINT
NICULESCU, MEDEA P.
NIELSEN, NIELSINE MATHILDE
OBENG, LETITIA
OCTAVIA
OGINO, G.
OKAMI, KAI
OKAMI, KYOKO
OLYMPIA OF ANTIOCH
OLYMPIAS OF THEBES
ORIGENIA

PHYSICIANS (cont'd)

PADMAVATI, S.
PAK, ESTHER KIM
PALMER, ALICE EUGENIA
PANAYOTATOU, ANGELIQUE
PANTHIA
PAPER, ERNESTINE
PARSONS, ELOISE
PAULA
PEARCE, LOUISE
PERAZA, GILDA
PERETTE
PERETTI, ZAFFIRA
PEREZ, ERNESTINA
PERNA
PEROVSKAYA, SOFIA
PEROZO, EVANGELINE RODRIGUEZ
PETRUCCINI, MARIA
PETTRACINI, MARIA
PHANOSTRATE
PHELIPPE
PHILOMELA, SAINT
PICK, RUTH HOLUB
PICOTTE, SUSAN LAFLESCHE
PINERO, DOLORES M.
PLEIKE, ROSSING
PODVYSOTSKAIA, OLGA NIKOLAEVNA
POLYDAMNA
POSSANNER-EHRENTHAL, GABRIELLE
PRESTON, ANN
PRIMILLA (000s-100s)
PRIMILLA (400s-500s)
PRITA, MARIA
PTAH, MERIT
PUCHTLER, HOLDE
PULCHERIA (Roman/Italian)
PULCHERIA (Italian)
PYE, JULIA
QUIMBY, EDITH HINCKLEY
QUINTIUS, JULIA
RADEGONDE
RAMSEY, ELIZABETH MAPELSDEN
RANNEY, HELEN M.
REBECCA VON SALERNO
REDDY, MUTHULAKSHMI
RICE-WRAY, EDRIS

RICHEUT
RITTLE, EDINA
RODRIGUEZ, MARIE LUISA
  SALDUNDE
RODRIGUEZ-DULANTO, LAURA
  ESTHER
ROPER, MARGARET
ROUDNEVA, MME. B.K.
  KACHEVAROVA
ROWLEY, JANET DAVIDSON
RUSIECKA, SALOMEA
RUYS, A. CHARLOTTE
SABIN, FLORENCE RENA
SALOME
SALPE
SALUZZIO, MARGUERITE
SALVAGGIA, NICHOLA
SALVINA
SAMITHRA
SARA
SARAH LA MIRGESSE
SARAH OF SAINT GILLES
SARAH OF WURZBURG
SARRE
SARROCHI, MARGARETA
SARTRE, MARQUISE DE
SATURNIA, JULIA
SAUER, MARIE ELIZABETH
SCHABANOFF, ANNA N.
SCHMIDT, INGEBORG
SCHOLASTICA, SAINT
SCHULZ, KAROLINE
SEDDON, MARGARET RHEA
SEGA, MONA
SELEKEID
SERINA, LAURA CERETA
SHABANOVA, ANNA
SHIH MAI-YU (DR. MARY STONE)
SIGEA, ALOYSIA
SINGER, ELIZABETH
SMITH, JOANNA
SOLIS, MANUELA
SOROR
SOSIS, VENULEIA
SOUSLOVA, NAJEDJA, MME.
SPANGBERG-HOLTH, MARIE
SPETTOWA, STANISAWA MARIA J.

STEELE, LOIS G. FISTER
STEEVENS, MADAME
STEPHENS, JEANNE
STEVENSON, SARAH HACKETT
STEWARD, SUSAN SMITH MCKINNEY
STOICHITA, MICHAELA PAPILIAN
STONE, CONSTANCE
STOWE, EMILY JENNINGS
STOWE-GULLEN, AUGUSTA
STUART, MIRANDA (aka JAMES
  BARRY)
SUBANDRIO, HURUSTIATI
SUBBOTINA, MISS
SUMMERSKILL, EDITH CLARA,
  BARONESS
SUNDQUIST, ALMA
SUSLOVA, NADEZHDA
SUYIN, HAN
SWAIN, CLARA A.
SWARUP, SUSHIELA SHYAM
SYLVAIN, YVONNE
TARZI, PAKIZE IZZET
TAUSSIG, HELEN BROOKE
TAYLOR, LUCY BEAMAN HOBBS
TERENTIA
TERENTIA PRIMA
TERESA DE JESUS, SANTA
TESSA, MONA
TETKA OF BOHEMIA
THELKA, SAINT
THEODOLNDE
THEODOSIA, SAINT
THOMAS, CAROLINE BEDELL
THOMAS, MARY FRAME MYERS
THOMPSON, MARY HARRIS
TIBURTIUS, FRANZISKA
TISHEM, CATHERINE
TOMASZEWICZOWNA, ANNA
TRACY, MARTHA
TRENTACAPILLI, LUISE
TROTULA
UGON, MARIA ARMAND
ULRICH, MABEL
URRACA
VALIAE
VAN HOOSEN, BERTHA
VAN TUSSENBROEK, CATHARINE

VEIJJABU, PIERRA HOON
VENKOVA, TOTA
VICTORIA THE GYNECIA
VICTORIA
VILLA, AMELIA CHOPITEA
VIRDIMURA
VIVAUT, SARRE
VOGT, MME.
VON CALISCH, BARONESS
VON HILDEN, MARIE COLINET
VON LOSER, MARGARET SIBYLLA
VON RODDE, DOROTHEA
VON SCHURMANN, ANNA MARIA
VON SIEBOLD, CHARLOTTE
VON SIEBOLD, REGINA JOSEPH
VON ZAY, MARIA VON CALISCH
WAGNER-FISCHER, ANNE-MARIE
WALKER, MARY EDWARDS
WALPURGA, SAINT
WALTHAM, MARGARET
WARNER, ESTELLA FORD
WARWICK, LADY
WEINTRAUBIN, BARBARA
WELSH, LILLIAN
WIDERSTROM, KAROLINA
WILLIAMS, ANNA WESSELS
WILLIAMS, CICELY
WILLOUGHBY, LADY
WILSON, LOIS
WOOLEY, ANN
WRIGHT, JANE C.
WYTTENBACH, JEANNE
XANITA
YA MEI KIN
YANG, MARION
YOSHIOKA, YA YOI
YSABEL
YSABIAU
ZAKRZEWSKA, MARIE ELIZABETH
ZALESKA, KATHERINA
ZENIAS, SAINT
ZERLIN
ZIPPORAH
ZOK KYONS CHANG

PHYSICISTS
See also ASTROPHYSICISTS,
BIOPHYSICISTS, GEOPHYSICISTS

AJZENBERG-SELOVE, FAY
ALLIN, ELIZABETH J.
ALSTON-GARNJOST, MARGARET
ANCKER-JOHNSON, BETSY
ANDERSON, ELDA EMMA
ANSLOW, GLADYS AMELIA
ARDINGHELLI, MARIA ANGELA
ARETE OF CYRENE
AYRTON, (SARAH) HERTHA MARKS
BALCELLS, MARIAM
BARANGER, ELIZABETH UREY
BARNOTHY, MADELINE FORRO
BARTON, VOLA PRICE
BASSI, LAURE MARIA CATARINA
BAYNARD, ANNE
BLANCHE, MARIE DE COSTE
BLEWETT, MYRTLE HILDRED
BLODGETT, KATHARINE BURR
BONNER, JILL CHRISTINE
BORROMEO, CLELIA GRILLO
BRANT, LAURA
BROOKS, HARRIET
BURNS, ELEANOR
BUSSEY, JOANNA
BYERS, NINA
CAROLINE OF BRANDENBERG
ANSPACH
CARTER, EDNA
CARTER, ELIZABETH
CHATELET, GABRIELLE-EMILIE DU
CLARK, BERTHA
CLEOPATRA THE ALCHEMIST
CONWELL, ESTHER MARLEY
CURIE, MARIE SKLODOWSKA
DAVIS, GRACE
DEWEY, JANE
DONNE, MARIA DALLE
DRESSELHAUS, MILDRED S.
REIF
DU SAULT, LUCILLE ANNE
EVANS, MARJORIE WOODARD
FELDMAN, JACQUELINE
FISCHER-HJALMARS, INGA
MARGRETE

FOOT, EUNICE
FRANZ, JUDITH ROSENBAUM
FREHAFER, MABEL
GAILLARD, MARY K.
GATES, FANNY COOK
GERMAIN, SOPHIE
GILROY, HELEN
GIURGEA, MARGARETA
ALEXANDRU V.
GOKSU-OGELMAN, YETER
GOLD, LORNE W.
GOLDHABER, GERTRUDE SCHARFF
GOLDHABER, SULAMITH
GRIFFITHS, MARY
GUERNSEY, JANET BROWN
GUTHRIE, JANET
HANSEN, LUISA FERNANDEZ
HAYNER, LUCY
HAYS, MARGARET
HAYWARD, EVANS VAUGHAN
HENIN, FRANCOISE GABRIELLE
HERFORTH, LIESELOTT
HERZENBERG, CAROLINE S.
LITTLEJOHN
HOWARD-LOCK, HELEN ELAINE
HSIEH, HILDA
HUFF, MRS. WILLIAM BASHFORD
HYPATIA
JACKSON, DAPHNE F.
JACKSON, DEBORAH JEAN
JACKSON, SHIRLEY ANN
JEZOWSKA-TRZEBIATOWSKA,
BOGUSLAWA
JOHNSON, DOROTHY DURFEE
MONTGOMERY
JOHNSON, KATHERINE
JOHNSON, KRISTEN
JOLIOT-CURIE, IRENE
JOSLIN, LULU
KARLIK, BERTA
KEESOM, MISS
KEITH, MARCIA
KELLER, EVELYN FOX
KISTIAKOWSKY, VERA
KLADIVKO, EILEEN
KOCHINA, PELAGEYA YAKOVLEVNA
KOLLER, NOEMIE BENCZER
KOLTAY, BORBALA GYARMATI

KRYNICKA-DROZDOWICZ, EWA
LAIRD, ELIZABETH REBECCA
LANGFORD, GRACE
LEPAUTE, HORTENSE
LIBBY, LEONA WOODS MARSHALL
LONSDALE, KATHLEEN YARDLEY
LOWATER, FRANCES
MACLIN, ARLENE
MAGNAC-VALETTE, DENYSE
  JULIETTE
MALTBY, MARGARET ELIZA
MAYER, MARIA GOEPPERT
MCDOWELL, LOUISE
MEITNER, LISE
MEYER-SCHUTZMEISTER, LUISE
MIELCZAREK, EUGENIE V.
MILLER, IRENE
NORWOOD, VIRGINIA
NOYES, MARY C.
O'BRIEN, RUTH
O'FALLON, NANCY MCCUMBER
PEREY, MARGUERITE
PHILLIPS, MELBA NEWELL
PKIKHOT'KO, ANTONINA
  FYODOROVNA
POCKELS, AGNES
RAND, MARIE GERTRUDE
RAUSCHER, ELIZABETH ANN
REAMES, ELEANOR
RIDE, SALLY K.
ROCCATI, CRISTINA
ROOKS, JUNE M.
ROSANOFF, LILLIAN
ROSS, MARION AMELIA SPENCE
ROTH, LAURA MAURER
ROYER, CLEMENCE AUGUSTINE
SAGALYN, RITA
SARACHIK, MYRIAM PAULA
SENGERS, JOHANNA M.H. LEVELT
SHIELDS, MARGARET
SHOAF, MARY LA SALLE
SHOHNO, NAOMI
SHRAUNER, BARBARA ABRAHAM
SIEBERT, KATHARINE BURR
SITTERLY, CHARLOTTE E. MOORE
SLATER, ROSE C.L. MOONEY
SMITH, ELSKE VAN PANHUYS

SOMERVILLE, MARY FAIRFAX
  GREIG
SPONER, HERTHA
STEARNS, MARY BETH GORMAN
STEWART, MAUDE
STONE, ISABELLE
SURKO, PAMELA TONI
THEANO
THOMAS, EVA MARIA B.
TONNELAT, MARIE ANTOINETTE
  BAUDOT
TRAPEZNIKOVA, OLGA
TURI, ZSUZSA F.
UHLENBECK, KAREN K.
WARGA, MARY ELIZABETH
WAY, KATHARINE
WHITING, SARAH FRANCES
WICK, FRANCES GERTRUDE
WIDGOFF, MILDRED
WIEBUSCH, AGNES TOWNSEND
WILSDORF, DORIS KUHLMAN
WILSON, LUCY
WINOGRADZKI, JUDITH
WOZNICKA, URSZULA
WRINCH, DOROTHY M.
WU, CHIEN SHIUNG
XIE XI-DE
YALOW, ROSALYN SUSSMAN
YUASA, TOSHIKO
ZORUBIN, R., MISS

PHYSIOLOGISTS

ALBE, DENISE
BAETJER, ANNA MEDORA
BAZANOVA, NAYLYA URAZGULOVNA
BEAUVALLET, MARCELLE JEANNE
BEKHTEREVA, NATALYA
  PETROVANA
BEZNAK, MARGARET
BOTELHO, STELLA YATES
BROOKS, MATILDA MOLDENHAUER
CAHOON, MARY ODILE, SISTER
CARSTEN, MARY E.
CHING, TE MAY TSOU
CLARK, JANET HOWELL

PHYSIOLOGISTS (cont'd)

CLARKE, NANCY TALBOT
COBB, JEWEL PLUMMER
CULLIS, WINIFRED CLARA
DAVIS, AUDREY KENNON
ECKERSON, SOPHIA H.
FARR, WANDA KIRKBRIDE
FELL, HONOR BRIDGET, DAME
FITZGERALD, MABEL PUREFOY
FRINGS, MABLE RUTH SMITH
GANTT, ELISABETH
GOCHOLASHVILI, MARIYA
  MIKIEVNA
GRANDJEAN, ETTIENNE P.
GREISHEIMER, ESTHER MAUD
GUTTMAN, RITA
HARTT, CONSTANCE ENDICOTT
HAYNES, LINDEN C. SMITH
HINRICHS, MARIE AGNES
HOUTZ, SARA JANE
HYDE, IDA HENRIETTA
JACKSON, MARGARET
JACOBSEN, CLARA
JOO, P. KIM
JORGENSEN-KROGH, MARIE
LEACH, CAROLYN
LE BRETON, ELAINE
LEWIS, LENA ARMSTRONG
LEWIS, MARGARET REED
LINDAHL-KIESSLING, KERSTIN
LONG, RUBY PAULINE KING
MCWHINNIE, MARY ALICE
MEDVEDEVA, NINA BORISOVNA
MINOT, ANN STONE
PANTELEEVA, SERAFIMA
PATTERSON, FLORA WAMBAUGH
PETROVA, MARIA KONSTANTINOVNA
PICKFORD, LILLIAN MARY
POOL, JUDITH GRAHAM
PORTER, HELEN KEMP
PRICHARD, MARJORIE MABEL LUCY
QUIROGA, MARGARITA DELGADO D.
ROLF, IDA
ROMIEU, MARIE
ROSOFF, BETTY
SCHMIDT-NIELSEN, BODIL MIMI

SCHWARTZ, NEENA BETTY
SHTERN, LINA SOLOMONOVNA
SMITH, CHARLOTTE R.
VARGA, MAGDOLNA
VEIL, CATHERINE
VOGT, MARTHE LOUISE
WELSH, LILLIAN
WHITE, FRANCES EMILY
ZUCKER, MARJORIE BASS

PLANT PATHOLOGISTS

ALLEN, RUTH FLORENCE
BROWN, NELLIE
BRYAN, MARY
ELLIOTT, CHARLOTTE
HART, HELEN
HASSE, CLARA
MOREAU, MIREILLE
NEWTON, MARGARET
QUIRK, AGNES
RICHARDS, C. AUDREY
SAVULESCU, I. ALICE
SMITH, ELIZABETH H.
SPALDING, EFFIE SOUTHWORTH
WATKINS, DELLA
WESTCOTT, CYNTHIA

PSYCHIATRISTS

BART, PAULINE
BENDER, LAURETTA
BIBRING, GRETE LEHNER
DE GROOT, JEANNE LAMPL
DUNBAR, (HELEN) FLANDERS
EL SAADAWI, NAWAL
FOX, RUTH
HARRISON-ROSS, PHYLLIS ANN
HORNEY, KAREN DANIELSSEN
JOSSELYN, IRENE MILLIKEN
MACALPINE, IDA
MONTESSORI, MARIA
PAVENSTEDT, ELEANOR
RICHARDS, ESTHER
SMITH, KATHLEEN

PSYCHOANALYSTS

ANDREAS-SALOME, LOU
BONAPARTE, MARIE
DEUTSCH, HELENE
FREUD, ANNA
HINKLE, BEATRICE
HORNEY, KAREN DANIELSSEN
KLEIN, MELANIE REIZES
MCLEAN, HELEN VINCENT

PSYCHOLOGISTS

ADAMS, GRACE
ADKINS, DOROTHY CHRISTINA
ALPER, THELMA G.
AMES, LOUISE BATES
ANDERSON, ROSE GUSTAVA
ARNOLD, MAGDA BLONDIAN
BABCOCK, HARRIET
BARRERA, OLIVA SABUCO
BAUMGARTEN-TRAMER, FRANZISKA
BAYLEY, NANCY
BEASELY, JULIE
BECKER, LYDIA E.
BIRJANDI, PARVIN
BOURDEL, LEONE
BREGMAN, ELSIE O.
BRODY, SYLVIA
BRONNER, AUGUSTA FOX
BROSSEAU, KATE
BULL, NINA
BUVINIC, MAYRA
CALKINS, MARY WHITON
CASE, MARY S.
CASTLE, CORA SUTTON
CIMINI, MARIA DOLORES
COBB, MARGARET
COLLINS, MARY
COX, RACHEL DUNAWAY
DANIELS, AMY
DEUTSCH, HELENE
DOUVIN, ELIZABETH
DOWNEY, JUNE ETTA
DUFFY, ELIZABETH
EDWARDS, MARIE

FERNALD, GRACE
FERNALD, MABEL
FERRERO, GINE LOMBROSO
FESHBACH, NORMA DEITCH
FIELD, JOANNA
FOLLETT, MARY PARKER
FRANKENHAEUSER, MARIANN VON W.
FRENKEL-BRUNSWIK, ELSE
FREUD, ANNA
FROMM, ERIKA
GAMBLE, ELEANOR A.M.
GIBSON, ELEANOR JACK
GILBRETH, LILLIAN EVELYN
    MOLLER
GLEASON, JOSEPHINE
GOODENOUGH, FLORENCE LAURA
GRAHAM, FRANCES KEELER
GUILD, ELIZABETH (BETSY)
HAMLIN, ALICE
HEIDBREDER, EDNA
HILDRETH, GERTRUDE
HOLLINGWORTH, LETA ANNA
    STETTER
HORACKOVA, EVA HEYROVSKA
HORNER, MATINA
HOWARD, RUTH
HOWES, ETHEL D. PUFFER
ILG, FRANCES
ISAACA, SUSAN
JAMESON, DOROTHEA
JOHNSON, VIRGINIA ESHELMAN
JONES, MARY COVER
KENT, GRACE
LADD-FRANKLIN, CHRISTINE
LEVY, JERRE MARIE
MALLORY, EDITH BRANDT
MANOOCHEHRIAN, MEHRANGUIZ
MARTIN, LILLIEN JANE
MCHALE, KATHRYN
MEEK, LOIS HAYDEN
MILES, CATHARINE COX
MILNER, BRENDA
MUELLER, KATE HEUVNER
MURPHY, LOIS BARCLAY
NEWTON, NILES RUMELY
NICE, MARGARET MORSE
NORSWORTHY, NAOMI

PSYCHOLOGISTS (cont'd)

PARKE, MARY
PEAK, HELEN
PFAFFLIN, SHEILA
PRESSEY, LUELLA COLE
RAND, MARIE GERTRUDE
RHINE, LOUISA ELLA
ROE, ANN
ROLAND, MANON JEANNE PHILIPON
RUBINSTEIN, SUSANNE
RUSSELL, OLIVE RUTH
RUSSO, NANCY FELIPE
SANDLER, BERNICE
SHINN, MILICENT WASHBURN
SPRAGUE, LUCY
STENDLER, CELIA BURNS
TAPP, JUNE L.
TERESA DE JESUS, SANTA
WASHBURN, MARGARET FLOY
WEISSTEIN, NAOMI
WEMBRIDGE, ELEANOR ROWLAND
WOLF, KATHERINE
WOOLLEY, HELEN BRADFORD
   THOMPSON
ZACHRY, CAROLINE BEAUMONT

SCHOLARS/SCIENTISTS (General)

AESARA OF LUCANIA
AMPHICIA
ANDREAS-SALOME, LOU
ANTHUSA
ARDINGHELLI, MARIA ANGELA
ARETE OF CYRENE
ARDITI, MICHELE
ARETHUSA
ARGIA
ARIA
ARRIA
ARTEMISIA
ARTEMISIA OF CARIA
ASCLEPIGENIA
ASPASIA OF MILETUS
ASTELL, MARY
ATRIA

AXIOTHEA
BAJEV, ALEXANDRA
BALELYMA
BARRERA, OLIVA SABUCO
BASSI, LAURE MARIA CATARINA
BEATRICE MEDICA OF CANDIA
BEAUFORT, MARGARET, COUNTESS
BECTOZ, CLAUDE DE
BERGQUIST, PATRICIA ROSE
BERONICE
BERTILE OF CHELLES
BORROMEO, CLELIA GRILLO
BUCCA, DOROTEA
BYO
CAERELLIA
CAROLINE OF BRANDENBURG
   ANSPACH
CARTER, ELIZABETH
CASSANDRA FIDELIS
CATHERINE OF ALEXANDRIA, SAINT
CATHERINE URSULA OF BADEN
CEAUSESCU, ELENA
CHRISTINA, QUEEN OF SWEDEN
CHRISTINA OF HESSE
CLEA
CLEAECHMA
CLEMENT, MARGARET
CLEOBULINA
CLIFFORD, ANN, LADY
COMNENA, ANNA
CORNERO, ELLENA LUCRETIA
CRANWELL, LUCY M.
CRUZ, JUANA INEZ DE LA
CURTIS, KATHLEEN M.
DE CASTRA, ANNA
DIOTIMA
DOMNA, JULIA
DUPRE, MARIAE
ECHECRATIA THE PHILASIAN
ELEANOR OF AQUITAINE, QUEEN
ELIZABETH OF BOHEMIA,
   PRINCESS
ERDMUTHE, SOPHIE
ERXLEBEN, DOROTHEA CHRISTIANE
EUDOCIA
EUDOCIA (ATHENAIS)
EURYDICE

EURYDICE OF ILLYRIUM
FANNIA
FAUSTINA
FELICITAS, CLAUDIA
GALINDO, BEATRIX
GARRETT, SUE ANDERSON
GEMINAE (MOTHER)
GEMINAE (DAUGHTER)
GOLDMAN, RACHEL
GOULD, ALICE BACHE
GREY, JANE, LADY
GRIEkSON, CONSTANTIA
HALKETT, ANNE, LADY
HARCOURT, HARRIET EUSEBIA
HARDY, MIRIAM PAULS
HASKOVA, VERA
HATSHEPSUT, QUEEN
HELMHOLTZ, ANNA
HELOISE
HELPES
HERRADE OF LANDSBERG
HESTIAEA
HILDEGARD OF BINGEN, SAINT
HIPPARCHIA OF MARONEIA
HODGSON, ELIZA AMY
HOLMAN, MOLLIE ELIZABETH
HROSVITHA OF GANDERSHEIM
HUXLEY, HENRIETTA HEATHORN
HYSPECKA, LUDMILA
KEDAR, JASSA
KEDEN, ORA
KOBILKOVA, JITKA
LASTHENIA OF ARCADIA
LEFEVRE, ANNE
LEONTIUM
LOUISE OF SAVOY
MAGNILLA
MAHOUT, COUNTESS OF ARTOIS
MANOOCHEHRIAN, MEHRANGUIZ
MCCORMICK, KATHERINE DEXTER
MENTUHETEP, QUEEN
MILDMAY, GRACE SHERRINGTON
MOLZA, TARQUINIA
MONICA, SAINT
MOORE, LUCY BEATRICE
MORIZAKI, H.
MYRO

NESTHEADUSA
NICARETE OF MEGARA
NOBLES, MILDRED K.
ONDRACKOVA, JANA
PAMPHYLA OF EPIDAURUS
PANTACLEA
PANYPERSEBASTA
PARTHENAY, CATHERINE DE
PENROSE, EDITH TILTON
PERICTIONE
PHAENARETE
PHINTYS
PISAN, CHRISTINE DE
PISCOPIA, ELENA CORNARO
PORCIA
PTOLEMAIS THE CYRENEAN
PUTNAM, MARY LOUISE DUNCAN
RAABE, MARIE
RASKOVA, HELENA
ROBINSON, MARION FRANCES
ROPER, MARGARET
ROSENTHAL, SINAIDA
SCHOBER, RITA
SERINA, LAURA CERETA
SIGEA, ALOYSIA
SKALKOVA-PROCHAZKOVA, JARMILA
SOPHIA ELIZABETH OF
  BRAUNSCHWEIG
SOPHIE, ELECTRESS OF HANOVER
SOPHIE-CHARLOTTE OF PRUSSIA
SORMOVA, ZORA
SOSIPATRA
STOWELL, LOUISA REED
STROZZI, LORENZA
SUYIN, HAN
THEANO
THEMISTO
THEODORA
THEOGNIDA
THEOPHILA
TISHEM, CATHERINE
TOLLET, ELIZABETH
TYRSENE OF SYBARIS
VON LOSER, MARGARET SIBYLLA
VON RODDE, DOROTHEA
VON SCHURMANN, ANNA MARIA
WEEKS, DOROTHY

SCHOLARS/SCIENTISTS (General)
(cont'd)

ZAMIR, AVA
ZENOBIA, QUEEN

SCIENCE AUTHORS

AESARA OF LUCANIA
ASPASIA
ASTELL, MARY
BEHN, APHRA
BOIVIN, MARIE ANNE VICTOIRE
BRYAN, MARGARET
CAERELLIA
CAVENDISH, MARGARET, DUCHESS
CLEOBULINA
CRUZ, JUANA INEZ DE LA
CUNITZ, MARIA
DE LA MARCHE, MARGUERITE
    DU TERTRE
DUMEE, JEANNE
DU PIERRY, MME.
EDGEWORTH, MARIA
ELIZABETH, COUNTESS OF
    KENT
FOQUET, MARIE, VICOMTESSE
    DE VAUX
FULHAME, ELIZABETH
FULLER, MARGARET
HALKETT, ANNE, LADY
HELPES
HENTSCHEL-GUERNTH, DOROTHEA
HERRADE OF LANDSBERG
HERZENBERG, CAROLINE S.
    LITTLEJOHN
HIPPARCHIA OF MARONEIA
HURSTON, ZORA NEALE
IBERIN, VERONICA
KEIL, ELIZABETH MARGARETA
KIRCH, MARIA MARGERITE
    WINCKELMANN
MARCET, JANE HALDIMAN
MARIA THE JEWESS
MEARS, MARTHA
MEDAGLIA, DIAMANTE

METRODORA
NECKER, ANNE GERMAINE
PAMPHYLA OF EPIDAURUS
PARTHENAY, CATHERINE DE
PERICTIONE
PHINTYS
PISAN, CHRISTINE DE
POTTER, BEATRIX
REBECCA VON SALERNO
RICHARDIS
RUBINSTEIN, SUSANNE
SHARP, JANE
SIGEA, ALOYSIA
STRACHEY, RAY
TAYLOR, JANET
THEOSEBEIA
VON HORENBURG, ANNA ELIZABETH
WEINTRAUBIN, BARBARA

SCIENCE EDUCATORS

ABELLA
ANGIOLINA OF PADUA
ARETE OF CYRENE
ASCLEPIGENIA
ASTELL, MARY
BARNARDINO, CONSUELO
BARROWS, ISABEL C.
BASS, ELIZABETH
BERTHAGYTA, ABBESS
BEVIER, ISABEL
BILLIG, FLORENCE GRACE
BIRJANDI, PARVIN
BLAKE, FLORENCE G.
BLUNT, KATHARINE
BRYAN, MARGARET
BUCCA, DOROTEA
BUNTING, MARY INGRAHAM
BURGESS, MARY AYRES
CAERELLIA
CALDERONE, MARY S.
CALDICOTT, HELEN
CALENDA, COSTANZA
CALENDA, LAURA
CALENDA, LAUREA CONSTANTIA
CARR, EMMA PERRY

CATHERINE THE SECOND, QUEEN
CLARK, BERTHA
CLAYTON, BARBARA
CLEOPATRA
COBB, JEWEL PLUMMER
DANIELLO, ANTONIA
DANTE, THEODORA
DE LA MARCHE, MARGUERITE DU
  TERTRE
DE LA MOTTE, MADAME
DI NOVELLA, MARIA
DIOTIMA
DOMNA, JULIA
DU COUDRAY, ANGELIQUE
  MARGUERITE
DU COUDRAY, LOUISE LEBOURSIER
EDGEWORTH, MARIA
ETHELDRIDA, QUEEN
FEODOROWNA, MARIA
FIELDS, EWAUGH FINNEY
FOQUET, MARIE, VICOMTESSE
FRANTZ, VIRGINIA KNEELAND
FULTON, MARY
GILCHRIST, MAUDE
GOKDOGEN, NUZHET
GOODRICH, ANNIE WARBURTON
GRIERSON, CECILIA
GRIFFIN, HARRIET MADELINE
GUARNA, REBECCA DE
GUARNA, SENTIA
GUION, CONNIE
HAMILTON, ALICE
HERRADE OF LANDSBERG
HERZENBERG, CAROLINE S.
  LITTLEJOHN
HILDA OF WHITBY, ABBESS
HUNSCHER, HELEN ALVINA
ISIS
JACARUSO, KAREN M.
JOBE, MARY L.
KALTENBEINER, VICTORINE
KLUCKHOHN, FLORENCE ROCKWOOD
LACEY, ELLA PHILLIPS
LYON, MARY
MACK, PAULINE BEERY
MADDISON, ISABEL
MARIA FEODOROWNA, QUEEN

MARIA THE JEWESS
MARLATT, ABBY LILLIAN
MEDAGLIA, DIAMANTE
MERCURIADA
MONTESSORI, MARIA
MOSHER, ELIZA M.
MURRAY, ROSEMARY
NUTTING, MARY ADELAIDE
PERETTI, ZAFFIRA
PETTRACINI, MARIA
PHELPS, ALMIRA HART LINCOLN
POLYDAMNA
REBECCA VON SALERNO
ROBERTS, LYDIA JANE
ROCCATI, CRISTINA
ROGERS, MARTHA ELIZABETH
RUYS, A. CHARLOTTE
SANDLER, BERNICE
SARAH OF SAINT GILLES
SERINA, LAURA CERETA
SHERRILL, MARY LURA
SIEGEMUNDIN, JUSTINE DITTRICHIN
SINKFORD, JEANNE C.
STERN, CATHERINE BRIEGER
STEWART, MAUDE
SWIFT, MARY
TALBOT, MARION
TALLIEN, MADAME
THILLAYAMPALAM, EVANGELINE
VAN HOOSEN, BERTHA
VAN WAGENEN, GERTRUDE
WALPURGA, SAINT
WHITING, SARAH FRANCES
YARROS, RACHEL
YOSHIOKA, YA YOI

SCIENCE HISTORIANS

ALDRICH, MICHELE L.
HALL, MARIA BOAS
HURD-MEAD, KATE CAMPBELL
METZGER, HELENE
NICHOLSON, MARJORIE HOPE
ROSSITER, MARGARET
SANFORD, VERA
SIMONS, LAO GENEVRA
UNZER, JOHANNA CHARLOTTE

SEISMOLOGISTS

LEHMANN, INGE
ROZOVA, EVDOKIA ALEKSANDROVNA

SOCIAL SCIENTISTS

ALLARD, ELIZABETH MAAJ
COBBE, FRANCES POWER
MARTINEAU, HARRIET
MYRDAL, ALVA REINER
NELKIN, DOROTHY
ROSSI, ALICE
TAEUBER, IRENE BARNES
THOMAS, DOROTHY SWAINE

SOCIOLOGISTS

BART, PAULINE
CHIANG KAI-SHEK, MADAME
ECKSTEIN-DIENER, BERTHA
EPSTEIN, CYNTHIA FUCHS
GILMAN, CHARLOTTE PERKINS
GLUECK, ELEANOR TOUROFF
HAGOOD, MARGARET LOYD JARMAN
HOLTER, HARRIETT
HUBBARD, RUTH
JACKSON, JACQUELYNE JOHNSON
KANTER, ROSABETH MOSS
KAPUR, PROMILA
KELLER, SUZANNE
KLOSKOWSKA, ANTONINA
KOMAROVSKY, MIRRA
LEE, ROSE HUM
MARRETT, CORA BAGLEY
MARTINEAU, HARRIET
MCAFEE, MILDRED
MERNISSI, FATIMA
MYERS, SARAH KERR
NECKER, ANNE GERMAINE
NELKIN, DOROTHY
PARSONS, ELSIE WORTHINGTON
   CLEWS
ROSE, HILARY
STRESHINSKY, NAOMI GOTTLIEB

TAEUBER, IRENE BARNES
THOMAS, DOROTHY SWAINE
WEBB, MARTHA BEATRICE POTTER
ZUCKERMAN, HARRIET

SPECTROSCOPISTS

CAUCHOIS, YVETTE
COWLEY, ANNE PYNE
DEWEY, JANE

STATISTICIANS

BAILAR, BARBARA ANN
BRYANT, LOUISE STEVENS
BRYANT, SOPHIE WILLOCK
BURGESS, MARY AYRES
CADE, RUTH ANN
CASTLE, CORA SUTTON
CELLIER, ELIZABETH
CLAGHORN, KATE HOLLODAY
COOK, MARGUERITE
COX, GERTRUDE MARY
ELDERTON, ETHEL MARY
GEIRINGER, HILDA
HAGOOD, MARGARET LOYD JARMAN
MARQUET, SIMONE
MERRELL, MARGARET
NIGHTINGALE, FLORENCE
NORWOOD, JANET
PENA, DEAGELIA M.
ROSENBLATT, JOAN RAUP
SALUTER, ARLENE
SCARPELLINI, CATERINA
SILVERMAN, HILDA FREEMAN
WHITNEY, JESSAMINE
WICKENS, ARYNESS JOY

STRATIGRAPHERS

BASCOM, FLORENCE

SURGEONS

AELFLEDA, ABBESS
ALCOCK, SARAH
ANDRE, VALERIE EDMEE
BALL, LOUISE CHARLOTTE
BARRINGER, EMILY DUNNING
BARROWS, ISABEL C.
BOURGEOISE, LOUYSE
BOWLES, CATHERINE
BRES, MADELEINE
CECELIA OF OXFORD
CUST, AILEEN
D'AUXERRE, JEANNE
DE ROMANA, FRANCOISE
DER WOLFF, FRAULEIN
DES WOLFFES, FRAULEIN
DICKENS, HELEN OCTAVIA
DIMOCK, SUSAN
DONNE, MARIA DALLE
DU LUYS, GUILLEMETTE
FABIOLA
FABRICIUS, MARIE
FARRAR, LILLIAN K.P.
FEARN, ANNE WALTER
FELICITAS, CLAUDIA
FRANCOISE
GERTRUDE
GUILLAMETTE DE LUYS
GUION, CONNIE
HALKETT, ANNE, LADY
HARWOOD, FANNY
HEBDEN, KATHERINE
HILDA OF WHITBY, ABBESS
HOBBS, LUCY B.
HOBY, LADY
HOLDER, MRS.
INCARNATA, MARIA
ISIAE, TOMASIA DE MATTEO DE
  CASTRO
KNOCK, FRANCES ENGELMANN
LA CHOPILLARDE, MARGUERITE
LOGAN, MYRA ADELE
LUXOSE, MARY POONEN
MARGARETA
MARILLAC, LOUISE
MARTHA, SISTER

MATTEO, THOMASIA DE
MCGEE, ANITA NEWCOMB
MERCURIADA
PACHAUDE, DAME LEONARD
RAMOS, SYLVIA M.
READ, LADY
ROUDNEVA, MME. B.K. KACHEVAROVA
RUSIECKA, SALOMEA
SAUER, MARIE ELIZABETH
SHAIBANY, HOMA
STEWARD, SUSAN SMITH MCKINNEY
STUART, MIRANDA (aka JAMES
  BARRY)
TARZI, PAKIZE IZZET
THEODOSIA, SAINT
THOMPSON, MARY HARRIS
VON CALISCH, BARONESS
VON HILDEN, MARIE COLINET
VON ZAY, MARIA VON CALISCH
WOODHOUSE, ELEANOR

SYSTEMS ENGINEERS

SANDI, ANA-MARIA

TECHNOLOGISTS

SEMIRAMIS, QUEEN
VISSCHER, ANNA ROEMERS

TOXICOLOGISTS

BAETJER, ANNA MEDORA
BINGHAM, EULA
BROOKS, MATILDA MOLDENHAUER
HAMILTON, ALICE
SICHELGAITA

VIROLOGISTS

DOWNS, CORA
GEY, MARGARET
HENLE, GERTRUDE SZPINGIER

VIROLOGISTS (cont'd)

LUND, EBBA
MELNICK, MATILDA BENYESH
MORGAN, ISABEL
POPESCU, GEORGETA
SHEININ, ROSE
TOU, JENNIE

ZOOLOGISTS

ACCAME-MURATORI, ROSANNA
ADAMS, ELIZABETH A.
AUSTIN, MARY LELLAH
BAI, A.R. KASTURI
BAILEY, ETHEL
BATTLE, HELEN IRENE
BECKWITH, CORA
BENNETT, MIRIAM FRANCES
BERGER, KATHARINA BERTHA
  CHARLOTTE
BOVERI, MARCELLA O'GRADY
BOWEN, SUSAN
BRADFORD, JANET MARY
BRATHCHER, TWILA
BRYAN, ELIZABETH LETSON
BUSH, KATHARINE JEANNETTE
CALVERT, ADELIA SMITH
CAROTHERS, E. ELEANOR
CARPENTER, ESTHER
CAUSEY, NELL BEVEL
CLAPP, CORNELIA MARIA
CLARK, CORA
CLARK, EUGENIE
COMSTOCK, ANNA BOTSFORD
CRAM, ELOISE BLAINE
CRANE, JOCELYN
DAVENPORT, GERTRUDE CROTTY
DE WOLFE, BARBARA BLANCHARD
EIGENMANN, ROSA SMITH
FOOT, KATHERINE
FOSSEY, DIAN
GAGE, SUSANNA S. PHELPS
GAIGE, HELEN THOMPSON
GOODALL, JANE
GUTHRIE, MARY JANE

HAYNES, LINDEN C. SMITH
HAYWOOD, CHARLOTTE
HIBBARD, HOPE
HINRICHS, MARIE AGNES
HOLLISTER, GLORIA
HUGHES-SCHRADER, SALLY
HYMAN, LIBBIE HENRIETTA
KENNEDY, SUZANNE
KING, HELEN DEAN
KING, JESSIE L.
KLEIMAN, DEVRA
LANGDON, FANNIE E.
LAW, ANNIE E.
LAWRENCE, BARBARA
LINDAHL-KIESSLING, KERSTIN
MACDOUGALL, MARY
MANTON, SIDNIE
MILLARD, NAOMI ADELINE HELEN
MILLER, AGNES E.
MOODY, AGNES CLAYPOLE
MORGAN, ANN HAVEN
MORGAN, LILLIAN SAMPSON
NICKERSON, MARGARET L.
PEEBLES, FLORENCE
PEREYASLAWZEWA, SOPHIA
PITELKA, DOROTHY RIGGS
RANDOLPH, HARRIET
RASMUSON, MARIANNE
RATHBUN, MARY JANE
RAY, DIXY LEE
REES, FLORENCE GWENDOLINE
RICHARDS, MILDRED HODGE
ROTHSCHILD, MIRIAM LOUIS A.
RUSSELL, ELIZABETH SHULL
SCHMIDT-NIELSEN, BODIL MIMI
SNETHLAGE, EMILIE
STEVENS, NETTIE MARIA
STICKEL, LUCILLE FARRIER
SZEGO, CLARA MARIAN
TALBOT, MARY
THILLAYAMPALAM, EVANGELINE
TURNER, ABBEY H.
TWITTY, GERALDINE WILLIAMS
WELSH, LILLIAN
WILDER, INEZ WHIPPLE
WILLCOX, MARY